# Designing Democracy

# DESIGNING DEMOCRACY

## What Constitutions Do

CASS R. SUNSTEIN

OXFORD
UNIVERSITY PRESS
2001

# OXFORD
UNIVERSITY PRESS

Oxford   New York
Athens   Auckland   Bangkok   Bogotá   Buenos Aires   Cape Town
Chennai   Dar es Salaam   Delhi   Florence   Hong Kong   Istanbul   Karachi
Kolkata   Kuala Lumpur   Madrid   Melbourne   Mexico City   Mumbai
Nairobi   Paris   São Paulo   Shanghai   Singapore   Taipei   Tokyo   Toronto   Warsaw

and associated companies in
Berlin   Ibadan

Published by Oxford University Press, Inc.
198 Madison Avenue, New York, New York 10016

Oxford is a registered trademark of Oxford University Press

Library of Congress Cataloging-in-Publication Data
Sunstein, Cass R.
Designing democracy : what constitutions do / Cass R. Sunstein.
p.   cm.
Includes bibliographical references and index.
ISBN 0-19-514542-9
1. Constitutional law.   2. Democracy.   I. Title.
K3165 .S86 2001
342'.02—dc21      00-069301

3   5   7   9   8   6   4   2
Printed in the United States of America
on acid-free paper

*For Stephen Holmes and Jon Elster*

*[T]he Constitution is not simply some kind of statutory codification of an acceptable or legitimate past. It retains from the past only what is acceptable and represents a radical and decisive break from that part of the past which is unacceptable. It constitutes a decisive break . . . to a constitutionally protected culture of openness and democracy and universal human rights for . . . all ages, classes, and colours. . . . The past was pervaded by inequality, authoritarianism, and repression. The aspiration of the future is based on what is justifiable in an open and democratic society based on freedom and equality. It is premised on a legal culture of accountability and transparency. The relevant provisions of the Constitution must therefore be interpreted to give effect to the purposes sought to be advanced by their enactment.*

—The Constitutional Court of South Africa,
Shaballala and Others v. Attorney General
of the Transvaal and Another, 1996
South Africa 725 (C.C.)

# Contents

Designing Democracy

# Introduction
## *Tales of Democracy and Law*

For many years, Israel's General Security Service has engaged in certain forms of physical coercion, sometimes described as "torture," against suspected terrorists. According to the General Security Service, these practices occurred only in extreme cases and as a last resort, when deemed necessary to prevent terrorist activity and significant loss of life. Nonetheless, practices worthy of the name "torture" did occur, and they were not rare. Suspected terrorists were repeatedly shaken, in a way that causes the head and neck to dangle and vacillate rapidly. They were tied in chairs for long periods of time, their heads covered in an opaque and foul-smelling sack, while loud music was played. They were deprived of sleep. They were subject to other forms of physical harassment, designed to elicit information about terrorist activities.

Those practices were challenged before the Supreme Court of Israel, on the ground that they were inconsistent with the nation's fundamental law. The government responded that abstractions about human rights should not be permitted to overcome real-world necessities, so as to ban a practice that was, in certain circumstances, genuinely essential to prevent massive deaths in an area of the world that was often subject to terrorist activity. According to the government, physical coercion was justified in these circumstances. A judicial decision to the opposite effect would be a form of unjustified activism, even hubris.

In deciding the case, the Supreme Court of Israel refused to resolve the most fundamental questions.[1] It declined to say that the practices of the security forces would be illegitimate if expressly authorized by a democratic legislature. But the Court nonetheless held that those practices were unlawful. The Court's principal argument was that if such coercion were to be accept-

3

able, it could not be because the General Security Service, with its narrow and potentially self-serving agenda, said so. At a minimum, the disputed practices must be endorsed by the national legislature, after a full democratic debate on the precise question. "[T]his is an issue that must be decided by the legislature branch which represents the people. We do not take any stand on this matter at this time. It is there that various considerations must be weighed."

Instead of deciding the fundamental issue, the Court relied on what it saw as the inadequacy, from the democratic point of view, of a judgment by the unelected General Security Service alone. To say the least, members of that organization do not represent a broad spectrum of society. It is all too likely that people who work with the General Security Service will share points of view and frames of reference. When such people deliberate with one another, they are likely to strengthen, rather than to test, their existing convictions—very possibly to the detriment of human rights. A broader debate, with a greater range of views, is a necessary (if not sufficient) precondition for permitting coercion of this sort.

Because of its narrowness, the Court's decision does not do all that might be done. It does not impose an unambiguous barrier to government action—to say the least, a special problem where torture is involved and where most of the victims lack the rights of citizens. But it is important to see that in protecting basic rights, liberty-protecting nations have often taken an approach of just this sort—requiring broad democratic debate, and clear legislative permission, before permitting liberty or equality to be invaded.

Consider an example from the United States. In the 1950s, when the United States was in the midst of the "Red Scare," the secretary of state banned members of the Communist Party from traveling abroad. The ban was challenged under the Constitution, on the ground that it violated both freedom of speech and the right to travel.[2] The central question in the case—whether the United States government could deny a passport to communists—was bitterly contested. But the Supreme Court of the United States refused to resolve it. Instead the Court said that if people were going to be banned from leaving the United States because of their political convictions, it was not sufficient for the executive branch to have inaugurated that ban on its own. It was necessary, at a minimum, that the national legislature, with its greater diversity and deliberative pedigree, should make the decision. In other words, the Supreme Court suggested that purely internal deliberations, involving only the executive branch itself, are an insufficient safeguard against oppression and abuse.

Invoking democratic constitutions, and in times of both war and peace, courts have said that such deliberations are inadequate to support government action. Liberty-protecting courts have shown great suspicion of liberty-invading judgments by one branch of government, or at the behest of deliberating groups of like-minded people. By showing that suspicion, they have linked the project of ensuring democratic deliberation with that of promoting rights, by saying that if the latter are at risk, the former is required.

Now let us expand the viewscreen:

1. A city in California adopts an ordinance authorizing same-sex marriage. Many citizens of California are alarmed by this ordinance, which they believe to be a threat to traditional moral values and a "caricature" of civil rights. A statewide referendum is held on a ballot measure that would forbid same-sex marriage. After an intense campaign, with much advertising on both sides, the referendum is approved as state law. It is promptly challenged in federal court. The Supreme Court eventually rules that the law violates the federal Constitution. Is the Court's decision undemocratic?

2. A religious school in a large city does not hire women teachers. It insists that it is permitted to discriminate in this way because the religion's deepest convictions prescribe "different social roles" for men and women. But many citizens have come to believe that no school should be allowed to discriminate against women. The local government enacts a law to forbid sex discrimination in education, even by religious institutions. The school contends that the new law violates religious freedom as guaranteed by the Constitution. Is it right?

3. A nation in eastern Europe is considering amendments to its Constitution. After years with an "interim" post-Communist constitution, it is time to produce a more permanent document. But debates are now stalling over two questions. Some people argue that the Constitution should guarantee a right to secede, as a protection against oppression and discrimination. Others fear that a right to secede would endanger national unity. Some people argue that the Constitution should protect "positive" rights to food, housing, and health care. Others think that such rights are beyond the state's financial capabilities, and in any case that their constitutional protection would entangle courts in impossible managerial judgments. Who is correct?

4. The newly elected governor of Minnesota is frustrated by his inability to enact new legislation, an inability he attributes to the state's bicameral legislature. He argues that if the legislature consisted of only one house, the system would be far more democratic. Invoking the idea of democracy, he argues for an amendment to the state constitution, designed to create a unicameral legislature. Does the idea of democracy support the amendment?

## Deliberative Democracy and the Constitution

We are in the midst of a period of dramatic new thinking about the relationship between democracy and constitutionalism. Much of the thinking has been spurred by the remarkable collapse of two political systems: communism in eastern Europe and apartheid in South Africa. New constitutions are in place in many nations all over the globe, including South Africa, Russia, the Czech Republic, Hungary, Bulgaria, Canada, Ukraine, Lithuania, and Slovakia. Constitutional provisions, and constitutionalism itself, are receiving fresh consideration in many more, including Germany, the United States, France, Brazil, and even nations lacking a written constitution, such as Israel and England. As of this writing, it appears possible that a Palestinian state might be created at some point; discussions are beginning about the contents of a constitution for that new nation. The writing, rewriting, interpretation, and reconsideration of constitutional provisions is taking place amid sharp debates about whether a written constitution is necessary to protect rights, helpful or harmful to democracy, valuable or dangerous to economic prosperity, or a safeguard of property rights or of the prospects of disadvantaged groups.

This book calls for a democratic understanding of the role of a constitution in political life. This understanding competes with prominent alternatives based on national traditions, or equality, or even justice. In my view, the central goal of a constitution is to create the preconditions for a well-functioning democratic order, one in which citizens are genuinely able to govern themselves. Self-government is a good in itself. It is an important aspect of freedom. But self-government is also associated with other valuable goals. Consider Amartya Sen's astonishing finding that in the history of the world, no famine has ever occurred in a country with democratic elections and a free press.[3] This finding should be seen as an illustration of the many ways that democracy can promote social well-being, by increasing the likelihood that government will act in the interest of the citizenry, rather than the other way around. A good constitution ensures democratic elections and a free press. It thus creates self-government on dual grounds: liberty requires self-government, and self-government makes it far more likely that citizens will have good lives.

Of course the ideal of democracy can be understood in many different ways. Some people think that democracy calls simply for majority rule; other people think that a democratic system qualifies as such if it is highly responsive to popular will. I reject these views. I contend that a constitution should promote *deliberative democracy*, an idea that is meant to combine political accountability with a high degree of reflectiveness and a general commitment to reason-giving. My principal aim is to link the project of constitutionalism with the notion of deliberative democracy, not to elaborate that notion on its own.[4] But to understand the link, it is important to see, in broad outline, what deliberative democrats seek both to avoid and to ensure.

Those who believe in deliberative democracy think that by itself the idea of "majority rule" is a caricature of the democratic aspiration. They insist that government is not a kind of Aggregating Machine, trying to uncover people's desires, to sum them up, and then to translate them into law. They claim that a democratic government is based on reasons and arguments, not just votes and power. Deliberative democrats believe that people tend to overstate the tension between democracy, properly understood, and individual rights. Democracy comes with its own internal morality—*the internal morality of democracy*. This internal morality requires constitutional protection of many individual rights, including the right of free expression, the right to vote, the right to political equality, and even the right to private property, for people cannot be independent citizens if their holdings are subject to unlimited government readjustment. Properly understood, democracy is not antagonistic to rights. It enthusiastically protects rights, thus constraining what majorities are able to do to individuals or groups. A democratic constitution is drawn up and interpreted with these ideas in mind.

Deliberative democrats emphatically reject the view that a government should be run on the basis of popular referenda. They seek constitutional structures that will create a genuine republic, not a direct democracy. They hope to create institutions to ensure that people will be exposed to many topics and ideas, including ideas that they reject, and topics in which they have, as yet, expressed little interest. A deliberative approach to democracy, and to a constitution, is closely attuned to the problems, even the pathologies, associated with deliberation among like-minded people. A good constitutional system makes space for deliberating groups of this kind while also limiting the risks of misunderstanding, and ultimately even violence, that come when people are exposed only to echoes of their own voices.

Under a democratic constitution, what is the role of national traditions? Democracy's constitution is not tradition bound; it looks forward as well as backward. Because deliberative democrats want to ensure rule by free and equal citizens, they refuse to honor traditions as such. A democratic constitution makes it more likely that people will look behind traditions in order to see what can be said on their behalf.

For similar reasons, a self-governing citizenry does not take existing preferences and beliefs as unalterable, as natural, or as "givens." A central point of deliberation, in the private and public domains, is to shape both preferences and beliefs, and frequently to alter them, by subjecting them to reasoned arguments. For the same reason, deliberative democrats are skeptical of social practices that form preferences, and especially children's preferences, in a way that inculcates beliefs that threaten free and equal citizenship. A democratic constitution creates structures that will promote freedom in the formation of preferences and not simply implement whatever preferences people happen to have.

## Disagreement and Deliberative Trouble

In any democracy that respects freedom, the process of deliberation faces a pervasive problem: widespread and even enduring disagreement. A central goal of constitutional arrangements, and constitutional law, is to handle this problem, partly by turning disagreement into a creative force, partly by making it unnecessary for people to agree when agreement is not possible.

Under good conditions, deliberation is likely to clarify the basis for disagreement. Sometimes it will bring people into accord with one another. Some people will have misunderstood the relevant facts. Or they might not have seen the likely consequences of proposed policies. Once it is shown that some policy will actually make things worse rather than better, those who initially supported it are likely to reconsider. If a high minimum wage really would increase unemployment, people who thought that they favored a high minimum wage might consider other ways of helping low-income employees. In some cases, people might even be convinced to reconsider what they thought were their priorities, or their judgments of value. They might have believed, for example, that the overriding social goal is to promote economic prosperity, but after discussion, they might come to think that it makes sense to sacrifice overall prosperity for other social goals. Shifts of this sort happen all the time.

In many cases, however, all the deliberation in the world will not dissolve disagreement. Many of the discussions here take up the question: In the face of intractable disagreements, how should constitutional democracies proceed? One of my principal themes is the danger posed by *group polarization*—a process by which groups of like-minded people move one another to increasingly extreme positions. This is a particular problem for heterogeneous or multicultural societies, especially if members of groups, defined in ethnic, religious, or political terms, are mostly speaking only with one another. Ethnic, religious, and racial conflicts are often a product of group polarization. Another of my principal themes is the value of *incompletely theorized agreements*—a process by which people agree on practices, or outcomes, despite disagreement or uncertainty about fundamental issues. Incompletely theorized agreements have a central role in constitution-making and constitutional interpretation; they are also a key part of democracy's constitution.

Group polarization is often the source of deliberative trouble. Incompletely theorized agreements are often the solution to deliberative trouble. And it is especially important for a diverse democracy to create institutions to ensure that governmental power is not available only to segments of society, and to promote deliberation among people who would otherwise like to talk only to like-minded people. A system of checks and balances, or separation of powers, is best understood in this light. One of the key goals of democracy's constitution is to solve the problem of enduring disagreement—by promoting exposure to multiple perspectives, by proliferating the points of access to government, and by finding productive courses of action when disagreements cannot be solved.

## Democracy's Constitution: Cases and Practices

To return to the cases with which I began: The decision of the Supreme Court of Israel is an incompletely theorized agreement, one that promotes democracy rather than undermining it. A democratic constitution should, in my view, ban torture under all circumstances; but judges and citizens who disagree on that question should be able to agree that it ought not to be imposed without democratic authorization. In the case of the statewide referendum on homosexual marriage, deliberative democrats fear that what has happened is a parody of democratic aspirations. Judicial invalidation of the outcome will promote democracy, properly understood.

In the case of the discriminatory schools, a deliberative democrat does not believe that religious institutions have automatic protection against laws designed to promote sex equality. Such laws are an outcome of deliberative processes; they might be necessary to ensure free and equal citizenship. In the case of the proposed right to secession, the twenty-first-century deliberative democrat (following nineteenth-century deliberative democrat Abraham Lincoln) is skeptical, because of a belief that the Constitution should promote a well-functioning political order and a fear that the suggested right would compromise that goal. In the case of the proposed rights to food, housing, and health care, the deliberative democrat is nervous about judicial entanglement in managerial issues—but also stresses that people in desperate conditions cannot have the independence and security that citizens require. The deliberative democrat does not think that a unicameral legislature is to be preferred, on democratic grounds, to a bicameral legislature; the latter might be better for reflection and reason-giving.

In these and other cases, a belief in deliberative democracy, and in a constitution that protects it, has concrete and sometimes radical implications. To be sure, this belief helps explain many practices in existing democracies. But it also suggests why many of those practices deserve to be changed.

### Adversaries

Against those who see a continuing conflict between constitutional law and democracy, I urge that there need be no such conflict at all. Whether a constitution conflicts with democracy depends on what kind of constitution we have, and what kind of democracy we seek. In a deliberative democracy, one of the principal purposes of a constitution is to protect not the rule of the majority but democracy's internal morality, seen in deliberative terms. A system in which many people cannot vote or vote equally, or in which some people have far more political power than others, violates that internal morality.

Against those who identify the contents of a good constitution with the requirements of justice, I suggest that constitutions are pragmatic instruments, not outlines of a just society, and hence there is a gap between what constitutions say and what justice requires. Against those who think that a democratic constitution is best understood by reference to traditions, I suggest that traditions do not come labeled for easy identification and that national traditions contain much that is bad as well as much that is good. Against those who favor a large role for the judiciary, I stress the value and omnipresence of incompletely theorized agreements by which courts (and sometimes citizens) avoid, when they can, the largest and most abstract issues. Against those who believe that a democratic constitution is best understood to promote freedom, I suggest that in a way this is correct but that judges have serious limitations in giving content to that large ideal, and hence they properly proceed in an incremental way, giving a large emphasis to the prerequisites for democratic self-government.

Against those who believe that the equality principle is violated whenever the government treats people differently on the basis of race and sex, I argue that democracy's constitution is best taken to embody an *anticaste principle*, which means that some of the time, government can indeed treat people differently on the basis of race and sex. It also means that a central obligation of a government committed to equality is to eliminate the caste-like features of contemporary society. The anticaste principle turns in large part on a notion of equal citizenship. It is therefore closely associated with the ideal of deliberative democracy. There are also close links between the anticaste principle and an understanding of the virtues (and limits) of deliberation within enclaves. And those who favor deliberative democracy are at least willing to consider constitutional protections designed to ensure decent conditions for all.

One of my major themes is that judges have both limited wisdom and limited tools. They are also participants in *systems*, and complex ones at that, in which a pull or a tug at one point can have large unanticipated consequences elsewhere. Hence the appropriate judicial role is catalytic rather than preclusive—an idea that I apply to a number of areas, including discrimination on the basis of sexual orientation and the separation of powers. But an appreciation of the limited role and capacity of the judiciary should not be confused with skepticism about rights. As we will see, the anticaste principle, as an understanding of both freedom and equality, helps place a number of democratic initiatives, combating both poverty and subjection to violence, in an emphatically constitutional light. Initiatives of this kind should not be compelled by the judiciary. But they too are part of democracy's constitution.

None of these points is meant to provide a blueprint for constitutional design. Nor do I attempt to specify the ingredients of well-functioning constitutions. Of course some ideals are universal; but there is room for considerable variety among reasonable nations. Nor do I mean to set out a comprehensive account of deliberative democracy or of the relationship between the idea of democracy and the idea of constitutionalism. But by focusing on a series of particular questions about that relationship, I do hope to advance understanding of both ideas. In my view, the route to future advances, in both theory and practice, will lie less through abstractions, and in discussions of the concepts themselves, and more through an appreciation of the concrete contexts in which a nation's diverse aspirations are tested and specified. At least that is a hope that pervades this book.

# Deliberative Trouble

*[handwritten: Herein of "enclave deliberation"]*

The differences of opinion, and the jarrings of parties in [the legis-
lative] department of the government . . . often promote deliberation and circumspection; and serve to check the excesses of the majority.

*[handwritten: True? Today?]*

Alexander Hamilton, The Federalist

In everyday life the exchange of opinion with others checks our
partiality and widens our perspective; we are made to see things
from the standpoint of others and the limits of our vision are
brought home to us. . . . The benefits from discussion lie in the fact
that even representative legislators are limited in knowledge and
the ability to reason. No one of them knows everything the others
know, or can make all the same inferences that they can draw in
concert. Discussion is a way of combining information and enlarg-
ing the range of arguments.

*[handwritten: (my Shapiro paper donuts)]*

John Rawls, A Theory of Justice

Each person can share what he or she knows with the others, making the whole at least equal to the sum of the parts. Unfortunately,
this is often not what happens. . . . As polarization gets underway,
the group members become more reluctant to bring up items of information they have about the subject that might contradict the
emerging group consensus. The result is a biased discussion in
which the group has no opportunity to consider all the facts, because the members are not bringing them up. . . . Each item they
contributed would thus reinforce the march toward group consensus rather than add complications and fuel debate.

Patricia Wallace, The Psychology of the Internet

Consider the following events:

- Affirmative action is under attack in the state of Texas. A number of professors at a particular branch of the University of Texas are inclined to be sup-

portive of affirmative action; they meet to exchange views and to plan further action, if necessary. What are these professors likely to think, and to do, after they talk?

- After a nationally publicized shooting at a high school, a group of people in the community, most of them tentatively in favor of greater gun control, come together to discuss the possibility of imposing new gun control measures. What, if anything, will happen to individual views as a result of this discussion?
- A jury is deciding on an appropriate punitive damage award in a case of recklessly negligent behavior by a large company; the behavior resulted in a serious injury to a small child. Before deliberating as a group, individual jurors have chosen appropriate awards, leading to an average of $1.5 million and a median of $1 million. As a statistical generalization, how will the jury's ultimate award tend to compare to these figures?
- A group of women are concerned about what they consider to be a mounting "tyranny of feminism." They believe that women should be able to make their own choices, but they also think that men and women are fundamentally different and that their differences legitimately lead to different social roles. The group decides to meet every two weeks to focus on common concerns. After a year, is it possible to say what its members are likely to think?

Every society contains innumerable deliberating groups. Church groups, political parties, women's organizations, juries, legislative bodies, regulatory commissions, multimember courts, faculties, student organizations, people participating in talk radio programs, Internet discussion groups, and others engage in deliberation. It is a simple social fact that sometimes people enter discussions with one view and leave with another, even on political and moral questions. Emphasizing this fact, many recent observers have embraced the aspiration to deliberative democracy, an ideal that is designed to combine popular responsiveness with a high degree of reflection and exchange among people with competing views.[1] But what are the real-world consequences of deliberation? In a constitutional democracy, how can deliberation be made to work well? When and why does it work poorly?

The standard view of deliberation is that of Hamilton and Rawls, given in the epigraph. Group discussion is likely to lead to better outcomes, if only because competing views are stated and exchanged. Aristotle spoke in similar terms, suggesting that when diverse groups "all come together . . . they may surpass—collectively and as a body, although not individually—the quality of the few best. . . . When there are many who contribute to the process of deliberation, each can bring his share of goodness and moral prudence; . . . some appreciate one part, some another, and all together appreciate all."[2] But under what circumstances is it really true that "some appreciate one part, some another, and all together appreciate all"?

My principal purpose in this chapter is to investigate a striking statistical regularity—that of *group polarization*—and to relate this phenomenon to underlying questions about the role of deliberation in the "public
sphere" of a heterogeneous democracy. In brief, group polarization means
that *members of a deliberating group predictably move toward a more extreme
point in the direction indicated by the members' predeliberation tendencies.*
Thus, for example, members of the first deliberating group are likely to
become more firmly committed to affirmative action; the second group will
probably end up favoring gun control quite enthusiastically; the punitive
damages jury is likely to come up with an award higher than the median,
perhaps higher than the mean as well, and very possibly as high as or higher
than that of the highest predeliberation award of any individual member;
the group of women concerned about feminism is likely to become very
conservative indeed on gender issues. Notably, groups consisting of individuals with extremist tendencies are more likely to shift, and likely to shift
more; the same is true for groups with some kind of salient shared identity (like Republicans, Democrats, and lawyers, but unlike jurors and experimental subjects). When like-minded people meet regularly, without sustained exposure to competing views, extreme movements are all the more
likely.

Two principal mechanisms underlie group polarization. The first points
to *social influences on behavior* and in particular to people's desire to maintain
their reputations and their self-conceptions. The second emphasizes the role
of reasons in deliberation—in particular, the limited "argument pools"
within any group, and the directions in which those limited pools lead group
members. An understanding of the two mechanisms provides many insights
into democratic institutions. It illuminates a great deal, for example, about
likely processes within multimember courts, juries, political parties, and legislatures—not to mention ethnic groups, extremist organizations, criminal
conspiracies, student associations, faculties, institutions engaged in feuds or
"turf battles," workplaces, and families.

One of my largest purposes is to evaluate the social role of *enclave deliberation*, understood as deliberation within small groups of like-minded
people. I suggest that enclave deliberation is, simultaneously, a potential danger to social stability, a source of social fragmentation, and a safeguard against
social injustice and unreasonableness. As I will show, group polarization helps
explain an old point, with clear foundations in constitutional law in many
nations, to the effect that social homogeneity can be quite damaging to good
deliberation. When people are hearing echoes of their own voices, the consequence may be far more than mere support and reinforcement.

Group polarization is naturally taken as a reason for skepticism about enclave deliberation and for seeking to ensure deliberation among a wide group of diverse people. But there is a point more supportive of enclave deliberation: Participants in heterogeneous groups tend to give least weight to the views of low-status members[3]—in some times and places, women, African Americans, less educated people. Hence enclave deliberation might be the only way to ensure that those views are developed and eventually heard. Without a place for enclave deliberation, citizens in the broader public sphere may move in certain directions, even extreme directions, precisely because opposing voices are not heard at all. The ultimate lesson is that deliberating enclaves can be breeding grounds for *both* the development of unjustly suppressed views and for unjustified extremism, indeed fanaticism. Group polarization thus explains why and when many groups—including legislative majorities, political dissenters, hate groups, and civil liberties organizations—go to extremes.[4]

## Social Influences and Cascades

### In General

People frequently think and do what they think and do because of what they think (relevant) others think and do.[5] Employees are more likely to file suit if members of the same workgroup have also done so[6]; those who know other people who are on welfare are more likely to go on welfare themselves[7]; the behavior of proximate others affects the decision whether to recycle[8]; a good way to increase the incidence of tax compliance is to inform people of high levels of voluntary tax compliance[9]; broadcasters tend to follow one another[10]; and students are less likely to engage in binge drinking if they think that most of their fellow students do not engage in binge drinking, so much so that disclosure of this fact is one of the few successful methods of reducing binge drinking on college campuses.[11]

Social influences can lead people to go quite rapidly in identifiable directions, often as a result of "cascade" effects, involving either the spread of information (whether true or false) or growing peer pressure. Sometimes cascade effects are highly localized and lead members of particular groups, quite rationally, to believe or to do something that members of other groups, also quite rationally, find to be silly or worse. Thus *local cascades* can ensure that different groups end up with very different, but entrenched, views about the same issues and events. With the rise of the Internet, local cascades are sometimes dampened, but they continue to be an extremely important phenomenon.

Social influences affect behavior via two different mechanisms. The first is informational. What other people do, or say, carries an *informational externality;*[12] if many other people support a particular candidate, or refuse to use drugs, or carry guns, observers, and particularly observers within a common group, are given a signal about what it makes sense to do. The second mechanism is reputational, as group members impose sanctions on perceived deviants, and would-be deviants anticipate the sanctions in advance.[13] Even when people do not believe that what other people do provides information about what actually should be done, they may think that the actions of others provide information about what other people *think* should be done. People care about their reputations; hence they have an incentive to do what (they think) other group members think they should do. Reputational considerations may, for example, lead people to obey or not to obey the law, urge a certain view in group discussions, buy certain cars, drive while drunk, help others, or talk about political issues in a certain way. A concern for reputation exerts a ubiquitous influence on behavior, including that of participants in democratic debate, who often shift their public statements in accordance with reputational incentives.

## Some Classic Experiments

In the most vivid experiments involving group influences, conducted by Solomon Asch, individuals were apparently willing to abandon the direct evidence of their own senses.[14] In the relevant experiments, a certain line was placed on a large white card. The task of the subjects was to "match" that line by choosing, as identical to it in length, one of three other lines, placed on a separate large white card. One of the lines on the second white card was in fact identical in length to the line to be matched to it; the other two were substantially different, with the differential varying from an inch and three-quarters to three-quarters of an inch. The subject in the original experiments was one of eight people asked to engage in the matching. But unbeknown to the subject, the other seven people apparently being tested were actually there as Asch's confederates, serving as part of the experiments.

Asch's experiments unfolded in the following way. In the first two rounds, everyone agreed about the right answer; this seemed to be an extremely dull experiment. But the third round introduced "an unexpected disturbance."[15] Other group members made what was obviously, to the subject and to any reasonable person, a clear error; they matched the line at issue to one that was obviously longer or shorter. In these circumstances the subject had the choice of maintaining his independent judgment or instead yielding to the crowd. A large number of subjects ended up yielding. In ordinary circumstances, subjects erred less than 1 percent of the time; but in rounds in which group pressure supported the incorrect answer, subjects erred 36.8 percent of the time. Indeed, in a series of twelve questions, no less than 70 percent of subjects went along with the group, and defied the evidence of their own senses, at least once.

Notably, susceptibility to group influence was hardly uniform; some people agreed with the group almost all of the time, whereas others were entirely independent in their judgments. Significantly, a small variation in the experimental conditions made a big difference: the existence of at least one compatriot, or voice of sanity, dramatically reduced both conformity and error. When just one other person made an accurate match, errors were reduced by three-quarters, even if there was a strong majority the other way. By contrast, varying the size of the group unanimously making the erroneous decision mattered only up to a number of three; increases from that point had little effect. Opposition from one person did not increase subjects' errors at all; opposition from two people increased error to 13.6 percent; and opposition from three people increased error to 31.8 percent, not substantially different from the level that emerged from further increases in group size.

More recent studies have identified an important feature of social influence, directly bearing on group behavior in democracies: Much depends on the subject's perceived relationship to the experimenters' confederates and in particular *on whether the subject considers himself part of the same group in which those confederates fall.* Thus conformity—hence error—is dramatically *increased,* in public statements, when the subject perceives himself as part of a reasonably discrete group that includes the experimenter's confederates (all psychology majors, for example).[16] By contrast, conformity is dramatically *decreased,* and error is also dramatically decreased, in public statements, when the subject perceives himself as in a different group from the experimenter's confederates (all ancient history majors, for example). Notably, private opinions, expressed anonymously afterward, were about the same whether or not the subject perceived himself as a member of the same group as others in the experiment. There is a big lesson here about both the risk of inaccuracy and insincerity of public statements of agreement with a majority view, when relevant speakers closely identify themselves as members of the same group as the majority.[17]

Both informational and reputational factors lead people toward errors. In Asch's own studies, several people said, in private interviews, that their own opinions must have been wrong. On the other hand, these statements may have been an effort to avoid the dissonance that would come from confessing that the statement was false but made only to protect reputation. Experimenters find some reduced error, in the same basic circumstances as Asch's experiments, when the subject is asked to give a purely private answer—a point suggesting that reputation is what is producing mistakes. And note that in the study described in the immediately preceding paragraph, people who thought that they were members of the same group as the experimenter's confederates gave far more accurate answers, and far less conforming answers, when they were speaking privately.[18]

In a statement of direct relevance to constitutional democracies, Asch concluded that his results raised serious questions about the possibility that "the social process is polluted" by the "dominance of conformity."[19] He added: "That we have found the tendency to conformity in our society so strong that reasonably intelligent and well-meaning young people are willing to call white black is a matter of concern." Asch's experiments did not involve deliberation, for people were not exchanging reasons; indeed, we might expect that reason-giving, on the part of Asch's confederates, would have severely weakened his results. What reasons could have been given for incorrect matches? But the existence of substantial numbers of mistakes, as a result of mere exposure to the incorrect conclusions of others, raises questions about whether and when deliberation within groups and institutions will lead people in the right directions.

### Social (and Law-Related) Cascades

Societies are vulnerable to cascade effects, in which law, policy, opinion, and behavior shift rapidly in one or another direction.[20] Consider issues involving race and sex equality, global warming, capital punishment, AIDS, the filing of lawsuits, or presidential candidates. Indeed, Asch's work demonstrates considerable individual susceptibility to cascade effects. What is striking about such effects is their epidemic-like nature, or the quality of apparent contagion. Group polarization is sometimes, but not always, a product of cascade effects. It will be useful to understand the former against the background of the latter.

*Informational cascades.* A puzzling question here is *why* individuals and social groups move so rapidly. A useful starting point is that when individuals lack a great deal of private information (and sometimes even when they have such information), they rely on information provided by the statements or actions of others. If B does not know whether abandoned waste sites are in fact hazardous, he may be moved in the direction of fear if A seems to think that fear is justified. If A and B both believe that fear is justified, C may end up thinking so too, at least if she lacks reliable independent information to the contrary. If A, B, and C believe that abandoned waste dumps are hazardous, D will have to have a good deal of confidence to reject their shared conclusion.

People typically have different "thresholds" for choosing to believe or do something new or different. Some people will require very convincing reasons to change their view; other people will require much less. As those with low thresholds come to a certain belief or action, people with somewhat higher thresholds will join them, possibly to a point where a critical mass is reached, making groups, possibly even nations, "tip."[21] The result of this process can be to produce snowball or cascade effects, as small or even large groups of people end up believing something—even if that something is false—simply because other people seem to believe that it is true. There is a great deal of experimental evidence of informational cascades, which are easy to induce in the laboratory;[22] real-world phenomena also seem to have a great deal to do with cascade effects.[23] Consider, for example, smoking, participating in protests, voting for third-party candidates, striking, recyling, using birth control, rioting, buying stocks,[24] choosing what to put on television,[25] even leaving bad dinner parties.[26]

The same processes influence views on political, legal, and moral questions; we can easily find political, legal, and moral cascades. Suppose, for example, that A believes that affirmative action is wrong and even unconstitutional, that B is otherwise unsure but shifts upon hearing what A believes, and that C is unwilling to persist in his modest approval of affirmative action when A and B disagree; it would be a very confident D who would reject the moral judgments of three (apparently) firmly committed others. Sometimes people are not entirely sure whether capital punishment should be imposed, whether a president should be impeached, whether the Constitution protects the right to have an abortion, whether it is wrong to litter or to smoke. Many people, lacking firm convictions of their own, may end up believing what (relevant) others seem to believe. Even judges are vulnerable to cascade effects.[27]

The same process is sometimes at work in the choice of political candidates, as a fad develops in favor of one or another—a cascade "up" or "down," with sensational or ruinous consequences. We can easily imagine cascade effects in the direction of certain judgments about the appropriate course of government regulation, environmental protection, or constitutional law. Note that a precondition for an informational cascade is a lack of much private information on the part of many or most people; if people have a good deal of private information, or are confident about their own judgments, they are unlikely to be susceptible to the signals sent by the actions of others.

*Reputational cascades.* Thus far the discussion has involved purely informational pressures and informational cascades, where people care about what other people think because they do not know what to think, and they rely on the opinions of others to show what it is right to think. But there can be reputational pressures and reputational cascades as well.[28]

The basic idea here is that people speak out, or remain silent, or even engage in certain expressive activity partly in order to preserve their reputations, even at the price of failing to say what they really think. Suppose, for example, that A believes that hazardous waste dumps pose a serious environmental problem; suppose too that B is skeptical. B may keep quiet or (like some of Asch's subjects) even agree with A, simply in order to preserve A's good opinion. C may see that A believes that hazardous waste dumps pose a serious problem and that B seems to agree with A; C may therefore voice agreement even though privately she is skeptical or ambivalent.

It is easy to see how this kind of thing can happen in political life with, for example, politicians expressing their commitment to capital punishment (even if they are privately skeptical) or their belief in God (even if they are privately unsure). People will typically have different thresholds for yielding to perceived reputational pressure; some people will follow perceived pressure only when it is very severe (for example, because a large number of people impose it, or because they care a great deal about those people who impose it), whereas others will follow when it is mild (for example, simply because a few relevant others impose it). Here too the consequence can be cascade effects—large social movements in one direction or another—as increasing numbers of people yield to a pressure that they simultaneously impose, eventually reaching a critical mass. At that stage a large number of people eventually appear to support a certain course of action simply because others (appear to) do so.

As in the context of the informational cascade, what is true for factual beliefs is true as well for moral, legal, and political judgments. People might say, for example, that affirmative action violates the Constitution simply because of perceived reputational sanctions against saying the opposite; they might support or oppose the death penalty largely in order to avoid the forms

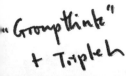
"Groupthink"
+ Triplek

of social opprobrium that might come, in the relevant community, from taking the opposing view. A precondition for reputational cascades is that for people in the relevant group, reputational considerations must be an important motivation for behavior. If people do not care about their reputations, or if reputation is a small component of the choice involved, the perceived intrinsic merits will be crucial, and cascades are unlikely to result.

Are social cascades good or bad? No general answer would make sense. Sometimes cascades are quite fragile, precisely because people's commitments are based on little private information; sometimes cascades are rooted in (and greatly fuel) blunders. Sometimes cascade effects will eliminate group or public neglect or indifference, by generating concern about serious though previously ignored problems. But sometimes cascade effects will make people far more worried than they ought to be or will otherwise produce large-scale distortions in private judgments, public policy, and law. The antislavery movement in America had distinctive cascade-like features, as did the environmental movement, the fall of Communism, and the antiapartheid movement in South Africa; so too with Mao's Cultural Revolution and the rise of Nazism in Germany. Cascades need not involve deliberation; but related problems infect processes of group deliberation, as we will now see.


## How and Why Groups Polarize

My basic interest here is the relationship between social processes within groups[29] and democratic theory and in particular that aspect of democratic theory that interacts with law and especially constitutional law. How do small groups of like-minded people differ from large groups of heterogeneous people? What is likely to happen within isolated deliberating enclaves? How does all this bear on deliberative democracy or the content of a democratic constitution? To answer these questions, it is necessary to understand group polarization.


### The Basic Phenomenon

Group polarization is among the most robust patterns found in deliberating bodies, and it has been found in many diverse tasks. Polarization occurs "when an initial tendency of individual group members toward a given direction is enhanced [by] group discussion."[30] The result is that groups often make more extreme decisions than would the typical or average individual in the group (where "extreme" is defined solely internally, by reference to the group's initial dispositions). There is a clear relationship between group polarization and cascade effects. As we will see, the former, like the latter, has a great deal to do with both informational and reputational influences. A key difference is that group polarization involves the effects of deliberation. In addition, it may or may not involve a cascade-like process; polarization can result simply from simultaneous independent decisions to move toward the group extreme.

Though standard within psychology, the term "group polarization" is somewhat misleading. It is not meant to suggest that group members will shift to two poles. Instead the term refers to a predictable shift *within* a group discussing a case or problem.[31] As the shift occurs, groups, and group members, move and coalesce, not toward the middle of antecedent dispositions but toward a more extreme position in the direction indicated by those dispositions. The effect of deliberation is both to decrease variance among group members, as individual differences diminish, and also to produce convergence on a relatively more extreme point among predeliberation judgments.

Consider some examples of the basic phenomenon, which has been found in over a dozen nations.[32] (1) A group of moderately profeminist women will become more strongly profeminist after discussion.[33] (2) After discussion, citizens of France become more critical of the United States and its intentions with respect to economic aid.[34] (3) After discussion, whites predisposed to show racial prejudice offer more negative responses to the question whether white racism is responsible for conditions faced by African Americans in American cities.[35] (4) After discussion, whites predisposed not to show racial prejudice offer more positive responses to the same question.[36] As statistical regularities, it follows, for example, that those moderately critical of an ongoing war effort will, after discussion, sharply oppose the war; that those who believe that global warming is a serious problem are likely, after discussion, to hold that belief with considerable confidence; that people tending to believe in the inferiority of a certain racial group will become more entrenched in this belief as a result of discussion.

The phenomenon of group polarization has conspicuous importance to the communications market, where groups with distinctive identities often engage in within-group discussion—as well as to the operation of many deliberating bodies of relevance to law and politics, including legislatures, commissions, multimember courts, and juries. I will return to this point shortly; for now, notice a few obvious possibilities. If the public is sharply divided, and if different groups design their own preferred communications packages, the consequence may be further division, as group members move one another toward more extreme points in line with their initial tendencies.

Different deliberating groups, each consisting of like-minded people, may be driven increasingly far apart, simply because most of their discussions are with one another.

In a similar vein, members of a political party, or of the principal political parties, may polarize as a result of internal discussions; party-line voting is sometimes explicable partly on this ground. Extremist groups will often become more extreme. A set of judges with similar predilections on a three-judge panel may well produce a more extreme ruling than any individual member would write if he were judging on his own. As we will soon see, the largest group polarization typically occurs with individuals already inclined toward extremes.

## Risky Shifts and Cautious Shifts

Group polarization was first found in a series of intriguing experiments involving risk-taking decisions. Before 1961, conventional wisdom had been that as compared with the individuals who compose it, a group of decision-makers—for example, a committee or board—would be likely to favor a compromise and thus to avoid risks. But the relevant experiments, originally conducted by Stoner, found otherwise; they identified what has become known as the "risky shift."[37] Deliberation tended to shift group members in the direction of greater risk-taking; and deliberating groups, asked to reach a unanimous decision, were generally more risk-inclined—sometimes far more risk-inclined—than the mean individual member, predeliberation.

It is important to distinguish at this point between two aspects of these findings, both of relevance to democracy and constitutional law. The first involves the movement of deliberating groups, when a group decision is necessary, toward the group's extreme end; call this (as it is sometimes described) a *choice shift*. This means that if a group decision is required, the group will tend toward an extreme point, given the original distribution of individual views. Undoubtedly the group's decision rule will matter here; a requirement of unanimity may well, for example, produce a shift toward the most extreme points, at least if those with the most extreme views are least tractable and most confident. The second involves the movement of (even private) individual judgments as a result of group influence; call this simply (as is standard) group polarization. This means that to the extent that the private judgments of individuals are moved by discussion, the movement will be toward a more extreme point in the direction set by the original distribution of views. It is possible to have one kind of movement without the other, though ordinarily the two accompany one another.

A possible (and contemporaneous) reading of Stoner's early studies would be that group dynamics are generally such as to move people—both groups and individuals within them—in the direction of greater risk-taking. But this conclusion would be wrong. Later studies showed that under certain conditions, it was possible, even easy, to induce a "cautious shift" as well. Indeed, certain problems reliably produced cautious shifts.[38] The principal examples involved the decision whether to marry and the decision whether to board a plane despite severe abdominal pain possibly requiring medical attention. In these cases, deliberating groups moved toward caution, as did the members who composed them. Burglars, in fact, show cautious shifts in discussions, though when they work together, the tendency is toward greater risk-taking.[39]

In Stoner's original data, subsequent researchers noticed, the largest risky shifts could be found when group members had an extreme initial position, in the sense that the predeliberation votes were weighted toward the risky end, whereas for the items that shifted a little or not at all, people started out near the middle of the scale. A group of very cautious individuals would produce a significant shift toward greater caution; a group of individuals inclined toward risk-taking would produce a significant shift toward greater risk-taking; and groups of individuals in the middle would produce smaller shifts in the direction indicated by their original disposition. Similar results have been found in many contexts with relevance to law and democracy, involving, for example, questions about economic aid, architecture, political leaders, race, feminism, and judgments of guilt or innocence. Polarization has been found for questions of obscure fact (e.g., how far Sodom on the Dead Sea is below sea level) as well as for evaluative questions, including political and legal issues and even the attractiveness of people in slides.

### Mechanisms

What explains group polarization? It is tempting to think that conformity plays a large role, and as the Asch experiments suggest, individual judgments can be greatly influenced by the desire to conform. Perhaps conformity is sometimes at work, but the data make clear that group polarization is not a matter of conformity; people do not shift to the mean of initial positions.[40] The relevant movement goes to one or another side. Indeed, this is what defines, and what is most distinctive about, group polarization.

There have been two main explanations for group polarization, both of which have been extensively investigated.[41] Massive support has been found on behalf of both explanations.

*Social comparison.* The first explanation begins with the claim that people want to be perceived favorably by other group members and also to perceive themselves favorably. Once they hear what others believe, they adjust their positions in the direction of the dominant position. They might want to signal, for example, that they are not cowardly or cautious, especially in an entrepreneurial group that disparages these characteristics. Hence they will frame their position so that they do not appear as such by comparison to other group members. With respect to risk-taking activity, people want to occupy a certain position in comparison to others, and before they hear what other people think, they assume that they do in fact occupy that position. But when they hear what other people think, they find, often, that they occupy a somewhat different position, and they shift accordingly. The result is to press the group's position toward one or another extreme, as well as to induce shifts in individual members. The same appears to happen in other contexts. People might wish, for example, not to seem too enthusiastic or too restrained in their enthusiasm for affirmative action, feminism, or an increase in national defense; hence their views may shift when they see what other group members think. The result will be both choice shifts and group polarization.

Thus individuals move their judgments in order to preserve their image to others and their image to themselves. A key claim here is that information alone about the actual positions of others—without discussion—will produce a shift. Evidence has confirmed this fact; mere exposure induces a substantial risky shift (though it is smaller than what is produced by discussion—about half as large).[42] This effect helps explain a shift toward caution (the "cautious shift") as well.

*Persuasive arguments.* The second explanation is based on a common-sense intuition: that any individual's position on an issue is partly a function of which arguments presented within the group seem convincing. The choice therefore moves in the direction of the most persuasive position defended by the group, taken as a whole. Because a group whose members are already inclined in a certain direction will have a disproportionate number of arguments supporting that same direction, the result of discussion will be to move individuals further in the direction of their initial inclinations. The key is the existence of a limited argument pool, one that is skewed (speaking purely descriptively) in a particular direction. Members of a group will have thought of some, but not all, of the arguments that justify their initial inclination. In discussion, arguments of a large number of individuals are stated and heard, but the total argument pool will be tilted in one or another direction, depending on the predispositions of the people who compose the group. Hence there will be a shift in the direction of the original tilt.

There is a related possibility, not quite reducible to either of the two standard arguments but borrowing elements of each. In their individual judgments, people are averse to extremes; they tend to seek the middle of the relevant poles.[43] When people are making judgments individually, they often err on the side of caution, expressing a view in the direction that they really hold but stating that view cautiously, for fear of seeming extreme. Once other people express supportive views, the inhibition disappears, and people feel free to say what, in a sense, they really believe. It is reasonable to believe that this phenomenon plays a role in group polarization and choice shifts.

## Refinements—and Depolarization

For purposes of understanding the relationship between the phenomenon just described and constitutional democracy, there are some further points, two with special importance. *First*, it matters a great deal whether people consider themselves part of the same social group as the other members; a sense of shared identity will heighten the shift, and a belief that identity is not shared will reduce and possibly eliminate it. *Second*, deliberating groups will tend to "depolarize" if they consist of equally opposed subgroups and if members have a degree of flexibility in their positions.

*Statistical regularities.* Of course not all groups polarize; some groups end up in the middle, not toward either extreme. Note that in Stoner's original experiments, one of the twelve deliberating groups showed no polarization at all. Nor is it hard to understand why this might be so. If the people defending the original tendency are particularly unpersuasive, group polarization is unlikely to occur. If the outliers are especially convincing, groups may even shift away from their original tendency and in the direction held by few or even one.

Sometimes, moreover, external constraints or an external "shock" may prevent or blunt group polarization. Group members with well-defined views on a certain issue (gun control, separation of church and state, intervention in foreign nations) may be prone to polarize; but in order to maintain political effectiveness, even basic credibility, they will sometimes maintain a relatively moderate face, publicly or even privately. Groups that have started to polarize in an extreme direction may move toward the middle in order to promote their own legitimacy or because of new revelations of one kind or another. In the United States, consider the Democrats in the early 1990s and the Republicans in the late 1990s.

*Affective factors and the role of confidence.*   Affective factors are quite important in group decisions. When manipulated, such factors will significantly increase or decrease polarization. If group members know and like each other, dissent is significantly less frequent.[44] The existence of affective ties thus reduces the number of divergent arguments and also intensifies social influences on choice. Hence people are less likely to shift if the direction advocated is being pushed by unfriendly group members; the likelihood of a shift, and its likely size, are increased when people perceive fellow members as friendly, likeable, and similar to them. A sense of common fate and within-group similarity increases group polarization, as does the introduction of a rival "outgroup."

The confidence of particular members also plays an important role. Indeed, part of the reason for group polarization appears to be that, as a class, extreme positions are less tractable and more confidently held. This point is an important complement to the persuasive arguments theory: The persuasiveness of arguments depends, not surprisingly, not simply on the grounds given but also on the confidence with which they are articulated. (Consider here legislatures, juries, and multimember courts.) Group polarization can also be fortified through "exit," as members leave the group because they reject the direction in which things are heading. If exit is pervasive, the tendency to extremism will be greatly increased.

*Identity and solidarity.*   In a refinement of particular importance to social deliberation, constitutionalism, and the theory of democracy, it has been found to matter whether people think of themselves, antecedently or otherwise, as part of a group having a degree of connection and solidarity. If they think of themselves in this way, group polarization is all the more likely and is likely, too, to be more extreme.[45] When the context emphasizes each person's membership in the social group engaging in deliberation, polarization increases. This finding is in line with more general evidence that social ties among deliberating group members suppress dissent and in that way tend to lead to inferior decisions.[46] This should not be surprising. If ordinary findings of group polarization are a product of social influences and limited argument pools, it stands to reason that when group members think of one another as similar along a salient dimension or if some external factor (politics, geography, race, sex) unites them, group polarization will be heightened.

*Depolarization and deliberation without shifts.* Is it possible to construct either groups that will depolarize—that will tend toward the middle—or groups whose members will not shift at all? Both phenomena are real in actual deliberating bodies. In fact the persuasive arguments theory implies that there will be depolarization if and when new persuasive arguments are offered that are opposite to the direction initially favored by group members. There is evidence for this phenomenon.[47] Depolarization, rather than polarization, will also be found when the relevant group consists of individuals drawn equally from two extremes.[48] Thus if people who initially favor caution are put together with people who initially favor risk-taking, the group judgment will move toward the middle.

Group members with extreme positions generally change little as a result of discussion or shift to a more moderate position. Consider a study[49] consisting of six-member groups specifically designed to contain two subgroups (of three persons each) initially committed to opposed extremes; the effect of discussion was to produce movement toward the center. One reason may be the existence of partially shared persuasive arguments in both directions.[50] Interestingly, this study of opposed subgroups found the greatest depolarization with obscure matters of fact (e.g., the population of the United States in 1900) and the least depolarization with highly visible public questions (e.g., whether capital punishment is justified). Matters of personal taste depolarized a moderate amount (e.g., preference for basketball or football or for colors for painting a room).[51]

These findings fit well with the persuasive arguments account of polarization. When people have a fixed view about some highly salient public issue, they are likely to have heard a wide range of arguments in various directions, producing a full argument pool, and an additional discussion is not likely to produce movement. With respect to familiar issues, people are simply less likely to shift at all. And when one or more people in a group know the right answer to a factual question, the group is likely to shift in the direction of accuracy.

*Several regularities.* It is now possible to suggest some general, commonsensical conclusions about how and when group discussion will move pre-deliberation opinions. Views based on a great deal of thought are least likely to shift; depolarization can occur with equal subgroups tending in opposite directions; groups will usually shift in the direction of an accurate factual judgment where one or more members knows the truth; where views are not firmly held, but where there is an initial predisposition, group polarization is the general rule. The effects of discussion are also likely to depend on members' perception of the group and of their relationship to it. If a group consists of "people," less polarization is likely than if it consists of "Republicans" or "defenders of the Second Amendment" or "opponents of American imperialism." Depolarization may well occur in groups with equal subgroups having opposite tendencies. But this is less likely and less pronounced (1) if subgroup members have fixed positions and (2) if subgroup members know that they are members of identifiable groups and that their codiscussants are members of different identifiable groups.

## Actual Deliberation within Identifiable Groups: Repeated "Polarization Games"

Studies of group polarization involve one-shot experiments. I will turn shortly to group polarization in the real world. But notice an intriguing implication of the experiments, an implication with special importance for democratic deliberation involving people who meet with each other not once but on a regular basis.

If participants engage in repeated discussions—if, for example, they meet each month, express views, and take votes—there should be repeated shifts toward, and past, the defined pole. Thus, for example, if citizens are thinking about genetic engineering of food, or the minimum wage, or the World Trade Organization, their discussions, over time, should lead them in quite extreme directions. In these repeated "polarization games," deliberation over time should produce a situation in which individuals hold positions more extreme than those of any individual member before the series of deliberations began. In fact the idea of iterated polarization games seems far more realistic than the processes studied in one-shot experiments. And it is not difficult to think of real-world groups in which the consequence of deliberation, over time, appears to be to shift both groups and individuals to positions that they could not possibly have accepted early on. Iterated polarization games are an important real-world phenomenon.

But this raises two questions: Why and when do groups stop polarizing? Why and when do they end up at a certain point or even shift in the opposite direction? It is reasonable to speculate that polarization often ends or reverses as a result of some *external shock*—as, for example, when new members add new arguments, or when the simple self-interest of political leaders produces a shift in direction, or when new circumstances, of fact or value, alter the perspectives and incentives of group members. Social cascades often change direction as a result of such external shocks, as through the release of new information; the same processes seem to terminate or to reverse group polarization.

### Rhetorical Asymmetry and the "Severity Shift": A Pervasive Phenomenon?

In a noteworthy qualification of the general literature on group polarization, the previously discussed study of punitive damage awards by juries found a striking pattern for dollar awards.[52] For *any* dollar award above zero, the general effect of deliberation was to increase awards to amounts above those sought by the median voter. This was a kind of "severity shift." Dollar awards did not simply polarize; while higher awards increased dramatically, as compared to the median of predeliberation votes, low awards increased as well. Why is this?

Both the original experiment and a follow-up experiment suggest that the severity shift is a product of a "rhetorical asymmetry" that favors, other things being equal and in any contest, the person or persons urging higher awards. Systematic increases in dollar awards strongly suggest a general tendency toward upward movement; a subsequent experiment confirmed this effect, with a substantial majority of subjects agreeing that it was easier, other things being equal, to argue for higher awards than for lower ones. In our culture, and in light of existing social norms, the person favoring the higher amount for punitive damages appears likely to be more convincing than the person favoring the lower amount. It is important to emphasize that this asymmetry operates independently of any facts about the individual case. The reason appears to be that with respect to dollar awards involving a corporate defendant, intuitively stronger arguments—"we need to deter this kind of conduct," "we need to send a powerful signal," "we need to attract their attention"—tend to favor higher awards.

This finding has general importance; it is an important component of deliberative trouble and the tendency toward extremism. Undoubtedly there are many other contexts containing rhetorical asymmetry, and undoubtedly the asymmetry can affect outcomes in democratic institutions, as it did in the jury study. Legislative judgments about criminal punishment may, for example, involve an asymmetry of exactly this kind; those favoring greater punishment for drug-related offenses appear to have a systematic advantage over those favoring lesser punishment. In certain settings, those favoring lower taxes or more aid for scholarship students or greater funding for environmental protection may have a similar rhetorical advantage. Much remains to be explored here. For my purposes here, the point is that when there is an initial distribution of views in a certain direction, and when existing norms give a more extreme movement in that direction a rhetorical advantage, quite extreme shifts can be expected.

## Polarization and Democracy

I now trace some of the implications of group polarization for participants in a deliberative democracy. I show how social groups are vulnerable to extremism, especially when polarization is combined with a conception of shared identity by group members. I also show how public institutions are subject to polarization, because of both internal dynamics and external influences. The result of the relevant processes can be to create serious trouble for deliberative bodies.

### Polarizing Events and Polarization Entrepreneurs

Group polarization has a large effect on many deliberating groups and institutions. Consider religious organizations. Such organizations tend to strengthen group members' religious convictions, simply by virtue of the fact that like-minded people are talking to one another. Religious groups amplify particular religious impulses, especially if group members are insulated from other groups, and on occasion people are led in quite bizarre directions. Whether or not this is so, political activity by members of religious organizations is undoubtedly affected by cascade-like effects and by group polarization. In a related vein, survey evidence shows that dramatic social events, like the assassination of Martin Luther King and civil rights disturbances, tend to polarize attitudes, with both positive and negative attitudes increasing within demographic groups.[53] Discussion will often harden attitudes toward outsiders and social change; thus proposals "for establishment of a halfway house or a correctional facility have typically elicited private apprehensions which, after discussion, become polarized into overt paranoia and hostility."[54]

In fact it is possible to imagine "professional polarizers," or "polarization entrepreneurs"—political activists who have, as one of their goals, the creation of spheres in which like-minded people can hear a particular point of view from one or more articulate people, and also participate, actually or vicariously, in a deliberative discussion in which a certain point of view becomes entrenched and strengthened. For those seeking to promote social reform, an extremely promising strategy is to begin by promoting discussions among people who tend to favor the relevant reform; such discussions are likely to intensify the underlying convictions and concerns. In fact the fields of environmental protection and civil rights are filled with leaders who take advantage of cascade-like processes and group polarization.

Polarization is also likely to be produced by magazines with identifiable political convictions; special television programs devoted to preferred causes; and talk radio hosts with distinctive positions, generally shared by the relevant audience. Because the results of group polarization cannot be evaluated in the abstract, nothing need be dishonorable in these efforts. What can be said, in the abstract, is that attempts to ensure discussion among people with similar predispositions may be strikingly successful in increasing the confidence of individual participants and also in moving them toward more extreme positions. In any society, would-be social reformers do well to create forums, whether in-person, over-the-air, cyberspace, or print, in which people with similar inclinations are frequently speaking with one another and can develop a clear sense of shared identity.

### "Outgroups"

Group polarization has particular implications for insulated "outgroups"; these might be political groups, or ethnic groups, or groups defined in any identifiable way. Recall that polarization increases when group members identify themselves along some salient dimension and especially when the group is able to define itself by contrast to another group. Outgroups are in this position—of self-contrast to others—by definition. Excluded by choice or coercion from discussion with others, such groups may become polarized in quite extreme directions, often in part because of group polarization. Extremism on the part of outgroups (not excluding murders and suicides) is a possible result, especially if we consider the fact that extreme groups show comparatively greater polarization.

The tendency toward polarization among outgroups helps explain special concern about "hate speech," where group antagonisms can be heightened. There is indeed reason to fear the consequences of such speech; group polarization shows why. An understanding of group polarization simultaneously raises some questions about the idea that certain group discussions produce "consciousness raising." It is possible, at least, that the consequence of discussion is not only or mostly to raise consciousness but to produce group polarization in one direction or another—and at the same time to increase confidence in the position that has newly emerged. This does not mean that consciousness is never raised; undoubtedly group discussion can identify and clarify problems that previously were repressed or were understood as an individual rather than social product. But nothing of this sort is established by the mere fact that views have changed and coalesced and are held, post-discussion, with a high degree of confidence.

### Feuds, Ethnic and International Strife, and War

Group polarization is at work in feuds of all kinds. One of the characteristic features of feuds is that members of feuding groups tend to talk only to one another, fueling and amplifying their outrage and solidifying their impression of the relevant events. Informational and reputational forces are extremely important here, typically producing cascade effects, and group polarization can lead members to increasingly extreme positions.

It is not too much of a leap to suggest that these effects are sometimes present within ethnic groups and even nations, notwithstanding the usually high degree of national heterogeneity. In the United States, sharp divergences between whites and African Americans, on particular salient events or more generally, can be explained by reference to group polarization. Racial and ethnic strife, or hostility amid "multiculturalism," is often affected by the same process.

The economist Timur Kuran has explored the broader international phenomenon of "ethnification."[55] Kuran's basic claim is that in many nations, including Turkey and the former Yugoslavia, ethnic strife is not a reawakening of long-suppressed resentments but instead a product of reputational cascades. In this process, a failure to engage in ethnically identified activity produces reputational sanctions, which grow in intensity over time, as increasing numbers of people join the cascade. Initially people may be asked to dress in an ethnically identifiable way; later they may be asked to engage in certain celebrations and to participate in meetings; still later they may be asked to segregate themselves. Hence "the fears and antagonisms that accompany high levels of ethnic activity may be a result of ethnification rather than its root cause."[56] Kuran does not refer to group polarization. But an understanding of this phenomenon would much fortify his analysis by showing how within-group discussion (which is, under conditions of ethnification, an increasingly large percentage of total discussion) can ensure that ethnic groups, and individual members of ethnic groups, end up with a far stronger ethnic identification than that of the median member before discussions began. Informational and reputational pressures have undoubtedly had effects in the Middle East. In the extreme case, the result might be war.[57] And when a war begins, group polarization, if it operates at the national level, can help ensure continued hostility and antagonism.

## The Internet, Communications Policy, and Mass Deliberation

There is good reason for concern about processes of social influence on the mass media and the Internet.[58] The general danger is one of fragmentation, with certain people hearing more and louder versions of their own preexisting commitments, thus reducing the benefits that come from exposure to competing views and unnoticed problems. With greater specialization, people are increasingly able to avoid general interest newspapers and magazines and to make choices that reflect their own predispositions. The Internet is making it possible for people to design their own highly individuated communications packages, filtering out troublesome issues and disfavored voices. Long before the Internet, it was possible to discuss the "racial stratification of the public sphere" by reference to divergences between white and African-American newspapers.[59] New communications technologies may increase this phenomenon.

An understanding of group polarization explains why a fragmented communications market may create problems. A "plausible hypothesis is that the Internet-like setting is most likely to create a strong tendency toward group polarization when the members of the group feel some sense of group identity."[60] If certain people are deliberating with many like-minded others, views will not merely be reinforced but instead shifted to more extreme points. This cannot be said to be bad by itself—maybe the increased extremism is good—but it is certainly troublesome if diverse social groups are led, through predictable mechanisms, toward increasingly opposing and ever more extreme views. As we have seen, group polarization is intensified if people are speaking anonymously and if attention is drawn, through one or another means, to group membership. Many Internet discussion groups have precisely this feature. The Internet is serving, for many, as a breeding ground for extremism.

An understanding of group polarization raises more general issues about communications policy. Under the "fairness doctrine," now largely abandoned,[61] broadcasters were required to devote time to public issues and to allow an opportunity for opposing views to speak. The second prong of the doctrine was designed to ensure that listeners would not be exposed to any single view. When the Federal Communications Commission (FCC) abandoned the fairness doctrine, it did so on the ground that this second prong led broadcasters, much of the time, to avoid controversial issues entirely and to present views in a way that suggested a bland uniformity.[62] Subsequent research has suggested that the elimination of the fairness doctrine has indeed produced a flowering of controversial substantive programming, frequently with an extreme view of one kind or another; consider talk radio.[63] Typically this is regarded as a story of wonderfully successful deregulation. But from the standpoint of group polarization, things are more complicated. The growth of issues-oriented programming with a strong, often extreme view may create group polarization, and all too many people might be exposed to louder echoes of their own voices, resulting in social fragmentation, en-mity, and often misunderstanding. Perhaps it is better for people to hear fewer controversial views than for them to hear a single such view, stated over and over again.

It is not clear what can be done about this situation. But it certainly makes sense to consider communications initiatives that would ensure that people would be exposed to a range of reasonable views, not simply one. This was the original inspiration for the fairness doctrine, and there is reason to encourage media outlets to implement the same goal today. An appreci-ation of group polarization suggests that creative approaches should be de-signed to ensure that people do not simply read their "Daily Me."[64]

### Deliberation and Polarization in Public Institutions

*Juries.*   Group polarization is well documented on juries; there is much di-rect evidence here. In experimental settings, polarization has been found in numerous settings with respect to guilt and innocence, and indeed this ap-pears to be an uncontradicted finding.[65] Outside of the experimental setting, we know that the predeliberation verdict predicts the final outcome 90 per-cent of the time in cases where juries do not hang; this provides "powerful presumptive evidence that group polarization occurs in real juries."[66]

*Independent regulatory commissions.*   The twentieth century saw the rise of a number of "independent" regulatory commissions, including the FCC, the Federal Trade Commission (FTC), and the National Labor Relations Board (NLRB). A striking but generally overlooked provision of the relevant statutes requires bipartisan membership: The independent commissions must be di-vided between Republicans and Democrats. A simple and undoubtedly cor-rect explanation of this unusual requirement is that Congress wanted to ensure that no commission would be dominated by any single party. But an understanding of group polarization would strengthen any such concern on

Congress's part. An independent agency—the FCC, the NLRB, the FTL—that is all Democratic, or all Republican, might polarize toward an extreme position, probably more extreme than that of the median Democrat or Republican and possibly more extreme than that of any member standing alone. A requirement of bipartisan membership can operate as a check against movements of this kind.

*Multimember courts.*   We hear many platitudes about judicial neutrality; but judges often have a great deal of latitude, sometimes in the ultimate outcome, even more often in determining the reach of their decision. If a court consists of three or more like-minded judges, it may well end up with a relatively extreme position, more extreme in fact than the position it would occupy if it consisted of two like-minded individuals and one of a different orientation.

There is little direct confirmation of this general proposition. But considerable support comes from two intriguing studies of judicial behavior on the D.C. Circuit.[67] Both of these studies suggest that when judges on three-member panels all come from the same political party, they are likely to reach far more extreme results than when the three judges include one member from a different party. The fact that like-minded judges go to extremes seems to provide clear evidence of group polarization in action.

*Legislatures.*   Legislators are highly susceptible to group polarization, partly because of the effects of limited argument pools, perhaps above all because of social influence (and the importance of conveying a proper signal to fellow legislators and, even more, constituents). Imagine, for example, that a group of Republicans and a group of Democrats are thinking about how to vote on a proposed law—perhaps involving military spending or an increase in the minimum wage or greater environmental protection. If Republicans are speaking mostly with Republicans, and if Democrats are speaking mostly with Democrats, we should expect a hardening of views toward the more extreme points. Undoubtedly this is part (certainly not all) of the explanation of party-line voting. And it is easy to imagine similar effects on Congress as a whole.

The mechanisms of group polarization affect constituents as well. We can imagine a society in which Republicans speak mostly with each other; we can imagine a society in which Democrats speak mostly with one another too. If this is the situation, polarization should occur within political camps. We might think that group polarization supplies one of the many factors behind the sharp split between Republicans and Democrats on the impeachment of President Clinton in 1998.

### The Electoral College: A Note

My last point is connected to many recent political events. Consider, for example, the closely contested 2000 presidential election in the United States. In that election, attention was newly focused on an apparently bizarre constitutional creature: the electoral college. For my purposes here, the central point is that the electoral college was originally supposed to be a deliberative institution, filtering popular will by ensuring discussion among a diverse set of informed people. In Alexander Hamilton's words,

> the immediate election should be made by men most capable of analyzing the qualities adapted to the station, and acting under circumstances favorable to deliberation and to a judicious combination of all the reasons and inducements, which were proper to govern their choice. A small number of persons, selected by their fellow citizens from the general mass, will be most likely to possess the information and discernment requisite to so complicated an investigation.[68]

This seems to be a self-conscious recognition of the need for institutions to ensure deliberation and to counteract the risk of polarization, by responding to "a judicious combination of all the reasons and inducements."

In the United States, we all now know, the president is chosen not by a majority of the people but by the majority of "electors," generally chosen by the state's political parties. The electors are apportioned to each state, in a number corresponding to the sum of the number of senators (always two) and the number of members of the House of Representatives (determined by population). A principal effect of this way of allocating electors is to strengthen the power of small states, which have more electoral votes than their population would justify. In all states (with tiny exceptions not relevant here), the majority vote within the state determines the candidate to whom all electoral votes will go.

In American debates in 2000, the electoral college was alternately criticized as an intolerably undemocratic body and supported as an indispensable way of ensuring protection of small states. But both the criticism and the support miss the original point. The founders of the United States Constitution were extremely proud of the electoral college, thinking of it as nearly perfect and indeed as one of the least criticized, and most approved, parts of the Constitution. For Hamilton, the method for selecting the president "is almost the only part of the system, of any consequence, which has escaped without severe censure." In Hamilton's view, "if the manner of it be not perfect, it is at least excellent," not least because it affords "as little opportunity as possible to tumult and discord."[69]

With the device of the electoral college, the framers sought to ensure a compromise between two extremes. The first would be to place the election of the president in the hands of Congress. The problem with that route is that it would make the president too dependent on the legislature. The second would be to allow direct popular election of the president. The problem with that route is that it would make the selection too dependent on uninformed, and manipulable, popular will. Thus it was expressly urged, at the convention itself, that a "popular election in this case is radically vicious. The ignorance of the people would put it in the power of some one set of men dispersed through the Union & acting in Concert to delude them into any appointment."[70] The electoral college would ensure independence, accountability to the public, and, best of all, broad deliberation among heterogeneous people, creating a situation where manipulation and group polarization could not occur.

The most important point here is that the electors were originally supposed to engage in deliberation, choosing the president independently, with regard for the views of constituents but without at all being bound by them. A large part of the founders' theory here was that the people would be most unlikely to know much about candidates for president, and that voters would be in a much better position to choose electors, who would be local figures, than remote aspirants to national leadership. In creating the electoral college, the founders sought to ensure that those choosing the president would be sufficiently independent to engage in their deliberative tasks. And in the early days of the republic, the electoral college did indeed function as a deliberative body. In this light we can see that the electoral college was, at its inception, of a piece with the many parts of the constitutional framework that attempted to combine responsiveness with reflectiveness.

Of course the electoral college is very different today. Not long after the founding, a practice developed by which the electors would not be independent but would be bound, in fact if not in law, by the votes of their constituents. The postframing rise of the party system was crucial here. For well over a century, people have voted for presidential candidates rather than electors, and political parties have selected the relevant slates of electors. It is therefore almost inevitable that electors will support the candidate of their own party. Indeed, a number of states legally bind electors to do exactly that. Members of the electoral college now follow the majority's vote rather than deliberating.

Under modern circumstances, this is as it should be. In an ironic reversal of the framers' expectations, people know far more about presidential candidates than about electors. It would be unacceptably undemocratic to allow comparatively anonymous people to choose the president on their own. Today the principal function of the electoral college is not to promote deliberation but to give considerable power to small states by allocating them more electors than their populations would allow. With these statements I do not mean to take a position on proposals to abolish the electoral college; to say the least, those proposals raise many complexities. The central point is that the electoral college was originally meant to promote deliberation in circumstances in which the public would be both insufficiently informed and prone to polarization.

## Deliberative Trouble?

Widespread error and social fragmentation are likely to result when like-minded people, insulated from others, move in extreme directions simply because of limited argument pools and parochial influences. In terms of designing institutions, and even constitutions, the best response is to ensure that members of deliberating groups, whether small or large, will not isolate themselves from competing views—a point with implications for multimember courts, open primaries, freedom of association, and the architecture of the Internet. Here, then, is a plea for ensuring that deliberation occurs within a large and heterogeneous public sphere and for guarding against a situation in which like-minded people are walling themselves off from alternative perspectives.

But there is a difficulty with this response: A certain measure of isolation will, in some cases, be crucial to the development of ideas and approaches that would not otherwise emerge and that deserve a social hearing. Members of low-status groups are often quiet within heterogeneous bodies. Deliberation, in such bodies, tends to be dominated by high-status members. Any shift—in technology, norms, or legal practice—that increases the number of deliberating enclaves will increase the diversity of society's aggregate "argument pool" while also increasing the danger of extremism and instability, ultimately even violence. Shifts toward a general "public sphere," without much in the way of enclave deliberation, will decrease the likelihood of extremism and instability—but at the same time produce what may be a stifling uniformity. And shifts toward more in the way of enclave deliberation will increase society's aggregate "argument pool," hence enrich the marketplace of ideas, while also increasing extremism, fragmentation, hostility, and perhaps even violence.

It is not simple to solve the resulting conundrums. But some general lessons do emerge. A democratic constitution ensures social spaces for deliberation by like-minded persons but also increases the likelihood that members of the relevant groups are not isolated from conversation with people having quite different views. The goal of that conversation is to promote the interests of those inside and outside the relevant enclaves, by subjecting group members to competing positions, by allowing them to exchange views with others and to see things from their point of view, and by ensuring that the wider society does not marginalize, and thus insulate itself from, views that may turn out to be right or at least informative. Ideas of this kind have a central place in the American constitutional framework—with the system of checks and balances, bicameralism, and the framers' explicit rejection of the "right to instruct" representatives. They also have an important emerging place on the Internet, where there are many current efforts to create a "public sphere" involving discussions among diverse people who would otherwise be in contact largely with those who are like-minded. In these ways, an understanding of group polarization is helpful in obtaining a better understanding of how institutions, both old and new, might be restructured in the service of democratic ideals.

## Doubts and Questions

*Why deliberate?* It should be clear that the phenomenon of group polarization, placed alongside the phenomenon of social cascades, raises severe doubts about the view that deliberation is a simple or unambiguous good. Of course deliberation might be justified on many different grounds. It may be that on the question at issue there is a truth of the matter—a correct answer—and deliberation might be the best way of reaching it. Perhaps group decisions, based on an exchange of reasons, are more likely to be right than decisions made by individuals. Or we might favor deliberation on a quite different ground; doubting whether there is a truth of the matter, a democracy might seek a deliberative process on the theory that this is the only reasonable and fair way to reach a decision that will be imposed on the group. Or deliberation might be seen as a way to reach shared understandings and to ensure a form of mutual respect. Group polarization does not create obvious difficulties for all of these accounts. But it does raise real questions about the widespread idea that deliberation is the best way of producing right answers.

If the effect of deliberation is to move people toward a more extreme point in the direction of their original tendency, why is it anything to celebrate? The underlying mechanisms do not provide much reason for confidence. If people are shifting their position in order to maintain their reputation and self-conception, within groups that may or may not be representative of the public as a whole, is there any reason to think that deliberation is making things better rather than worse? If shifts are occurring as a result of partial and frequently skewed argument pools, the product of deliberative judgments may be far worse than the product of simply taking the median of predeliberation judgments.

To be sure, those who emphasize the ideals associated with deliberative democracy tend to emphasize its preconditions, which include political equality, an absence of strategic behavior, full information, and the goal of "reaching understanding."[71] In real-world deliberations, behavior is often strategic; people lack full information; and equality is absent. But group polarization is likely to occur even in the face of equality and entirely conscientious efforts at reaching both truth and understanding. The existence of a limited argument pool, strengthening the existing tendency within the group, will operate in favor of group polarization even if no one behaves strategically and by itself will produce group polarization whether or not social influence is operating.

In any case, social influences need not be inconsistent with the effort to produce truth and understanding. When people attempt to position themselves in a way that fits with their best self-conception, or their preferred self-presentation, nothing has gone wrong, even from the standpoint of deliberation's most enthusiastic defenders. Perhaps group polarization could be reduced or even eliminated if we emphasized that good deliberation has full information as a precondition; by hypothesis, argument pools would not be limited if all information were available. But the requirement of full information is extremely stringent, and if there is already full information, the role of deliberation is greatly reduced. In any case the group polarization phenomenon suggests that in real-world situations, deliberation is hardly guaranteed to increase the likelihood of arriving at truth.

*Movements right and wrong.* Of course we cannot say, from the mere fact of polarization, that there has been a movement in the wrong direction. Perhaps the more extreme tendency is better; recall that group polarization is likely to have fueled the antislavery movement and many others that deserve to meet with widespread approval. Extremism should not be a word of opprobrium; everything depends on what extremists are arguing *for*. In addition, group polarization can be explained partly by reference to the fact that people who are confident are likely to be persuasive; and it is sensible to say that as a statistical matter, though not an invariable truth, people who are confident are more likely to be right. But when group discussion tends to lead people to more strongly held versions of the same view with which they began, and when social influences and limited argument pools are responsible, there is little reason for great confidence in the effects of deliberation.

We can go further. If it is possible to identify a particular viewpoint as unreasonable, it is also possible to worry about group discussion among people who share that viewpoint. This is a basis for justifying the decision to make criminal conspiracy an independent crime; the act of conspiring itself raises the stakes, and by hypothesis the actions ultimately at issue are unlawful and beyond the pale. An analogy can be found in discussions among hate groups, on the Internet, and elsewhere. If the underlying views are unreasonable, it makes sense to fear that these discussions may fuel increasing hatred. This does not mean that the discussions can or should be regulated in a system dedicated to freedom of speech. But it does raise questions about the idea that "more speech" is necessarily an adequate remedy.

## The Virtues of Heterogeneity

The simplest lesson here involves the need to design good institutions, through constitutions and otherwise. Institutions might well be designed to ensure that when shifts are occurring, it is not because of arbitrary or illegitimate constraints on the available range of arguments. This is a central task of constitutional design. A system of checks and balances might itself be defended, not as an undemocratic check on the will of the people but as an effort to protect against potentially harmful consequences of group discussion.

We have seen that the system of bicameralism, often challenged on populist grounds, might be defended by reference to the risk of group polarization. Indeed the great lectures on law of the American founder James Wilson spoke of bicameralism in just these terms, referring to "instances, in which the people have become the miserable victims of passions, operating on their government without restraint" and seeing a "single legislature" as prone to "sudden and violent fits of despotism, injustice, and cruelty."[72] Efforts to assure a plurality of views, on regulatory commissions and courts, can be defended on similar grounds. As supporting evidence, consider the findings that cohesive groups of like-minded people, whose members are connected by close social ties, often suppress dissent and reach inferior decisions—whereas heterogeneous groups, building identification through focus on a common task rather than through other social ties, tend to produce the best outcomes.[73]

To explore some of the advantages of heterogeneity, imagine a deliberating body consisting of all citizens in the relevant group; this may mean all citizens in a community, a state, a nation, or the world. By hypothesis, the argument pool would be very large. It would be limited only to the extent that the set of citizen views was similarly limited. Social influences would undoubtedly remain. Hence people might shift because of a desire to maintain their reputation and self-conception by standing in a certain relation to the rest of the group. But to the extent that deliberation revealed to people that their private position was different, in relation to the group, from what they thought it was, any shift would be in response to an accurate understanding of all relevant citizens and not a product of an accidental, skewed group sample.

This thought experiment does not suggest that this deliberating body would be ideal. Perhaps all citizens, presenting all individual views, would offer a skewed picture from the point of view of what is right or what is just. In a pervasively confused or unjust society, a deliberating body consisting of everyone may produce nothing to celebrate. Perhaps weak arguments would be made and repeated and repeated again, while good arguments would be offered infrequently. As we will see below, it is often important to ensure enclaves in which polarization will take place precisely in order to ensure the emergence of views that are suppressed, by social influences or otherwise, but reasonable or even right. But at least a deliberating body of all citizens would remove many of the distortions in some settings, where generally like-minded people, not exposed to others, shift in large part because of that limited exposure. Hence the outcomes of these deliberations will not be a product of the arbitrariness that can be introduced by skewed argument pools.

This is in fact a way of vindicating the passages from Hamilton and Rawls with which I began. On this view, Hamilton and Rawls are not naïve enthusiasts for deliberation, oblivious to empirical realities, but should be taken to be insisting on the advantages of heterogeneity, in which a wide argument pool is placed before the deliberators. This is a central part of the design of democracy's constitution. Consider here Hamilton's enthusiasm for the "jarring of parties" within a bicameral legislature, a process that, Hamilton contended, would "check the excesses of the majority"—excesses that can be reinterpreted in terms of the phenomena I have been describing. The framers of the Bill of Rights originally rejected a "right to instruct," by which constituents could tell their representatives how to vote; the rejection was based on the idea that one job of the representative was to "consult" with people from different states of the union, and to make decisions only after that consultation.[74] The rejection of the right to instruct, on the theory that deliberators should be talking to people with different experiences and viewpoints, shows an appreciation of the risks of group polarization.

As I have suggested, central features of the constitutional design, including the system of checks and balances, can be understood in similar terms. Indeed James Madison defended his preference for large election districts and long length of service as a way of counteracting polarization-type forces within particular constituencies. Rawls's reference to the need to "combin[e] information and enlarg[e] the range of arguments" through discussion with a range of people strikes precisely the same note.


## Enclave Deliberation and Suppressed Voices

I have not yet explored the potential vices of heterogeneity and the potentially good effects of deliberating "enclaves" consisting of groups of like-minded individuals. It seems obvious that such groups can be extremely important in a heterogeneous society, not least because members of some demographic groups tend to be especially quiet when participating in broader deliberative bodies. A special advantage of "enclave deliberation" is that it promotes the development of positions that would otherwise be invisible, silenced, or squelched in general debate. In numerous contexts, this is a great advantage. Many social movements have been made possible through this route (as possible examples, consider feminism, the civil rights movement, environmentalism, and the movement for gay and lesbian rights). The efforts of marginalized groups to exclude outsiders, and even of political parties to limit their primaries to party members, can be justified in similar terms. Even if group polarization is at work—perhaps *because* group polarization is at work—enclaves can provide a wide range of social benefits, not least because they greatly enrich the social "argument pool."

The central empirical point here is that in deliberating bodies, high-status members tend to initiate communication more than others, and their ideas are more influential, partly because low-status members lack confidence in their own abilities, partly because they fear retribution.[75] For example, women's ideas are often less influential and sometimes are "suppressed altogether in mixed-gender groups,"[76] and in ordinary circumstances, cultural minorities have disproportionately little influence on decisions by culturally mixed groups.[77] It makes sense to promote deliberating enclaves in which members of multiple groups may speak with one another and develop their views—a point that bears on the constitution of multicultural societies.

But there is a serious danger in such enclaves. The danger is that members will move to positions that lack merit but are predictable consequences of the particular circumstances of enclave deliberation. In the extreme case, enclave deliberation might even put social stability at risk (for better or for worse). And it is impossible to say, in the abstract, that those who sort themselves into enclaves will generally move in a direction that is desirable for society at large or even for its own members. It is easy to think of examples to the contrary, as, for example, in the rise of Nazism, hate groups, and numerous "cults" of various sorts.

There is no simple solution to the dangers of enclave deliberation. Sometimes the threat to social stability is desirable. As Thomas Jefferson wrote, turbulence can be "productive of good. It prevents the degeneracy of government, and nourishes a general attention to . . . public affairs. I hold . . . that a little rebellion now and then is a good thing."[78] Turbulence to one side, any judgments about enclave deliberation are hard to make without a sense of the underlying substance—of what it is that divides the enclave from the rest of society. From the standpoint of designing institutions, the problem is that any effort to promote enclave deliberation will ensure group polarization among a wide range of groups, some necessary to the pursuit of justice, others likely to promote injustice, and some potentially quite dangerous. In this light we should be able to see more clearly the sense in which Edmund Burke's conception of representation—rejecting "local purposes" and "local prejudices" in favor of "the general reason of the whole"[79]—is not accidentally but is instead *essentially* conservative (speaking purely descriptively, as a safeguard of existing practices). The reason is that the submersion of "local purposes" and "local prejudices" into a heterogenous "deliberative assembly"[80] will inevitably tend to weaken the resolve of groups—and particularly low-status or marginalized groups—whose purely internal deliberations would produce a high degree of polarization.

Hence James Madison—with his fear of popular passions producing "a rage for paper money, for an abolition of debts, for an equal division of property, or for any other improper or wicked project"[81]—would naturally be drawn to a Burkean conception of representation, favoring large election districts and long length of service to counteract the forces of polarization. By contrast, those who believe that "destabilization" of current practices is an intrinsic good, or that the status quo contains sufficient injustice that it is worthwhile to incur the risks of encouraging polarization on the part of diverse groups, will, or should, be drawn to a system that enthusiastically promotes insular deliberation within enclaves.

In a nation in which most people are confused or evil, enclave deliberation might be the only way to develop a sense of clarity or justice, at least for some. But even in such a nation, enclave deliberation is unlikely to produce change unless its members are eventually brought into contact with others. In constitutional democracies, the best response is to ensure that any such enclaves are not walled off from competing views, and that at certain points there is an exchange of views between enclave members and those who disagree with them. It is total or nearly total self-insulation, rather than group deliberation as such, that carries with it the most serious dangers, often in the highly unfortunate (and sometimes deadly) combination of extremism with marginality.

An appreciation of group polarization helps show why a constitutional democracy takes steps to protect deliberation within enclaves, to ensure that those inside enclaves hear alternative views, and to ensure as well that those outside of particular enclaves are exposed to what enclave members have to say. Above all, it is important to avoid a situation in which people are exposed only to softer and louder echoes of their own voices. In a diverse society, this form of self-insulation can create serious deliberative trouble, in the form of mutual incomprehension or much worse. Constitutional arrangements will inevitably increase or reduce that trouble. What is necessary is to design approaches ensuring that heterogeneity, far from being a source of social fragmentation, will operate as a creative force, helping to identify problems and even solutions that might otherwise escape notice.

# Constitutional Principles without Constitutional Theories

Consider the following problems:

1. In its constitution, now in early draft, a nation bans "cruel and unusual punishment." A large segment of society believes that capital punishment is necessarily "cruel and unusual"; many people want to insert an explicit ban on capital punishment into the constitution. But many other people disagree, and many more are unsure what they think. What should constitution-makers do about the problem?

2. A new law bans the transmission of "indecent" materials on the Internet to "anyone under the age of eighteen." The law is challenged on the ground that it violates the right to free speech. Those challenging the law argue that the Internet is no different from any other place where speech occurs and that the ordinary constitutional protections should apply. Those who defend the law argue that the Internet raises unique problems, because it is so easy to send materials to thousands or even millions of people. How should a court respond to the challenge to this law?

3. In response to a history of racial discrimination, an American university adopts a complicated system of "affirmative action," unambiguously giving a preference to African Americans in the admissions process. The preference is challenged on constitutional grounds. Should the Court invalidate the admissions system? If so, what should it say?

4. Public officials are supporting a law that would provide significant new protections for endangered species. Many people are defending the law in religious terms, as a way of ensuring that human beings do not disrupt "God's creation." Other people are defending the law as a way of ensuring against disruption of delicate ecological systems. How should public officials explain their support for this law?

In most democratic nations, citizens must proceed in the face of conflict and disagreement on the most fundamental matters. The existence of diverse values—of pluralism and even multiculturalism—seems to threaten the very possibility of a constitutional order. People disagree on rights, on the good life, on equality and liberty, on the nature and the existence of God. How can constitutionalism be feasible in these circumstances?

Deliberative trouble is an obvious risk here. People might find themselves unable to bridge intractable disagreements; if so, the project of constitution-making could well break down. In some nations, such as Israel, the failure to produce a constitution at all is largely a result of this problem. As in democratic discussion in general, group polarization can play an important part in debates over constitution-making and constitutional interpretation. At the phase of constitutional design, people who find themselves members of one camp might talk themselves into a fixed position, one that moves increasingly far away from the views of others. The astonishing success of constitutional design in South Africa was possible largely because people of one view were constantly in discussion with people of opposing views. Respect for reasonable disagreement could produce outcomes acceptable to all.

Something very different has often happened with debates about constitutional interpretation, at least in the United States. Partly because they talk mostly among themselves, some people think that it is obvious that any reasonable person would favor their own method of interpretation—say, the idea that the Constitution should be construed in accordance with the framers' "original understanding." Perhaps they are right. But I think that they are wrong, and in any case I am sure that they are too sure of their position. If, as Learned Hand wrote, the spirit of liberty is that spirit that "is not too sure that it is right," like-minded people, in both constitutional design and constitutional interpretation, often violate the spirit of liberty.

My basic suggestion is that people can often agree on constitutional *practices*, and even on constitutional rights, when they cannot agree on constitutional *theories*. In other words, well-functioning constitutional orders try to solve problems, including problems of deliberative trouble, through reaching *incompletely theorized agreements*. Sometimes these agreements involve abstractions, accepted amid severe disagreements on particular cases. Thus people who disagree on incitement to violence and hate speech can accept a general free speech principle, and those who argue about homosexuality and sex equality can accept an abstract antidiscrimination principle. This is an important phenomenon in constitutional law and politics; it makes constitution-making possible. But sometimes incompletely theorized agreements involve concrete outcomes rather than abstractions; people can agree that a certain practice is constitutional or is not constitutional, even when the theories that underlie their judgments sharply diverge.

*Pragmatism
(Dewey
not in
index.)*

The latter phenomenon suggests that when people or groups disagree or are uncertain about an abstraction—Is equality more important than liberty? Does free will exist?—they can often make progress by moving to a level of greater particularity. They can attempt a *conceptual descent*—a descent to the lower level of abstraction. This phenomenon has an especially notable feature: It enlists silence, on certain basic questions, as a device for producing convergence despite disagreement, uncertainty, limits of time and capacity, and (most important of all) heterogeneity. Incompletely theorized agreements are thus an important source of successful constitutionalism and social stability; they also provide an important way for people to demonstrate mutual respect.

Consider some examples. People might believe that it is important to protect religious liberty while having quite diverse theories about why this is so. Some people might stress what they see as the need for social peace; others might think that religious liberty reflects a principle of mutual respect and a recognition of human dignity; others might invoke utilitarian considerations; still others may think that religious liberty is itself a theological command. Similarly, people may invoke many different grounds for their shared belief that the Constitution should ensure the separation of powers. Some may think that separation helps ensure against tyranny; others may think that it makes government more democratic; still others may think that it leads to greater efficiencies.

The agreement on these points, more particular than their supporting grounds, is incompletely theorized in the sense that the relevant participants are clear on the practice or the result without agreeing on the most general theory that accounts for it. Often people can agree on a rationale offering low-level or midlevel principles. They may agree that a rule—protecting political dissenters, allowing workers to practice their religion—makes sense without entirely agreeing on the foundations of their belief. They may accept an outcome—perhaps affirming the right to marry or protecting sexually explicit art—without understanding or converging on an ultimate ground for that acceptance. What accounts for the outcome, in terms of a full-scale theory of the right or the good, is left unexplained.

*Sort of Dworkin—esp over analysis*

There is an extreme case of incomplete theorization: *full particularity.* This phenomenon occurs when people agree on a result without agreeing on any kind of supporting rationale. Any rationale—any reason—is by definition more abstract than the result it supports. Sometimes people do not offer any reasons at all—because they do not know what those reasons are, or because they cannot agree on reasons, or because they fear that the reasons that they have would turn out, on reflection, to be inadequate and hence would be misused in the future. This is an important phenomenon in Anglo-

American law. Juries usually do not offer reasons for outcomes, and negotiators sometimes conclude that something should happen without concluding why it should happen. I will not emphasize this limiting case here and shall focus instead on outcomes accompanied by low-level or midlevel principles.

My emphasis on incompletely theorized agreements is intended partly as descriptive. These agreements are a pervasive phenomenon in constitution-making and constitutional law. But I mean to make some points about constitutionalism amid pluralism as well. In short, there are special virtues to avoiding large-scale theoretical conflicts. Incompletely theorized agreements can operate as foundations for both rules and analogies, and such agreements are especially well suited to the limits of many diverse institutions, including courts. And incompletely theorized agreements can be especially helpful as a check on the kinds of intractability, and error, that often result from social cascades and group polarization. Such agreements play a central role in the constitution of a democratic social order.

## How People Converge

It is clear that outside of law, people may agree on a *correct* outcome even though they do not have a theory to account for their judgments. You might know that dropped objects fall, that bee stings hurt, that hot air rises, and that snow melts without knowing exactly why these facts are true. The same is true for justice and morality, both in general and insofar as they bear on constitutional law. You might know that slavery is wrong, that government may not stop political protests, that every person should have just one vote, and that it is bad for government to take your land unless it pays for it without knowing exactly or entirely why these things are so. Judgments about justice or morality may be right or true even if they are reached by people who lack a full account of those judgments (though people might well do better if they try to offer such an account, a point to which I will return). A judge might know that if government punishes religious behavior, it has acted unlawfully, without having a full account of why this principle has been enacted into law or why religious liberty is part of the Constitution. We can thus offer an epistemological point: People can know *that* X is true without entirely knowing *why* X is true.

There are points about politics and constitutional law as well. Sometimes people agree on individual judgments even if they disagree on general theory. You and your neighbor might support a particular candidate or party for quite different reasons. In American constitutional law, diverse judges may agree that *Roe v Wade*, protecting the right to choose abortion, should not be overruled, though the reasons that lead each of them to that conclusion sharply diverge. Some people think that the Court should respect its own precedents; others think that *Roe* was rightly decided as a way of protecting women's equality; others think that the case was rightly decided as a way of protecting privacy; others think that the decision reflects an appropriate judgment about the social role of religion; still others think that restrictions on abortion are unlikely to protect fetuses in the world and so the decision is good for pragmatic reasons. In South Africa, judges of the Constitutional Court believe that the death penalty violates the nation's Constitution; but they do not all agree on the reasons for that conclusion. It would be easy to multiply examples.

### Rules and Analogies

Rules and analogies are the two most important methods for resolving constitutional disputes without obtaining agreement on first principles. Both of these devices—keys to public law in many nations—attempt to promote a major goal of a heterogeneous society: *to make it possible to obtain agreement where agreement is necessary and to make it unnecessary to obtain agreement where agreement is impossible.* Achievement of this goal is a crucial way of ensuring that democratic debate does not become intractable.

People can often (though not always) agree on what constitutional rules mean even when they agree on very little else. A chief advantage of constitutional rules is that they create a kind of "focal point" around which diverse people can bracket their debates. And in the face of persistent disagreement or uncertainty about what justice requires, people can reason about particular constitutional cases by reference to analogies. They point to cases in which the legal judgments are firm. They proceed from those firm judgments to the more difficult ones. This is how ordinary people tend to think.

We might consider in this regard United States Supreme Court Justice Stephen Breyer's discussion of one of the key compromises reached by the seven members of the United States Sentencing Commission.[1] As Breyer describes it, a central issue was how to proceed in the face of highly disparate philosophical premises about the goals of criminal punishment. Some people asked the commission to follow an approach to punishment based on "just deserts"—an approach that would rank criminal conduct in terms of severity.

But different commissioners had very different views about how different crimes should be ranked. In these circumstances, there could be an odd form of deliberation in which criminal punishments became ever more, and more irrationally, severe, because some commissioners would insist that the crime under consideration was worse than the previously ranked crimes. Group polarization might well aggravate this process. In any case agreement on a rational system would be unlikely to follow from efforts by the seven commissioners to rank crimes in terms of severity.

Other people urged the commission to use a model of deterrence. There were, however, major problems with this approach. We lack empirical evidence that could link detailed variations in punishment to prevention of crime, and the seven members of the commission were highly unlikely to agree that deterrence provides a full account of the aims of criminal sentencing. An approach based on deterrence seemed no better than an approach based on just deserts.

In these circumstances, what route did the commission follow? In fact the commission abandoned large theories altogether. It adopted no general view about the appropriate aims of criminal sentencing. Instead the commission adopted a rule—one founded on precedent, basing the guidelines mostly on average past practice. Consciously articulated explanations, not based on high theory, were used to support particular departures from the past.

Justice Breyer sees this effort as a necessary means of obtaining agreement and rationality within a multimember body charged with avoiding unjustifiably wide variations in sentencing. Thus his more colorful oral presentation:

> Why didn't the Commission sit down and really go and rationalize this thing and not just take history? The short answer to that is: we couldn't. We couldn't because there are such good arguments all over the place pointing in opposite directions. . . . Try listing all the crimes that there are in rank order of punishable merit. . . . Then collect results from your friends and see if they all match. I will tell you they don't.[2]

The example suggests a more general point. Through both analogies and rules, it is often possible for participants in constitutional law to converge on both abstract principles and particular outcomes without resolving large-scale issues of the right or the good. People can decide what to do when they disagree on exactly how to think. Indeed this is a crucial fact about law, including constitutional law. Some positions about legal interpretation are

best defended with the claim that they make it easier to put intractable disagreements to one side and to ensure that diverse groups, with their diverse
positions, can unify around a view about what the law is. The problem is
that diverse groups often disagree about interpretive method as well as everything else. In these circumstances, a completely theorized agreement about
how to interpret the law is unlikely, and people are more likely to converge
on particular outcomes than on method.

## Agreements and Justice

It might be asked at this point: Why is agreement so important, in democracy, constitutional interpretation, or elsewhere? The fact that people can
obtain an agreement of this sort—about the value and meaning of a right
or about the existence of a sound analogy—is no guarantee of a good outcome. Agreements may be confused or unjust. This is so whatever our criteria
may be for deciding whether an outcome is good. Perhaps an agreement on
a certain constitution would lead to a bad constitution; perhaps the constitution will be better if the agreement is deeply theorized. Perhaps the Sentencing Commission incorporated judgments that were based on ignorance,
confusion, or prejudice.

Some of the same doubts can be raised about analogies. Any analogical
argument depends on an account of some kind, and the account may be
wrong. People in positions of authority may agree that a ban on same-sex
marriages is constitutionally acceptable, because it is analogous to a ban on
marriages between uncles and nieces, which is constitutionally acceptable by
general agreement. But the analogy may be misconceived, because there are
relevant differences between the two cases and because the similarities are
far from decisive. The fact that people agree that some constitutional case A
is analogous to case B does not mean that case A *or* case B is rightly decided.
Perhaps case A should not be taken for granted. Case A might be wrong;
perhaps it forbids some practice (campaign finance regulation or restrictions
on abortion?) that should be permitted. Or maybe case A should not be
selected as the relevant foundation for analogical thinking; perhaps case Z is
more pertinent. Perhaps case B is far less like case A than case C. Problems
with analogies and low-level thinking might lead us to be more ambitious.
We may well be pushed in the direction of general theory—and toward
broader and perhaps more controversial claims—precisely because analogical
reasoners offer an inadequate and incompletely theorized account of relevant
similarities or relevant differences.

All this should be sufficient to show that the virtues of decisions by rule and by analogy are partial. Sometimes we will be pressed to be more ambitious, both in making and interpreting constitutions and in discussing matters democratically. But no system of politics and law is likely to be either just or efficient if it dispenses with rules and analogies. In fact it is not likely even to be feasible.

### Constitutions, Cases, and Incompletely Theorized Agreements

Incompletely theorized agreements play a pervasive role in constitutional law and in democracy generally. It is quite rare for a person or group completely to theorize any subject, that is, to accept both a general theory and a series of steps connecting that theory to concrete conclusions. Thus societies often have an *incompletely theorized agreement on a general principle*—incompletely theorized in the sense that people who accept the principle need not agree on what it entails in particular cases. This is the sense emphasized by the United States Supreme Court justice Oliver Wendell Holmes in his great aphorism "General principles do not decide concrete cases."[3] The agreement is incompletely theorized in the sense that it is *incompletely specified*. Much of the key work must be done by others, often through casuistical judgments, specifying the abstraction at the point of application.

Very frequently constitution-making becomes possible through this form of incompletely theorized agreement. Many constitutions contain incompletely specified standards and avoid rules, at least when it comes to the description of basic rights. Consider the cases of eastern Europe and (especially remarkably) South Africa, where constitutional provisions include many abstract provisions on whose concrete specification there has been sharp dispute. Abstract provisions protect "freedom of speech," "religious liberty," and "equality under the law," and citizens agree on those abstractions in the midst of sharp dispute about what these provisions really entail. Much lawmaking also becomes possible only because of this phenomenon. And when agreement on a written constitution is difficult or impossible—in Israel, for example, and apparently in England as well—it is because it is hard to obtain consensus on the governing abstractions.

Let us turn to a second phenomenon. Sometimes people agree on a midlevel principle but disagree about both more general theory and particular cases. People might believe, for example, that government cannot discriminate on the basis of race, without having a large-scale theory of equality and also without agreeing whether government may enact affirmative action programs or segregate prisons when racial tensions are severe. People may think that government may not regulate speech unless it can show a clear and present danger—but disagree about whether the basis for this principle (e.g., whether it is founded in utilitarian or Kantian considerations) and disagree too about whether the principle allows government to regulate a particular speech by members of a fascist political party.

To understand democratic constitutionalism, we should place particular emphasis on a third kind of phenomenon, of special interest for constitutional law in courts: incompletely theorized agreements on particular outcomes, accompanied by agreements on the narrow or low-level principles that account for them. Of course there is no algorithm by which to distinguish between a high-level theory and one that operates at an intermediate or lower level. We might consider, as conspicuous examples of high-level theories, Kantianism and utilitarianism, and see illustrations in the many distinguished (academic) efforts to understand such areas as free speech, religious liberty, property rights, and the law of equality as undergirded by highly abstract theories of the right or the good. By contrast, we might think of low-level principles as including most of the daily material of low-level constitutional justification or constitutional "doctrine"—the general class of principles and justifications that are not said to derive from any particular large theories of the right or the good, that have ambiguous relations to large theories, and that are compatible with more than one such theory.

By the term "low-level principles" I refer to something relative, not absolute; I mean to do the same thing by the terms "theories" and "abstractions" (which I use interchangeably). In this setting, the notions "low-level," "high," and "abstract" are best understood in comparative terms, like the terms "big" and "old" and "unusual." Thus the "clear and present danger" standard for regulation of speech in American law is a relative abstraction when compared with the claim that government should not stop a website counseling violence or that members of the Nazi Party should be allowed to march in Skokie, Illinois. But the "clear and present danger" idea is relatively particular when compared with the claim that nations should adopt the constitutional abstraction "freedom of speech." The term "freedom of speech" is a relative abstraction when measured against the claim that campaign finance laws are acceptable, but the same term is less abstract than the grounds that justify free speech, as in, for example, the principle of personal autonomy. What I am emphasizing here is that when people diverge on some (relatively) high-level proposition, they might be able to agree when they attempt a conceptual descent and lower the level of abstraction.

In analogical reasoning, this phenomenon occurs all the time. People might think that A is like B and is covered by the same low-level principle, without agreeing on a deep theory to explain why the low-level principle is sound. They agree on the matter of similarity without agreeing on a large-scale account of what makes the two things similar. In the law of discrimination, for example, many people think that sex discrimination is "like" race discrimination and should be treated similarly, even if they lack or cannot agree on a general theory of when discrimination is unacceptable. In the law of free speech, many people agree that a ban on speech by a communist is "like" a ban on speech by a member of a fascist political party and should be treated similarly—even if they lack or cannot agree on a general theory about the foundations of the free speech principle.

## Incomplete Theorization and the Constructive Uses of Silence

What might be said on behalf of incompletely theorized agreements about the content of a constitution, or incompletely theorized judgments about particular constitutional cases, or incompletely theorized judgments in democratic debate? Some people think of incomplete theorization as quite unfortunate—as embarrassing, or reflective of some important problem, or even philistine. When people theorize, by raising the level of abstraction, they do so to reveal bias, or confusion, or inconsistency. Surely participants in politics and constitutional law should not abandon this effort.

There is important truth in these usual thoughts; it would not be sensible to celebrate theoretical modesty at all times and in all contexts. Sometimes incompletely theorized agreements produce a mess. Sometimes participants in constitutional law and politics have sufficient information, and sufficient agreement, to be very ambitious. The attack on slavery is an example; so too, perhaps, the attack on sex discrimination. But incompletely theorized judgments are an important and valuable part of both private and public life. They help make constitutions and constitutional law possible; they even help make social life possible. Most of their virtues involve *the constructive uses of silence*, an important social and legal phenomenon. Especially in a diverse society, silence—on something that may prove false, obtuse, or excessively contentious—can help minimize conflict, allow the present to learn from the future, and save a great deal of time and expense. What is said and resolved is no more important than what is left out. Let us explore why this is so.

The first and most obvious point is that incompletely theorized agreements about constitutional principles and cases are well suited to a world—and especially a legal world—containing social disagreement on large-scale issues and subject to group polarization and social cascades. By definition, such agreements have the large advantage of allowing a convergence on particular outcomes by people unable to reach anything like an accord on general principles. This advantage is associated not only with the simple need to decide cases but also with social stability, which could not exist if fundamental disagreements broke out in every case of public or private dispute.

Second, incompletely theorized agreements can promote two goals of a constitutional democracy and a liberal legal system: to enable people to live together and to permit them to show each other a measure of reciprocity and mutual respect. The use of low-level principles or rules allows judges on multimember bodies and also citizens generally to find commonality and thus a common way of life without producing unnecessary antagonism. Both rules and low-level principles make it unnecessary to reach areas in which disagreement is fundamental.

Perhaps even more important, incompletely theorized agreements allow people to show each other a high degree of mutual respect, or civility, or reciprocity. Frequently ordinary people disagree in some deep way on an issue—what to do in the Middle East, pornography, homosexual marriages—and sometimes they agree not to discuss that issue much, as a way of deferring to each other's strong convictions and showing a measure of reciprocity and respect (even if they do not at all respect the particular conviction that is at stake). If reciprocity and mutual respect are desirable, it follows that public officials or judges, perhaps even more than ordinary people, should not challenge their fellow citizens' deepest and most defining commitments, at least if those commitments are reasonable and if there is no need for them to do so.

To be sure, some fundamental commitments might appropriately be challenged in the legal system or within other multimember bodies. Some such commitments are ruled off-limits by the constitution itself. Many provisions involving basic rights have this function. Of course it is not always disrespectful to disagree with someone in a fundamental way; on the contrary, such disagreements may sometimes reflect profound respect. When the defining commitments are based on demonstrable errors of fact or logic, it is appropriate to contest them. So too when those commitments are rooted in a rejection of the basic dignity of all human beings (see the treatment of the anticaste principle in chapter 7) or when it is necessary to undertake the contest to resolve a genuine problem. But many cases can be resolved in an incompletely theorized way, and this is the ordinary stuff of constitutional law; that is what I am emphasizing here.

For people acting as arbiters of social controversies, incompletely theorized agreements have the crucial function of reducing the political cost of enduring disagreements. If participants in constitutional law disavow large-scale theories, then losers in particular cases lose much less. They lose a decision but not the world. They may win on another occasion. Their own theory has not been rejected or ruled inadmissible. When the authoritative rationale for the result is disconnected from abstract theories of the good or the right, the losers can submit to legal obligations, even if reluctantly, without being forced to renounce their largest ideals.

In constitutional law, incompletely theorized agreements are especially valuable when a society seeks moral evolution and progress over time. Consider the area of equality, where many democracies have seen considerable change in the past and will inevitably see much more in the future. A completely theorized judgment would be unable to accommodate changes in facts or values. If a culture really did attain a theoretical end-state, it would become too rigid and calcified; we would know what we thought about everything. This would disserve posterity. Hence incompletely theorized agreements are a key to debates over equality in both law and politics, with issues being raised about whether gender, sexual orientation, age, disability, and other differences are analogous to race; such agreements have the important advantage of allowing a large degree of openness to new facts and perspectives. At one point, we might think that homosexual relations are akin to incest; at another point, we might find the analogy bizarre. Of course a completely theorized judgment would have many virtues if it were correct. But at any particular moment in time, this is an unlikely prospect for human beings, not excluding judges in constitutional disputes or those entrusted with the task of creating constitutional provisions. Recall here Learned Hand's suggestion that the spirit of liberty is "not too sure that it is right."

Compare practical reasoning in ordinary life. At a certain time, you may well refuse to make decisions that seem foundational in character—about, for example, whether to get married within the next year, or whether to have two, three, or four children, or whether to live in San Francisco or New York. Part of the reason for this refusal is knowledge that your understandings of both facts and values may well change. Indeed, your identity may itself change in important and relevant ways, and for this reason a set of commitments in advance—something like a fully theorized conception of your life course—would make no sense. Legal systems and nations are not very different.

## Conceptual Ascents for Constitutional Law?

Borrowing from Henry Sidgwick's writings on ethical method,[4] a critic might insist that constitutional law should frequently use ambitious theories.[5] For example, there is often good reason for people interested in constitutional rights to raise the level of abstraction and ultimately to resort to large-scale theory. As a practical matter, concrete judgments about particular cases can prove inadequate for morality or constitutional law. Suppose, for example, that there is a controversy about the existence of a right to engage in a certain kind of speech on the Internet. Sometimes people do not have clear intuitions about how such cases should come out. Sometimes seemingly similar cases provoke different reactions, and it is necessary to raise the level of theoretical ambition to explain whether those different reactions are justified, or to show that the seemingly similar cases are different after all. Sometimes people simply disagree. By looking at broader principles, we may be able to mediate the disagreement.

In any case there is a problem of explaining our considered judgments about particular cases, in order to see whether they are not just a product of accident. When a modest judge joins an opinion that is incompletely theorized, he or she has to rely on a reason or a principle, justifying one outcome rather than another. The opinion must itself refer to a reason or principle; it cannot just announce a victor. Perhaps the low level principle is wrong, because it fails to fit with other cases or because it is not defensible as a matter of (legally relevant) political morality.

In short, the incompletely theorized agreement may be nothing to celebrate. It may be wrong or unreliable. If a judge is reasoning well, she should have before her a range of other cases, C through Z, in which the principle is tested against others and refined. At least if she is a distinguished judge, she will experience a kind of "conceptual ascent," in which the more or less isolated and small low-level principle is finally made part of a more general theory. Perhaps this would be a paralyzing task, and perhaps this judge need not often attempt it. But it is an appropriate model for understanding law and an appropriate aspiration for evaluating judicial and political outcomes. Judges who insist on staying at a low level of theoretical ambition are philistines—even ostriches.

There is some truth in this response. At least if they have time, moral reasoners thinking about basic rights should try to achieve vertical and horizontal consistency, not just the local pockets of coherence offered by incompletely theorized agreements. In democratic processes, it is appropriate and sometimes indispensable to challenge existing practice in abstract terms. But this challenge to incompletely theorized agreements should not be taken for more than it is worth, for any interest in conceptual ascent must take account of the distinctive characteristics of the arena in which real-world judges must do their work.

As I have noted, incompletely theorized agreements have many virtues, including the facilitation of convergence, the reduction of costs of disagreement, and the demonstration of humility and mutual respect. All this can be critical to successful constitution-making in a pluralistic society. The points bear on constitutional cases as well. In a well-functioning constitutional democracy, judges are often reluctant to invoke philosophical abstractions as a basis for invalidating the outcomes of electoral processes. They are reluctant because they know that they may misunderstand the relevant philosophical arguments, and they seek to show respect to the diverse citizens in their nation.

There are many lurking questions here. How we do know whether moral or political judgments are right? How do moral and political judgments bear on the content of law? What is the relation between provisional or considered judgments about particulars and corresponding judgments about abstractions? Sometimes people interested in constitutional law write as if abstract theoretical judgments, or abstract theories, have a kind of reality and hardness that particular judgments lack, or as if abstract theories provide the answers to examination questions that particular judgments, frail as they are, may pass or fail. On this view, theories are searchlights that illuminate particular judgments and show them for what they really are. But we might think instead that there is no special magic in theories or abstractions and that theories are simply the means by which people make sense of the judgments that constitute their ethical, legal, and political worlds. The abstract deserves no priority over the particular; neither should be treated as foundational.[6] A (poor or crude) abstract theory may simply be a confused way of trying to make sense of our considered judgments about particular constitutional cases, which may be much better than the theory. In fact it is possible that moral judgments, including the distinctive kinds that result in constitutional law, are best described not as an emanation of a broad theory but instead as a reflection of prototypical cases, or "precedents," from which moral thinkers—ordinary citizens and experts—work.

## Are Incompletely Theorized Agreements Conservative?

At this point it would be possible to object that incompletely theorized agreements are too conservative, too respectful of existing practice. Sometimes a good theory might show that it is important to produce large-scale changes. Why should constitutional law be so cautious?

There is some truth in the objection. Sometimes incompletely theorized agreements take the form of incremental decisions, building carefully on what has been said before. Incrementalism is unlikely to produce large changes quickly. But the objection is mostly rooted in confusions, because it does not make important distinctions. Note, first, that constitutional provisions taking the form of incompletely specified abstractions—"equal protection of the law," "unfair discrimination"—can operate as a basis for large challenges to longstanding practices. In South Africa, for example, the constitutional ban on "unfair discrimination" was incompletely specified, and the nation lacked a single understanding of what lay behind it; but everyone agrees that the ban is designed to challenge old practices and to establish new ones. The South African courts have interpreted the provision in exactly this spirit.[7] In the United States, the equal protection clause has had a similar role, having been used as a basis for invalidating discrimination on the basis of sex, sexual orientation, disability, and the marital status of one's parents.

Note, second, that insofar as judicial decisions are incompletely theorized agreements, they often work by analogy; and nothing need be conservative about analogical reasoning. Everything depends on the cases from which analogizers begin, and the process of reasoning by which they extract principles from those cases.[8] Consider, for example, the United States Supreme Court's decision in *Brown v. Board of Education*, invalidating school segregation. By analogy, the ban on school segregation was invoked to ban all racial segregation; to strike down laws forbidding racial intermarriage; to draw sex discrimination into question; to challenge race-conscious child custody decisions; to question affirmative action programs; and more. In fact *Brown* inaugurated a kind of legal revolution, not because the Court adopted a general theory but because subsequent courts used that incompletely theorized decision as a basis for other incompletely theorized decisions, most of them highly critical of longstanding practices.

Of course it is true that incompletely theorized decisions that are incremental and narrow produce less change than decisions, whether or not incompletely theorized, that call for immediate, large-scale revisions in existing practices. Judges drawn to incomplete theorization are nervous about such revisions, mostly because they are not sure that they are right, because they know that they are sometimes intervening into complex systems, and because they fear unintended consequences.[9] To this extent, a judiciary that favors incompletely theorized agreements will indeed be conservative, and sensibly so. But because constitutional abstractions can call for significant change and because analogical reasoning can do the same thing, it would be a big mistake to identify enthusiasm for incompletely theorized agreements with constitutional conservatism (see chapter 3 for more details).

## Incompletely Theorized Agreements and Disagreement

Incompletely theorized agreements have many virtues; but their virtues are partial. Stability, for example, is brought about by such agreements, and stability is usually desirable; but a constitutional system that is stable and unjust should probably be made less stable. I have shown that group polarization can lead to desirable social movements. Deliberation among insulated enclaves might lead to a perspective, or a truth, that will destabilize society, and this might be all for the good. Sometimes the instability will lead to a long overdue change in understandings, even constitutional understandings.

With this point in mind, I will end by qualifying what has been said thus far. Some cases cannot be decided *at all* without introducing a fair amount in the way of theory. Some constitutional cases cannot be decided *well* without introducing theory. If a good theory (involving, for example, the right to free speech) is available, if the theory is relevant to the issue at hand, and if judges can be persuaded that the theory is good, there should be no taboo on its judicial acceptance. The claims on behalf of incompletely theorized agreements are presumptive rather than conclusive.

What of disagreement? My discussion thus far has focused on the need for convergence. There is indeed such a need; but it is only part of the picture. In law, as in politics, disagreement among individuals and groups can be a productive and creative force, revealing error, showing gaps, moving discussion and results in good directions. Deliberative trouble can be good. The American constitutional order has placed a high premium on "government by discussion," and when the process is working well, this is true for the judiciary as well as for other institutions. Agreements may be a product of coercion, subtle or not, or of a failure of imagination. Indeed this is one reason for the protection, even the welcoming, of deliberating enclaves.

Constitutional disagreements have many legitimate sources. Two of these sources are especially important. First, people might share general commitments but disagree on particular outcomes. Second, people's disagreements on general principles might produce disagreement over particular outcomes and low-level propositions as well. People who think that an autonomy principle accounts for freedom of speech might also think that the government cannot regulate truthful, nondeceptive commercial advertising—whereas people who think that freedom of speech is basically a democratic idea, and is focused on political speech, may have no interest in protecting commercial advertising at all. Theorizing can have a salutary function in part because it tests low-level principles by reference to more ambitious claims. Disagreements can be productive by virtue of this process of testing.

Certainly if everyone having a reasonable general view converges on a particular (by hypothesis reasonable) judgment, nothing is amiss. But if an agreement is incompletely theorized, there is a risk that everyone who participates in the agreement is mistaken, and hence that the outcome is mistaken. There is also a risk that someone who is reasonable has not participated and that if that person were included, the agreement would break down. Over time, incompletely theorized agreements should be subject to scrutiny and critique, perhaps from members of deliberating enclaves. That process may result in more ambitious thinking than constitutional law ordinarily entails.

Nor is social consensus a consideration that outweighs everything else. Usually it would be much better to have a just outcome, rejected by many people, than an unjust outcome with which all or most agree. A just constitution is more important than an agreed-on constitution. Consensus or agreement is important largely because of its connection with stability, itself a valuable but far from overriding social goal. An unjust constitutional order should probably be made a lot less stable.

It would be foolish to say that no general theory about constitutional law or rights can produce agreement, even more foolish to deny that some general theories deserve support, and most foolish of all to say that incompletely theorized agreements warrant respect whatever their content. What seems plausible is something no less important for its modesty: except in unusual situations, abstract theories are an unlikely foundation for constitution-making and constitutional law, and caution and humility about high theory are appropriate at least when multiple theories can lead in the same direction. This more modest set of claims helps us to characterize incompletely theorized agreements as important phenomena with their own special virtues. Such agreements help make constitutions and constitutional law possible, even within nations where like-minded people speak mostly to one another and where citizens disagree on many of the most fundamental matters. Incompletely theorized agreements thus help illuminate an enduring constitutional and indeed social puzzle: how members of diverse societies can work together on terms of mutual respect amid sharp disagreements about both the right and the good. If there is a solution to this puzzle, incompletely theorized agreements are a promising place to start.

# 3

## Against Tradition

*[handwritten note: Right - Best Chapter so far.]*

Incompletely theorized agreements are not the only possible response to divisions on basic principles or to a situation of polarization among diverse social groups. Many people have argued that in a situation of this kind, it is best to follow traditions.

In fact traditionalism has often been urged precisely on the ground that if we follow our ancestors, we will not have to resolve the hard issues that divide us. People who tend to disagree, or who are not sure what they think, might be able to agree to follow the past. Long-standing practices might command assent, and deserve to command assent, precisely because they are long-standing. Those who have different views about liberty or equality might be willing to accept the authority of long-standing practices. And if diverse people are willing to listen to tradition, perhaps they will not go to unjustified extremes, even if like-minded people are speaking mostly to one another. Two central advantages of traditionalism seem to be its modesty and its anchoring effect—making it unnecessary for people to think anew about what should be done. If fresh thinking is a recipe for instability and error, traditionalism, in democracy and constitutional law, seems to be quite attractive.

Following Lawrence Lessig, we might distinguish between two kinds of constitutions: *preservative* and *transformative*.[1] Preservative constitutions attempt to protect long-standing practices that, it is feared, will be endangered by momentary passions. England has no written constitution; but insofar as it is ruled by unwritten understandings that produce constitutional law, the English constitution is thoroughly preservative. Many people read the United States Constitution in the same way. To the extent that it followed many English traditions, it does have important preservative dimensions, and many of its provisions continue to be understood in preservative terms. The same is true of eastern European constitutions postcommunism, especially insofar as these constitutions attempt to build on national understandings that predate communism.

By contrast, transformative constitutions attempt not to preserve an idealized past but to point the way toward an ideal future. On this view, the point of a democratic constitution is to hold a nation up to a mirror so as to reveal its flaws. The transformative constitution calls the nation to account. In the modern era, the most striking example of a transformative constitution can be found in South Africa. Self-consciously rejecting the legacy of apartheid, the South African constitution is rooted in principles of equality that extend far beyond racial hierarchy to ban discrimination on the basis of sex and sexual orientation—and also to create social and economic guarantees, similarly understood as a response to racial apartheid. The South African constitution

> constitutes a decisive break from a culture of apartheid and racism to a constitutionally protected culture of openness and democracy and universal human rights for South Africans of all ages, classes, and colours. There is a stark and dramatic difference between the past in which South Africans were trapped and the future on which the Constitution is premised.[2]

Indeed, constitutional law in South Africa has been developing with close reference to the goal of extirpating anything resembling apartheid; constitutional cases are decided with careful attention to what is necessary to eliminate apartheid's legacy.[3]

The United States Constitution itself has transformative elements, both in the original rejection of the monarchical heritage[4] and in the constitutional reforms of the Civil War era, rejecting slavery and authorizing the national government to do a great deal to promote equality. Some justices on the United States Supreme Court have seen the Constitution in transformative terms; William Brennan and Thurgood Marshall are examples. They form a sharp contrast with justices who have thought of the Constitution as essentially preservative; Felix Frankfurter and Antonin Scalia are examples.

Those who believe in a preservative constitution are often trying to find a corrective to sharp social divisions and to what they see as a kind of faddishness in constitutional thinking. Usually they urge that rights themselves should be rooted in traditions. More particularly, many people interested in United States constitutional law have said that constitutional rights should be developed with close reference to American traditions. My goal in this chapter is to challenge these claims. I argue that the enterprise of defining rights, including constitutional rights, should not be founded on an inquiry into tradition. Traditions should be assessed, not replicated. Social divisions, and the potential for error, should not be taken to disable people, including judges, from making that assessment.

Moreover, traditions do not come prepackaged for easy identification. They lack labels. Even the identification of traditions requires evaluation, not merely description. I conclude that courts thinking about what a constitution requires should be cautious about disrupting long-standing practices, but that apart from this simple cautionary note, traditionalism has little to offer to those thinking about the appropriate content of rights or the mandates of a constitution.

## Sources of Constitutional Rights *Bolivia? Power*

Where do constitutional rights come from? Once a constitution is in place, *Basic* the usual answer is: the words of the constitution. The answer is right so far as it goes, but it is ludicrously incomplete. The rights-conferring provisions of most constitutions are vague and apparently open-ended; they are hardly self-interpreting. What is "the freedom of speech"? When have people been deprived of "the equal protection of the laws"? When has government "taken private property"? And what counts as "liberty"? Some constitutional terms are clear, and when terms are clear, it is honorable to follow them. But it is less honorable to treat ambiguous legal texts as self-defining or to contend that such texts have a single meaning without the aid of interpretive tools.

The conventional lawyer's tools include not just text but also constitutional structure and history. From the structure of the United States Constitution, for example, we might conclude that there is a right to travel. After all, the system of federalism would be defeated without a right of interstate mobility. And in figuring out the meaning of an ambiguous constitutional provision, judges should certainly attend to the history behind it, so as to discipline themselves and to respect past democratic judgments. For example, the equal protection clause was an outgrowth of a belief that the states were not protecting the newly freed slaves from public and private violence. Undoubtedly judges should use this history to limit and shape current interpretations of the equal protection clause.

Sometimes, however, these conventional sources of interpretation run out, in the sense that they leave large gaps and ambiguities. Constitutional structure hardly answers the question whether commercial speech is protected by the first amendment, whether discrimination against homosexuals is forbidden by the equal protection clause, or whether the fourteenth amendment protects the right to die. Preratification history leaves equally hard issues. Should the historical understanding be described narrowly or broadly? If defined narrowly, why should it be binding? How do we deal with changed circumstances?

The conventional sources of interpretation therefore yield a number of open questions. Perhaps political philosophy can help us; certainly political philosophy has played an occasional role in decisions about the content of constitutional rights. Perhaps judges should try to bring the best philosophical thinking to bear on the interpretation of unclear provisions protecting rights. But in a famous opinion Justice Oliver Wendell Holmes, Jr., said that "the Constitution does not enact Mr. Herbert Spencer's Social Statics,"[3] and the same might be said for any effort to invoke any other kind of ambitious thinking to define constitutional rights. Holmes's point seems to be twofold. First, a constitution is best understood to allow majorities to choose among a range of political philosophies rather than to require the nation to select any particular one (though this very understanding is a product of a kind of political philosophy and of course requires an independent defense). Second, those of us who live in a heterogeneous society should distrust our judges, who may well be unresponsive, ignorant, parochial, or confused; we should therefore seek to disable them from invalidating statutes on the basis of the political philosophy they find most congenial.

In the history of United States constitutionalism, and in many other nations as well, tradition has often been invoked to fill the gaps left by text, structure, history, and philosophical argument. In judge-made constitutional law in the United States, tradition has been an extraordinarily important source of constitutional rights, especially in the interpretation of the due process clause of the Fourteenth Amendment. Dissenting from the Court's aggressive use of that clause in the early twentieth century, Justice Holmes said that a law should be held to violate that clause only if it "would infringe fundamental principles as they have been understood by the traditions of our people and our law."[6] The modern privacy cases have built on this foundation. For example, the Court held in *Griswold v. Connecticut* that married people had a right to use contraceptives,[7] thus invalidating a Connecticut law forbidding such use. In doing this, the Court relied heavily on what it saw as the "tradition" of marital privacy. Some justices stressed the novelty of the ban on use of contraceptives; for them it was critical that in Anglo-American history there had never been bans on *use* of contraceptives within marriage.

To be sure, the use of tradition was far more attenuated in some of the other privacy cases. Consider *Eisenstadt v Baird*,[8] where the Court invalidated, as "irrational" under the equal protection clause, the state's prohibition of the distribution of contraceptives to unmarried people. Here tradition did not support those who sought to attack the law. Surely unmarried people have no traditional right to purchase contraceptives. In invalidating the law, the *Eisenstadt* Court began the process of judicial definition of fundamental rights not by reference to tradition but by reference to something like a tentative account of what sorts of rights are most important to individual self-determination. Some such account underlay the conception of privacy in *Roe v. Wade*,[9] the famous (or infamous) case establishing the abortion right. This case was not fundamentally a case about tradition. Instead *Roe* depended above all on a conception of what individual liberty properly included and about the boundaries that communities could not legitimately cross.

But the life of tradition, as a source of constitutional rights, is hardly over, and in fact the last several decades have seen an unmistakable rebirth of the idea that constitutional rights should be defined by close reference to traditions. Tradition initially reemerged as a defining idea in *Bowers v. Hardwick*,[10] where the Court upheld a ban on same-sex sodomy. There the Court emphasized that sodomy was a criminal offense at common law and that thirty-two of the thirty-seven states outlawed sodomy in 1868, when the Fourteenth Amendment was ratified. "Against this background, to claim that a right to engage in such conduct is 'deeply rooted in this Nation's history and tradition' or 'implicit in the concept of ordered liberty' is, at best, facetious." Chief Justice Burger underlined the importance of tradition in his separate opinion, as he wrote in concurrence that "[d]ecisions of individuals relating to homosexual conduct have been subject to state intervention throughout the history of Western Civilization."

One of the most important modern uses of tradition can be found in *Michael H. v. Gerald D.*,[11] in which the Court denied an adulterous father's claim of a constitutional right to visit his child, who had been conceived by a woman who was married to someone else. The plurality of the Court relied heavily on the absence of any such right in tradition. The plurality emphasized "the historic respect—indeed, sanctity would not be too strong a term—traditionally accorded to the relationships that develop within the unitary family." Writing in dissent, Justice Brennan argued that tradition should be construed as a general respect for parental rights, that the privacy cases involved general aspirations rather than concrete practices, and that the plurality's approach would unravel the Constitution's protection of liberty. In a key and much-discussed footnote offered in response to Justice Brennan, the plurality defended its reliance on "historical traditions specifically relating to the rights of an adulterous natural father, rather than inquiring more generally 'whether parenthood is an interest that traditionally has received our attention and protection.' " The plurality said:

> Why should the relevant category not be even more general—perhaps "family relationships"; or "personal relationships"; or even "emotional attachments in general"? Though Justice Brennan has no basis for the level of generality he would select, we do: We refer to the most specific level at which a relevant tradition protecting, or denying protection to, the asserted right can be identified. . . . Because general traditions provide such imprecise guidance, they permit judges to dictate rather than discern the society's views. Although assuredly having the virtue (if it be that) of leaving judges free to decide as they think best when the unanticipated occurs, a rule of law that binds neither by text nor by any particular, identifiable tradition, is no rule of law at all.

Tradition has reemerged as a key issue in cases involving the patient's right to withdraw life-saving medical equipment and the right to die. Suicide has been banned by tradition. Should this count decisively against the alleged right to die? So Justice Scalia argued, in a separate opinion concluding that the Constitution does not constrain the state's power over individual choice in this area.[12] Justices Scalia and Thomas have increasingly insisted that where the constitutional text is unclear, judicial decisions should be made by reference to long-standing traditions. The Court itself endorsed Justice Scalia's point in its important decision rejecting the view that the Constitution creates a right to physician-assisted suicide.[13] Some justices have claimed that tradition has guarded against "state incursions into the body" and that therefore people have a right to resist invasive medical treatment even when necessary to save their lives.[14] Tradition continues to play a central role in establishing the meaning of the Constitution's basic liberty guarantee, and perhaps in other areas of constitutional law as well. In its only decision striking down a law discriminating on the basis of sexual orientation, the Court emphasized the oddity of the particular law in question: "The resulting disqualification of a class of persons from the right to seek specific protection from the law is unprecedented in our jurisprudence. . . . It is not within our constitutional tradition to enact laws of this sort."[15]

## Tradition and the Puzzling Search for an Antonym

At first glance, it might seem trivial to suggest that traditions are a source of rights. To decide on the appropriate category of rights, human beings have to rely on what other human beings think or have thought. For people in a particular nation, it is natural to ask about the present and past judgments of other people, in that nation or elsewhere. No one disagrees with that claim. Against whom is traditionalism directed?

Perhaps the answer is _metaphysical realists_—people who believe that with respect to rights (or anything else), human beings can have access to something wholly external to human judgment and cognition. To say the least, the issues underlying metaphysical realism are extremely complex.[16] Fortunately, those issues do not have to be resolved here. Many people believe in natural or God-given rights. But as participants in a constitutional culture, few people seriously believe that constitutional rights should be identified by exploring a point of view that is external to human perceptions, needs, and interests. If traditionalists are concerned to emphasize the fact that the origins of constitutional rights lie in human interests, and in human perceptions of human interests, they are not offering anything really distinctive. Those who reject constitutional traditionalism are not claiming to be metaphysical realists.

Perhaps traditionalism has other targets. Perhaps traditionalists mean to root constitutional rights in national and local practices and thus oppose _cosmopolitanism_ or _universalism_. Some people think that any community should decide on rights by reference to its own particular practices rather than to claims that come from elsewhere. On this view, Chinese traditionalism is good for China, South African traditionalism is good for South Africa, French traditionalism is right for France, Russian traditionalism makes sense for Russia, United States traditionalism is good for the United States, and so on. Practices of constitution-making and constitutional interpretation should be done with close reference to local traditions. Certainly ideas of this kind have played a role in constitution-making in eastern Europe, where documents have been drawn up with close reference to national traditions and values, historically defined. Those traditions are an important source of constitutional commitments.

In the American constitutional order, traditionalism might also be opposed to _nationalism_, in favor of respect for judgments of localities and small communities. Opposition to nationalism in favor of local traditions has a distinguished history in American federalism. Some forms of modern constitutional thinking are localist in character. They stem from the concern that definitions of rights imposed from the center will be unresponsive to local traditions and practices. In the constitutional context, we might think that the United States should resist judgments of the world community and that the Supreme Court should be reluctant to interpose national norms on a large nation having heterogeneous subunits.

There are many possible implications. On one view, for example, we should reassess the "incorporation" movement, which applied most provisions of the Bill of Rights to the states on the same terms as it was applied to the national government. Maybe the incorporation of the Bill of Rights was a large mistake. Perhaps some rights should not have been incorporated at all; or perhaps they should have been incorporated, but in more modest form, setting basic floors for rights without making the Bill of Rights, as applied to the states, equivalent to the Bill of Rights guaranteed against the more remote and less accountable national government. Whether or not incorporation makes sense, perhaps the Supreme Court should be more respectful than it now is of local traditions, refusing to impose national rights unless they are a clear or unmistakable inference from constitutional structure.

There is much to be said on behalf of this view. With freedom of movement, people who are unhappy with the activities of a local unit have the ability to leave. The power of exit creates a before-the-fact deterrent and an after-the-fact corrective to rights violations or other forms of oppression. In addition, democratic processes are reinforced by allowing a large degree of local self-determination. Because they are more closely responsive to democratic will, loyalists might have less need for safeguards in the form of judicially enforceable rights. There are of course countervailing considerations; small communities might well be more subject to factional influence, as James Madison feared. But we might well think that within a heterogeneous nation, localities should be permitted to impose, for example, more stringent regulations on obscene materials if this is their choice. There is no sufficient reason to have the same rules for obscenity in New York as in Utah.

So far so good. But it is equally correct to say that many rights are properly taken as national, because they represent the minimal guarantees of national citizenship or basic goods that all people deserve to have. The relation between basic minima and basic goods on the one hand and constitutional rights on the other is a complex business. As I have emphasized throughout, constitutional rights are practical instruments, with concrete purposes, and for this reason they might not match the set of minima and goods that would be identified by the best political theory. But some constitutional rights are rightly taken to embody principles that cannot be abridged anywhere. The prohibition on governmental race discrimination in the Fourteenth Amendment is a core example; so too with rights of political speech. If we expand the viewscreen a bit, we might see an analogy in the entirely reasonable suggestion that international human rights, minimally defined, should be enjoyed everywhere, not only in nations whose traditions support them.

In this light the problem with constitutional traditionalism, understood as a challlenge to cosmopolitanism or universalism, is not that it is wrong but that it is too vague and broad-gauged. It does not help us to make the necessary distinctions between universal rights and national rights or between national rights and local self-determination. To make such distinctions, we have to say much more, and the more that must be said will involve distinctions between goods and rights that all people should have on the one hand and appropriate local and national distinctions on the other. To make these distinctions we must think about the right mix between universal and local rights. The notion of "tradition" is unhelpful in supplying those criteria. What has been done in the past need not be a secure guide.

Perhaps the target of traditionalism is not cosmopolitanism or nationalism but *independent moral argument. Traditionalism is thus opposed* to one form of *rationalism*. We might think that human beings (or at least judges) are not especially good at evaluating our practices and that our practices are themselves the best guide to what should be done. In general, we should do what has been done before. If a practice has endured, many people have endorsed it, or at least not seen fit to change it. If a practice has endured, it has been found acceptable by numerous people over long periods, which is itself a reason to think that it is good. The tradition is therefore likely to serve important social functions that people at a particular point may not be able to perceive. Constitutional traditionalism therefore makes decisions simpler at the same time that it makes them less likely to go wrong. If economic terminology is thought to be helpful here, the use of traditions, by imperfect human beings, might not be perfect, but it is the best way to go because it minimizes both "decision costs," taken as the burdens of deciding what to do, and "error costs," taken as the problems introduced by making mistakes.

In this form, the inspiration for constitutional traditionalism can be found in the work of political theorist Edmund Burke, and in particular in Burke's enthusiasm for common-law processes of incremental development, based on precedents, as opposed to thinking on the basis of first principles. As a creed for constitutional law, traditionalism respects common-law processes of case-by-case judgment and sees them as a model for legal and even social development. It finds its antonym in the (hubristic?) belief that human beings should try to evaluate their practices by reference to principles of freedom and equality that give us an independent, critical purchase on what we have done. To some extent, traditionalists who speak in these terms are urging incompletely theorized agreements, indeed urging such agreements on traditional practices.

If traditionalism is designed to offer a cautionary note about the potentially harmful consequences of social change, it makes a lot of sense. It is a familiar but often overlooked point that particular social changes—minimum wage increases, health care laws, environmental protection—may have unanticipated systemic effects. A society is not an ecological system. But a change in a particular aspect of society may well have effects on other parts of the system, and those effects may be both hard to anticipate and harmful. It is also important for people to be humble about their ability to evaluate long-standing practices. Those practices may well have virtues that particular people are unable to see, or they may fit with a range of other practices in a complex way.

From these considerations we have some important reasons for caution in constitutional law and democracy generally. Those who emphasize the political and legal virtue of _prudence_ urge an appreciation of those reasons. But prudence is a limited virtue, not an overriding one; rapid and large movements can be warranted. Indeed, constitutional law is sometimes based on the judgment that our practices may offend our own aspirations and commitments. South African constitutional law, with its explicitly transformative goals, attests to the point. In any constitutional system, people do and should use their aspirations as the basis for moral argument. In the United States, the attack on chattel slavery is perhaps the most vivid example, but there are many others. Consider the challenges to sex discrimination, to restrictions on political speech, to violations of religious liberty (including compulsory school prayer), to maldistributions of political power, as through the poll tax and apportionment schemes that allocate votes on a discriminatory basis.

Frequently moral and political argument takes the form of a search for "reflective equilibrium," in which we try to align our various moral judgments at levels of both generality and specificity.[17] In this process, some traditional practices, and some particular convictions, may not survive reflection. Respect for traditions because they are traditions is inconsistent with the search for reflective equilibrium as an aspect of moral reasoning. This point undermines traditions as a source of rights, because many traditions cannot be shown to cohere with our best judgments about what is true or right.

To be sure, constitutional argument is not a search for reflective equilibrium. Constitutional text, structure, and history discipline the process of legal argument, creating "fixed points" that cannot be rejected and that have no clear analogue in the search for reflective equilibrium. Moreover, judges must take precedents as fixed or relatively fixed points even if they disagree with them. There are large differences between the search for reflective equilibrium and the process of constitutional argument.[18] But the differences do not mean that traditions should be immune from attack in the process of constitutional argument. A significant part of constitutional law, in most nations, is emphatically transformative. It involves the critical assessment of tradition by reference to sources of law and the moral arguments to which such sources, properly interpreted, draw attention. The equal protection clause is best understood to embody a principle of equality that forbids race and sex discrimination, even if those forms of discrimination are long-standing. The principle will have more weight if it can be found in the history behind the clauses and if it is reflected in previous judicial precedents. But the principle does not need to be justified by reference to traditional practices. Indeed, the principle operates as a sharp critique of traditional practices.

Now traditionalists do have a response here. They might insist that we should hesitate in attempting to change practices merely because they do not survive critical reflection. Perhaps we have overlooked something. Perhaps those who engage in critical reflection are wrong. Perhaps change would be futile or counterproductive. Points of this kind do support a mood of caution and humility; but they hardly make tradition into a good foundation for rights, constitutional or otherwise. If we are trying to figure out what rights people have, some traditions will have to yield, because they cannot survive moral or legal scrutiny. Of course it is true that for many people the search for reflective equilibrium will include, as fixed points, many traditional practices, and it may therefore be quite difficult to dislodge their (or our) approval of much that is long-standing. But the fact that a view is long-standing, and approved, is no guarantee that it is right.

Consider in this light the remarks of Anthony Kronman, traditionalist and dean of Yale Law School:

> The past is not something that we, as already constituted human beings, chose for one reason or another to respect; rather, it is such respect that establishes our humanity in the first place. We must, if we are to be human beings at all, adopt toward the past the custodial attitude that Burke recommends. That attitude is itself constitutive of our membership in the uniquely human world of culture, as opposed to animals or thinkers.[19]

Now Kronman is an intelligent and distinguished scholar. But this passage is a tangle of confusions. The fact that we are "already constituted" does not mean that we must "respect" some abstraction called "the past." People who have a skeptical attitude toward past practices, thinking that they must be shown to be sensible or just, hardly cease "to be human beings at all."

Of course human beings cannot evaluate the past without resort to something that some human beings think. But that point is banal. Kronman's uncontroversial descriptive claim, that people are "already constituted," cannot support his exceedingly controversial suggestion that we should adopt Burke's "custodial attitude" toward "the past."

## Tradition and the Constitution: Background

Thus far I have attempted to criticize the view that tradition is an appropriate source of rights, by suggesting that it is hard to figure out what traditionalists are seeking to oppose, and that once we disentangle their possible targets, we will uncover the virtue of prudence and little else. Certainly we have no good reason to challenge the view that basic rights, discovered on grounds independent of tradition, ought to be enjoyed nationally or universally. It is now time to turn to some particulars, and especially to the suggestion that tradition should have an honored place in the interpretation of the Constitution.

For constitutions with a transformative dimension, constitutional traditionalism seems positively perverse. As I have emphasized, the South African constitution is not understood by reference to long-standing practices; instead its meaning is gathered from the effort to eliminate the apartheid legacy. The Constitutional Court roots its decisions in principles of "human dignity" that repudiate, rather than accept, central local traditions.[20] "The people of South Africa are committed to the attainment of social justice and the improvement of quality of life for everyone."[21] Hence the Constitutional Court has held that capital punishment is forbidden by the Constitution, notwithstanding the extended use of capital punishment in South African history. In what might be its most dramatic ruling, the Court has concluded that the Constitution's social and economic guarantees must be understood in the context of the revolution against apartheid and that so understood, those guarantees are judicially enforceable, requiring government to take "progressive steps" to ensure decent shelter (see chapter 10).[22] The Court ruled that the government "failed to make reasonable provision within its available resources for people . . . with no access to land, no roof over their heads, and who were living in intolerable conditions or crisis situations." It should be clear that in many nations on the globe, including wealthy nations, a constitutional right of this sort would require large-scale transformations in current practices and would repudiate rather than follow traditions.

Or consider the rulings of the Constitutional Court of Germany. Of course the German Constitution was written against the backdrop of the Nazi experience, and much of its goal has been transformative, through the identification of ideals of universal human dignity.[23] The German commitment to those ideals rests on a belief that they are good ideals, not on a belief that they mirror German traditions (though to be sure the ideal of dignity does have strong roots in some aspects of German tradition). And in many ways the Constitutional Court has taken the Constitution to require approaches that have no clear foundation in German traditions. In the area of communications, for example, the Court has long held that it is not enough to prevent government from censoring opinions, though this is indeed important. The "guarantee of broadcast freedom" also imposes "a duty on the state to see to it that broadcasting facilities" are "controlled by a broad spectrum of interests" and also provide "a forum for a broad spectrum of opinion."[24] In other words, it is not enough for government to cede the ground to private broadcasters and allow them to provide whatever they wish, subject to market constraints. The government is under an affirmative obligation to ensure that broadcasters provide a broad spectrum of opinion, a requirement that has entangled the Constitutional Court in occasional supervision of the communications industry. What is operating here is a set of aspirations about democracy—about deliberative democracy in fact—and a judgment about the need for constitutional law to protect those aspirations. Tradition is irrelevant.

In some areas in American constitutional law, the same points hold. For example, the free speech principle has been taken to forbid states from using their ordinary libel law to protect people's reputations—even though libel law is well established by tradition.[25] In fact the American free speech principle overrides long-standing traditions in many areas, by protecting sexually explicit materials and commercial advertising, as well as potentially dangerous political dissent of the kind often not tolerated by our traditions. As I will urge at many places in this book, the equality principle of the United States Constitution is hardly understood by reference to traditions; it is treated as a self-conscious attack on traditions and hence is the largest symbol of transformative constitutionalism in American law. But traditionalism is now having a rebirth within the American judiciary, and to get a sense of the relationship between traditions and courts, it will be useful to explore that development.

First some background. The current emphasis on tradition has a particular source in history and indeed tradition: the Supreme Court's unfortunate experience with "economic liberties" in the first third of the twentieth century. In this period, the Court held that the due process clause of the Fourteenth Amendment created a right to freedom of contract, subject to interference only under special and highly limited conditions. The great case of the period was *Lochner v. New York*,[26] where the Court invalidated a maximum hour law. It was here that Justice Holmes, writing in dissent, said that the due process clause would not be violated unless "the statute proposed would infringe fundamental principles as they have been understood by the traditions of our people and our law." (Note Holmes's emphasis not only on judicial restraint but also and in his view equivalently on tradition as a source of rights.)

Many things contributed to the demise, in the New Deal period, of the *Lochner* era understanding, and *Lochner*'s legacy remains sharply contested.[27] Some people think that there is no room at all for "substantive due process," that is, for the idea that the due process clause imposes substantive limits on governmental power. The Court has never accepted this view. But eventually the Court concluded that it had indeed exceeded its authority and abused its constitutional role. It held that so long as the government behaved "rationally," the government behaved constitutionally; and in the economic arena, almost everything counts as rational. Government regulation of the economy is generally legitimate, even if it interferes with freedom of contract.

The shadows of the *Lochner* era, and of Holmes's famous dissent, loom over American constitutional law, especially over cases decided under the due process clause. At the time *Griswold*, the Connecticut birth control case, purported not to be an interpretation of the due process clause at all but instead of "penumbras" from other provisions. The right of privacy is now thought to be an inference from the due process clause, and in retrospect, *Griswold* is indeed understood as a due process case. But the textual basis of "substantive" due process is dubious; the constitutional text seems to refer to procedure and not to call for judicial oversight of the reasonableness of laws. In any case this textual awkwardness, and the perceived disaster of the *Lochner* era, threaten the legitimacy of all the privacy cases and indeed of all substantive liberty cases. I think that it is right to question substantive due process as a matter of first principle, and the problems with the legitimacy of substantive due process should push us to cabin its reach so long as it exists.[28]

The Court's current emphasis on tradition, read at a level of great specificity, must be understood in light of this background. Justice Scalia, and to

*But That, like Lewellyn's warry canons, traditions can be found to support whatever you want.*

some extent the Court as a whole, are now using tradition as a means of limiting judicial interference with democratic processes at the state and local levels. We might speculate that there are two motivations here. First is the belief that the United States Constitution is preservative—or at least that courts do best to take it as preservative, so as to ensure that when they are protecting rights, they do so in the name of long-standing social judgments rather than their own views about what is right and good. Second is the belief that substantive due process is itself illegitimate and the use of tradition, as a source of rights, will minimize the damage posed by substantive due process—not by eliminating it altogether but by understanding it in an exceedingly narrow way, so as to reduce the likelihood of an illegitimate judicial role. The value of tradition is that it operates to confine judicial discretion and to limit the occasions for invalidation of democratically enacted measures.

In the view of some of *Lochner*'s critics—and they could be liberal, conservative, or somewhere in between— tradition properly plays a defining role under the due process clause; but it might not be the appropriate source of rights under (say) the equal protection and free speech clauses. Tradition has a particular constitutional role, designed for a particular provision with a particular history. Tradition deserves a place under the due process clause as a way of preventing abuses under that otherwise open-ended clause or because that clause is best understood as designed to safeguard old practices from myopic or ill-considered practices. But tradition is not an all-purpose source of rights. It is not, for example, a good guide to the meaning of the equal protection clause, which was specifically designed as a check on traditions, most notably the tradition of racial inequality. (I deal with this point in more detail in chapter 7.)

## Tradition and the Constitution: The Main Question

Even with all this said, the main question remains: What can be said on behalf of invoking tradition as the foundation of constitutional rights under the due process clause if not elsewhere? There are several possibilities.

First, tradition might be a good source of constitutional rights for Americans, simply because our particular traditions are good. We might think, for example, that Anglo-American traditions of liberty can be defended in principle; these are wonderful traditions. Use of traditions to define rights—by the Supreme Court or others—is good not because traditions are good as such but because our particular traditions turn out to to be good. Traditionalism might even be urged on the simple grounds traced earlier: Judges who use traditions might simplify their jobs while also making fewer mistakes than they would through other approaches. Even if our traditions are imperfect, a general use of traditions to define rights might be best because it produces better overall outcomes than any plausible alternative. This conclusion might not hold for, say, South Africa, Cuba, and China, which have had oppressive governments for long periods. But the conclusion does hold for Americans.

I think that this is the most plausible basis for traditionalism in constitutional law. It draws increased strength if we emphasize that judges are mere human beings and if we fear that if they are unmoored from either text or traditions, they might well make mistakes. In fact we could imagine a society, different but not unrecognizably so from our own, in which this defense of traditionalism would be quite convincing. Suppose, for example, that political processes functioned extremely well, in the sense that unjust or ill-considered outcomes were highly unlikely and were corrected politically when they occurred. Suppose too that in such a nation, judges were likely to make big blunders, in the form of decisions that were confused or even invidious, and very hard to fix once made. In such a society, traditions might well be the best foundation of constitutional rights where text is unclear. Perhaps other bright-lines rules—such as a strong presumption in favor of upholding enacted law—would be better still. The point is that an evaluation of traditionalism, as of any other interpretive method, is partly empirical, and based on an assessment of how different institutions are likely to perform under the various alternatives. Without some empirical projections, it is hard to venture sensible answers.

Even so, there are serious problems with rooting constitutional rights in traditions. American traditions are multiple, not unitary, and if we investigate them on their merits, we will find much that is bad as well as much that is good. Our traditions include race and sex discrimination as well as considerable censorship of political dissent and disregard for the interests of the poor—alongside mounting freedom of political speech and religion and an anticaste principle, used to attack race and sex discrimination (see chapter 7). This basic claim—that our traditions contain much that is bad as well as much that is good—itself fits with American traditions. Indeed, a large part of the American tradition is critical rather than celebratory, transformative rather than preservative. A problem with Burkeanism for America is that Burkeanism is, in crucial ways, un-American. Burkeanism does not conform to American traditions, which have been punctuated by periods of critical self-consciousness, in which even long-standing practices are challenged on political and legal grounds, as failing to conform to our general aspirations. In areas including race and sex equality, the environment, rights of workers, and much more, our political and legal practices have been revised after inspection.

There is another problem. If our traditions are a source of rights because they turn out to be good on independent grounds and not just because they are traditions, why not move to those independent grounds and eliminate the middleman? If traditions are a source of rights because our traditions are right or good, we should proceed directly to the right or the good and put traditions to one side. This inquiry is subject to the general requirements of humility and prudence; but if those requirements are all there is to traditionalism, traditions become a simple and somewhat boring cautionary note and hardly a source of rights in any interesting sense.

These points leave open the possibility of defending traditionalism as likely to minimize complexity and to lead to better outcomes than any alternative. But without a lot more detail, that defense is highly speculative. It might be right, but we do not know whether it is right. Maybe judges can theorize pretty well on such issues as reproduction, sexual privacy, and the right to physician-assisted suicide. Perhaps they can do this precisely because of their training, the mode of their selection, and their insulation from politics. Perhaps judges can proceed on the basis of rules, analogies, and precedents and without making high-level or complex philosophical arguments on their own. Perhaps our traditions are very hard to describe; perhaps too many of our traditions, insofar as they bear on hard cases of this sort, contain injustice.

There is a final point. I have suggested that traditions may be a good source of rights because any practice that has lasted for a long time must have something to offer. If people have done a certain thing for a long period, their practice probably serves some important social function, hard as it may be for outsiders (or even insiders) to see what that function is. On this view, the real reason for constitutional traditionalism is that traditions are good, but not because we usually have an independent argument on their behalf. The whole point is that we may well lack any such argument—and that this does not mean that traditions are not good.

This argument too rests on fragile ground. Undoubtedly it is true that some practices have lasted because they serve desirable social goals, and undoubtedly it is true too that it is often hard to figure out how they do this. Here too we have a reason for prudence, humility, and caution. But some practices persist not because of their salutary functions but because of inertia, myopia, bias, power, and confusion. The defense of traditions is much too coarse-grained; it verges on a form of sentimentalism or even willful blindness. It approves of traditions without giving an adequate sense of what sorts of traditions warrant approval.


## Against Tradition

Thus far I have tried to identify the grounds for basing constitutional law on tradition, and I have tried to challenge those grounds. The argument has been largely defensive. In this section, I take the offensive. There are three basic problems with using traditions as sources of rights.

The first problem has to do with the existence of changed circumstances. Sometimes facts change. Sometimes values, or perceptions of facts, change as well. If they do, the role of tradition becomes far less clear. When facts and values change, it is sensible to insist that traditions have to be characterized and hence evaluated rather than simply "applied." The category of changed facts and values is a large one. It severely complicates the enterprise of constitutional traditionalism.

Return, for example, to the *Michael H.* case, and suppose that the question arises whether the father of a child conceived in an adulterous relationship has a constitutional right to see the child on some regular basis. As the plurality of the Court said, there is no specific tradition to support the father, at least if we ask whether rights of the sort he seeks to vindicate have been recognized in the past. Children of a mother in an intact marriage were conclusively presumed to be the children of the husband and wife. But the reasons for the tradition may be obsolete. Both facts and values have changed.

Facts first. An important basis of the conclusive presumption was the state of technology. It used to be impossible to know whether someone alleging that he was the father of a child was in fact the father of the child. Human beings lacked the means to find out. In light of that fact, the tradition made a lot of sense. If science could not tell us whether someone alleging that he was the father was in fact the father, it would probably be best to presume that he was not, so as to protect intact families from external assaults when the legal system lacked the means to distinguish true allegations from false ones. But the situation has changed. We can now figure out whether the alleged father is really the father. Must the old tradition be binding if it rested on assumptions that fail to hold? If the foundations of the tradition are missing, does the tradition still bind? How should the tradition be conceived under present conditions? To answer such questions, we cannot simply identify past practices. We have to engage in an act of constructive interpretation—that is, we have to understand the basis for the practice, to see whether it makes sense under our circumstances.

Now turn to values, or perhaps better, the interaction between facts and values. It used to be true that children conceived out of wedlock were subject to extreme social opprobrium and to a series of legal disabilities as well. Both the opprobrium and the disabilities have diminished—in part because of the perceived mandate of the equal protection clause, which is taken to forbid most discrimination on the basis of illegitimacy. This change means that another of the foundations of the tradition is absent: The old conclusive presumption may have made sense as a way of protecting the child against social hostility, but the need for the protection is sharply diminished.

Perhaps this change should make us revisit or recharacterize the tradition, whose founding assumption has become obsolete. It might make sense to have a conclusive presumption of the old kind when the consequences of conception in adultery would be so damaging for the child. But if the consequences are no longer so damaging, should the tradition remain?

These problems are hardly limited to the *Michael H.* case. Changing facts and values can be found in debates over contraception, abortion, the right to withdraw life-saving equipment, and euthanasia. In each of these areas, we could identify changes quite similar to those in *Michael H.* itself. In the last decades, abortion has come to involve far safer medical procedures, available in the context of sharply changed understandings about the relation between men and women. All this complicates the claim that "tradition" condemns or does not protect abortion (a controversial claim in any case). Medical technologies have changed so rapidly, and the availability of invasive life-prolonging equipment is so novel, that past traditions about euthanasia rest on palpably anachronistic assumptions. The assumptions that underlie traditions often become obsolete.

There is a second and related problem for constitutional traditionalists, referred to earlier but now requiring more detailed discussion: How do we describe any tradition? Traditions do not come in neat packages. In the United States, there are of course multiple traditions with respect to most contested issues, including free speech, sexual privacy, and individual choices about whether to live or to die. Traditions can be described at high levels of generality or low levels of specificity. We might think, for example, that there is a tradition of respect for freedom of contract and that laws forbidding the sale of marijuana violate that tradition. Or we might think that there is a tradition of respect for sexual privacy and that laws forbidding heterosexual or homosexual sodomy offend that tradition. How do we characterize a tradition?

Justice Scalia is quite alert to this problem, and he explicitly attempts to overcome the problems of multiplicity of traditions and conflicting levels of generality. A tradition that includes inconsistency and multiplicity is not, in his view, usable for constitutional purposes. To be usable, a tradition must be both consistent and unitary. Moreover, traditions should be described at a low level of generality—at the most specific level possible. This is so for several reasons. If traditions are described at a high level of generality, the judge's use of tradition is fraudulent. Described broadly, traditions do not exist as such. There is no tradition of respect for freedom of contract or sexual privacy. If we look at the details, we will see that no such traditions exist. In addition, if tradition is relevant because traditions are good and because their use disciplines the judges, it seems silly to read traditions at high levels of generality. At such levels, the discipline is removed, and we have no (real) long-standing practice on which we can rely. In Justice Scalia's view, the basic defense of constitutional traditionalism thus calls for highly specific readings of tradition. Specific readings tend to discipline judges. Specific readings also tend to draw on actual practices that have persisted over time.

Especially for critics of judicial use of substantive due process, Justice Scalia's argument has much to be said in its favor. If we are seeking to control the damage of having courts use substantive due process at all, Justice Scalia's route seems as good an approach as any. But there are problems with his approach as well. As I have urged, changed circumstances complicate the use of tradition, because specific old practices often rest on assumptions that no longer hold. Perhaps an old right was based on grounds that no longer make sense. Moreover, the notion of a "most specific" understanding of tradition is itself ambiguous. Defined at the highest level of specificity, every case is one of first impression and sui generis.[29] No case is exactly like a case that has come before. We can always identify features of a current case that distinguish it from the specific tradition invoked on the plaintiff's behalf.

Justice Scalia seems to think that we can identify a "most specific" tradition without making evaluations of any sort and that we can "read" traditions off practices without indulging interpretative assumptions. But this is false. When we say that there is a tradition of banning suicide, we are not simply reporting on the facts but also reading the past in a certain way. Sometimes suicides were not banned in practice. Sometimes extenuating circumstances were found, at least as a practical matter.

In addition, we should not be too skeptical about the reasoning capacities of the judges, disciplined as they will inevitably be by the system of precedent, the need to think analogically, and the judges' own awareness of their limited institutional role. When evaluated, specific traditions sometimes emerge as products of ignorance or bigotry. In *Bowers v. Hardwick*, the Georgia sodomy case, the court might have read from our tradition a general respect for consensual sexual activity, and carefully assessed any specific departure from that tradition, to make sure that it is based on something legitimate and reasonable. Or return to the approach of the German Constitutional Court to the free speech principle. Whether we think that approach right or wrong, it exemplifies the possibility that a court might understand its constitution to set out a principle of democracy, or self-rule, that operates as a check on regulations that compromise that principle.

*More like Llewellyn+Intin not just* (handwritten margin note)

The third problem is the largest. We have seen that any nation's traditions contain both good and bad. By itself, the fact that some practice is long-standing is no reason to allow it to guide us. For example, no one thinks that tradition is a good guide to the meaning of the equal protection clause. Old traditions of race and sex discrimination cannot plausibly be invoked in defense of current practices of race and sex discrimination. Nor is the problem limited to these contexts of inequality. When traditional practices are challenged on constitutional grounds, we cannot know whether those practices are defensible until we have done some investigating. Constitutional traditionalism truncates the analysis much too quickly.

Nothing in these notions supports the idea that courts should feel free to invoke an ambiguous constitutional provision to overrule practices with which they disagree or that they should invoke their own conceptions of the good and the right to test legislation. Indeed, I will shortly urge approaches to the privacy cases that are quite narrow and that allow the Court to avoid large-scale pronouncements about "privacy" or "liberty." But I hope I have said enough to explain why tradition is an unpromising source of rights, constitutional or otherwise.

## A Note on Originalism, Hard and Soft

Should the Constitution be understood to mean what it originally meant? In the United States, there has been a remarkable rise of interest in "originalism" as a possible method of constitutional interpretation. Justice Scalia believes in tradition. He also insists that the Constitution should be taken to mean what it meant when the relevant provisions were ratified.[30]

This is not the place for a full discussion of the topic.[31] But at this point the basic considerations should be clear. Originalism is a particular approach to constitutional interpretation; it is hardly the only approach. Those who choose originalism must defend that choice against the alternatives. Now no one believes that the original understanding is irrelevant. As I suggest throughout this book, the general goals of the Constitution's authors and ratifiers deserve considerable respect and attention. We should distinguish here between "soft originalism," captured in this view, and "hard originalism," captured in Justice Scalia's claim that the particular understandings of those authors and ratifiers are decisive and not merely relevant.

What can be said on behalf of hard originalism? Two points might be urged. First, hard originalism constrains judges, by limiting their discretion and room to maneuver, thus securing clarity in the law over time. This is an important virtue, particularly if we distrust judges. Second, it might be urged, hard originalism produces a tolerable or even excellent set of results, certainly compared with any other method of interpreting the Constitution. To the extent that hard originalists do not create rights that go beyond the original meaning, it remains open to the democratic process to do exactly that.

The most sophisticated defenses of originalism speak in exactly these terms.[32] But on both points, originalism is quite vulnerable. First, the "original understanding" is often ambiguous. Any decision about its content will require answers to hard questions, akin to those that must be asked by those who seek to identify traditions. What if the original understanding is not unitary? How should we handle changed circumstances of fact or value? Should the original understanding be described at a high level of particularity or at a high level of generality? For example, should the Fourteenth Amendment's equality principle be taken to ban only particular forms of discrimination against newly freed slaves, such as exclusion from juries? Or to ban race discrimination in general? Or to set out an anticaste principle? Or to ban all unjustified forms of discrimination? History alone is most unlikely to answer these questions; more probably, it contains complex and competing strands.

Now perhaps originalists can show that the problems here are overstated, or at least that hard originalism has a strong disciplining effect. But even if this is so, the more fundamental problem remains. American constitutional law would be worse, in fact much worse, if it adopted a form of originalism that would make constitutional meaning turn on the original answers to very particular questions. If constitutional law depended on those answers, it is highly likely that racial segregation would be entirely permissible at the state level; that the national government could discriminate on the basis of race however it chose; that sex discrimination would be entirely acceptable; that the free speech principle would be sharply limited; that many of the most cherished constitutional advances of the last century would not have occurred; and that the United States would no longer enjoy the fabric of rights that have made the United States Constitution a reference point for much of the world.

Constitutional rights, as Americans understand them, are very much a product of interpretive practices that begin with the original understanding but do not end there. If a proposed method of constitutional interpretation would make a constitutional democracy much worse, why should anyone adopt it? Courts do far better with soft originalism, alongside incompletely theorized agreements, analogical reasoning, a general posture of humility, and concern for the goal of ensuring a well-functioning system of deliberative democracy.

### The Privacy Cases Revisited: Desuetude, Discrimination, Democracy

Now let us put originalism to one side, at least in its "hard" form. The Supreme Court's privacy cases are notoriously difficult, and the Court's own analysis has been notoriously incomplete. I now present two narrower arguments, both applicable to several of the relevant cases. The two arguments are designed to show how constitutional rights might be founded on something other than traditional practice without fundamentally threatening democratic values.

The first argument invokes the old notion of desuetude.[33] If a law is founded on a social norm that no longer has much support, we should expect it to be enforced not at all or only on rare occasions. It is therefore a tool for harassment and not an ordinary law at all—in fact a violation of the rule of law itself. The rare enforcement occasions might well involve arbitrary or discriminatory factors. They might result from a police officer's mood or personal animus or bias of some kind. A prosecution for fornication or adultery, brought today, would be likely to have such features. In my view, the prosecution would be unconstitutional for *procedural* reasons having to do with the rule of law, not (necessarily) for substantive reasons having to do with the right to do as one chooses, with one's body or otherwise. The prosecution would be unconstitutional not because there is any general right to privacy but because the state may not enforce a law unsupported by public judgments—and no longer taken seriously as a law—in a few, randomly selected cases.

In a world in which prosecutions for fornication or adultery were common and accepted, perhaps no privacy right would be at stake; perhaps there would be no constitutional violation. At least a separate and harder question would be raised. But in a world in which such prosecutions cannot meet with public approval, an arrest or indictment would be the occasion for invalidation on procedural grounds.

*Griswold* itself should be understood in this way. The ban on contraception within marriage was not enforced by prosecutors, and the public would not stand for any such enforcement efforts. The ban served principally to deter clinics from dispensing contraceptives to poor people. The problem with the ban was not that it was unsupported by old traditions but that it had no basis in modern convictions. Few people believed that sex within marriage was legitimate only if it was for purposes of procreation, and those people could not possibly have commanded a legislative majority or even made it possible to bring many actual prosecutions against married couples. Notably, the law was not defended on its obvious foundational ground: a religious or quasi-religious judgment about when sexual activity is appropriate. It was defended instead as a means of preventing extramarital relations. So defended, the law made at best little sense, for it remained to be explained why the prohibition applied to *use* of contraceptives by married people and not just to distribution of contraceptives. Because of the absence of real enforcement, and its lack of foundation in anything like common public sentiment, the law offended a form of procedural due process, not substantive due process. *Griswold* should have been decided on this basis, which is narrower, more plausible as a textual matter, and more democratic; and as I will soon urge, the notion of desuetude covers many other cases as well. It is worthwhile to underline the democratic nature of this use of constitutional principles. The ban on use of laws that are rarely enforced is designed to ensure that if enforcement is going to take place at all, there must be democratic support for it.

Alternatively, we might understand the privacy cases as not principally or only about privacy but as closely connected with sex equality. It should not be hard to see that many of these cases involved women's rights—more particularly, they raised the question whether and when women should face a risk of an unwanted pregnancy. Of course all of the justices were well aware that the burdens of an unwanted pregnancy are borne disproportionately by women. Perhaps all of the justices believed as well that bans on the use or distribution of contraceptives would not have been likely if the consequences of an unwanted pregnancy were borne by men. In any case issues of sex equality come to the foreground once it is clear that the burdens of legal barriers to use of contraception—as well as to abortion—are faced disproportionately by women. The Court spoke in terms of privacy, but its subtext was equality. Notably, the Court did not say that the laws forbidding adultery and fornication were unconstitutional; on the contrary, it went out of its way to say that they might well be legitimate. (There is a connection with the anticaste principle, as discussed in chapter 7.)

We might therefore understand the Court in the following way. Perhaps the state may legitimately punish extramarital sexual activity directly (so long as the public will permit it to do so). This is a question that need not be decided. What the state may not do is to take the step of punishing extramarital sexual activity through the indirect, far less accountable, and discriminatory means of foreclosing access to contraception. It may not choose this route, because the indirect route is not very well connected with achievement of the relevant goal; because that route harms children (many of whom will be unwanted); and because that route imposes disproportionate burdens on women, who must bring children to term (or face the prospect of abortion if it is available). If the state is really concerned about extramarital relations, it must proceed through an adultery or fornication prosecution, which has the comparative advantages of sex neutrality, of refusing to create unwanted children as a punishment, and of exposing to public scrutiny and review the real interest at stake. The Court was telling the states: "If you are really invoking public morality, your remedy is to invoke public morality directly in favor of the interest at stake, through punishing extramarital sexual relations. We doubt that you yourselves take this interest seriously enough to prosecute anybody." In an important sense, this rationale is also democracy promoting.

The privacy cases might, then, be approached most narrowly as cases about desuetude, and more ambitiously as cases about sex discrimination; various combinations of the two ideas, both with democratic roots, are easily imaginable. On this view, tradition would be irrelevant. With these foundations, we can understand the subsequent decisions as well. Here as well it would be unnecessary to speak of tradition. *Bowers v. Hardwick* was a repeat of *Griswold*, and for this reason it was wrongly decided. The ban on homosexual sodomy is rarely enforced against consenting adults. Prosecutors simply do not initiate proceedings, since prevailing social norms would not permit many prosecutions of this kind. Realistically speaking, the ban on consensual homosexual sodomy is instead a weapon by which police officers and others might harass people on invidious grounds. The existence of unenforced and unenforceable sodomy laws, used for purposes of harassing American citizens, is an affront to the rule of law and democracy itself and objectionable for that reason, whatever we may think of privacy.

In this light the strongest constitutional argument on behalf of a right to physician-assisted suicide is not that laws forbidding that practice intrude on autonomy. It is instead that many states forbid physician-assisted suicide almost by accident and without a clear democratic judgment on behalf of the prohibition. That is, they generally ban both suicide and assisted suicide, with the latter being understood as an ordinary attempt to help someone do away with himself. The laws that embody these prohibitions were not enacted with anything like a self-conscious judgment that physician-assisted suicide should be banned under modern conditions. Perhaps courts should hold that if states are to prohibit physician-assisted suicide, it must be a product not of a decision hundreds of years old and directed to other issues but of contemporary decisions reflecting current values. On this view, laws forbidding physician-assisted suicide, like those forbidding sodomy between consenting adults, are invalid on grounds of desuetude.

Alternatively, and more ambitiously, we might approach *Hardwick* (though not physician-assisted suicide) as an equality case, in which the state was proceeding against homosexuals rather than heterosexuals. The state does not in fact oppose heterosexual sodomy, even when the law does so as a technical matter. The objectionable inequality consists of enforcement policies through which the police (and not the prosecution, which refuses to act at all) harass homosexuals and leave heterosexuals alone. As I will urge in chapter 8, this form of discrimination is objectionable because discrimination on grounds of sexual orientation is usually illegitimate and because such discrimination is a form of sex discrimination.

What of *Roe v. Wade*, sometimes taken to establish a general right to "control one's body" under the due process clause? So understood, the case was wrong. If it was right, it is because of sex equality. Bans on abortion are targeted at women. Moreover, men are not generally required to devote their bodies to the protection of others, even when the lives of innocent third parties are at stake, indeed even when the lives at stake are of innocent third parties for whose existence they are responsible. (Fathers are not compelled to give up kidneys or even blood when the lives of their children are on the line.) There is impermissible selectivity in the imposition of this burden on women alone. Moreover, the ban on abortion is closely entangled, as a matter of real-world politics, with the desire to maintain traditional gender roles. To be sure, there is no inevitable connection between opposition to abortion and commitment to those traditional roles. It is fully possible to oppose abortion while also opposing traditional gender roles. But such restrictions on abortions as are enacted exist partly because of the commitment to traditional roles, and this dooms the restrictions as a constitutional matter. A literacy test motivated by a discriminatory purpose is invalid, even though a literacy test need not be motivated by a discriminatory purpose.[34]

These are inadequate and brief remarks on some complex issues. I offer these remarks here not to resolve the relevant issues but to suggest the possibility of other sources of constitutional rights, useful for the so-called privacy cases and not relying on tradition at all. One of the most appealing arguments for constitutional traditionalism involves the apparent inadequacy of the alternatives: If not tradition, then what? I hope that these remarks are enough to show that this is hardly a rhetorical question—and that it is possible to devise arguments for constitutional rights that operate to catalyze democracy, not to oppose it.

Of course there is much to be said on behalf of constraining judges, whose role in society should be modest. But it is revealing that the case for a modest judiciary itself depends not on tradition but on considerations of democracy and hence of judgments about the rights that the people have, all things considered. When constitutionalism is working well, rights are a product of critical reflection, suitably disciplined and constrained in the way a legal system requires. Constitutionalism is not a search for tradition.

# 4

# What Should Constitutions Say?
# Secession and Beyond

Thus far I have been dealing with the problems that call for a democratic constitution, with methods for achieving constitutional agreements, and with sources of constitutional principles. I have said very little about the substance of a democratic constitution—about what, specifically, belongs in a founding document. What rights should a constitution protect? How should we go about answering that question? In this chapter I attempt to make some progress on that issue, mostly by discussing a problem that seems exotic but that contains a number of general lessons: the status of the right to secede.

The old Soviet constitution created a right to secede. The United States Constitution does not. Although some secessionists in the American South, invoking state sovereignty, claimed to find an implicit right to secede in the founding document, it was more common to invoke an extratextual "right to secede" said to be enshrined in the Declaration of Independence.[1] In any case, no serious scholar or politician now argues that a right to secede exists under United States constitutional law. It is generally agreed that such a right would undermine the spirit of the original document, one that encourages the development of constitutional provisions that prevent the defeat of the basic enterprise of democratic self-government.

Many countries recently writing constitutions have vigorously debated the question whether to create a right to secede. Within countries, many subunits have pressed claims for secession, whether or not they have a legal right to leave. It is likely that these claims will continue to be pressed in the future, especially in light of the power of nationalist, ethnic, or regional sentiments in so many places in the world. The claims for secession, or for a right to secede, also raise exceptionally large questions about the theory and practice of constitutionalism. Indeed secession movements are highly likely to reflect processes of group polarization, as like-minded people, speaking and listening mostly to one another, end up with increasingly extreme positions.

My principal claim here is that whether or not secession might be justified as a matter of politics or morality, constitutions ought not to include a right to secede. In fact nations should adopt an incompletely theorized agreement against the secession right. To place such a right in a founding document would increase the risks of ethnic and factional struggle; reduce the prospects for compromise and deliberation in government; raise dramatically the stakes of day-to-day political decisions; introduce irrelevant and illegitimate considerations into those decisions; create dangers of blackmail, strategic behavior, and exploitation; and, most generally, endanger the prospects for long-term self-governance. Constitutionalism, understood as a vehicle for promoting democracy, is frequently directed against risks of precisely this sort. Political or moral claims for secession are frequently powerful, but they do not justify constitutional recognition of a secession right. There are general lessons here for the theory of constitutionalism in general and also for the relationship between democracy and constitutionalism. An understanding of secession also illuminates a range of issues about federalism and local self-rule, and I will explore those issues here.

## Constitutions as Precommitment Strategies

It is often said that constitutionalism is in considerable tension with democracy. Thomas Jefferson was emphatic on the point, arguing that constitutions should be amended by each generation in order to ensure that the dead past would not constrain the living present.[2] Many contemporary observers echo the Jeffersonian position, claiming that constitutional constraints often amount to unjustified, antidemocratic limits on the power of the present and future. Responding to Jefferson, James Madison argued that a constitution subject to frequent amendment would promote factionalism and provide no firm basis for republican self-government.[3]

Madison envisioned firm and lasting constitutional constraints as a precondition for democratic processes rather than a check on them. This vision captures a central goal of constitutionalism: to ensure the conditions for the peaceful, long-term operation of democracy in the face of often persistent social differences and plurality along religious, ethnic, cultural, and other lines. This goal bears on constitutional developments in the many nations in which religious and ethnic hostilities are potentially intense. Madison saw differences and diversity as democratic strengths rather than weaknesses, if channeled through constitutional structures that would promote deliberation and lead groups to check, rather than exploit, other groups.

To approach the question of secession, it will be useful to provide a brief outline of some of the reasons for entrenching institutional arrangements and substantive rights. On such questions, constitutional theory remains in a surprisingly primitive state. I begin by examining what sorts of considerations might lead people forming a new government to place basic rights and arrangements beyond the reach of ordinary politics. The crucial idea here is that for various reasons, people in a newly formed nation might attempt to do so as part of a *precommitment strategy*—a strategy in which they commit themselves, in advance, to a certain course of action.[4]

1. Some rights might be entrenched because of a belief that they are in some sense pre- or extrapolitical, that is, because individuals ought to be allowed to exercise them regardless of what majorities might think. Some of these rights are entrenched for reasons entirely independent of democracy. Here constitutionalism is indeed a self-conscious check on self-government, attempting to immunize a private sphere from public power. Plausible examples include the rights to private property, freedom from self-incrimination, bodily integrity, protection against torture or cruel punishment, and privacy.

2. Many of the rights that are constitutionally entrenched actually derive from the principle of democracy itself. Their protection against majoritarian processes follows from democratic premises and creates no tension with the goal of self-government through politics. The precommitment strategy permits the people to protect democratic processes against their own potential excesses or misjudgments, sometimes associated with group polarization. The right to freedom of speech and the right to vote are the most familiar illustrations. Constitutional protection of these rights is not at odds with the commitment to self-government but instead a logical part of it. Here constitutional rights are part of the internal morality of democracy. Majority rule should not be identified with democracy itself. If a political majority restricts dissenters, or disenfranchises people, it is behaving inconsistently with democracy, and a constitution that forbids those actions is justified on democratic grounds.

In the same basic vein, constitutional rights might be designed to protect groups that are too weak to protect themselves in ordinary political life. Aware of this risk, those involved in constitutional design might create correctives. A constitution's equality principle might stem from this idea. So too with constitutional provisions guaranteeing decent food and shelter. Such provisions are absent from the United States Constitution, but they are the rule rather than the exception in constitutions written since 1950. The South African Constitution, for example, creates minimum economic guarantees, on the apparent theory that ordinary politics cannot be trusted to protect the interests of those on the margins of society (see chapter 10). An anticaste principle, designed to ensure against second-class citizenship for anyone, can similarly be understood as a way of protecting groups at risk in daily political life (see chapter 7).

3. Institutional arrangements can also be understood as an effort to protect a private sphere from majority rule. Often this effort stems from a fear of unrestrained democratic processes, perhaps because of a fear of popular passions, perhaps because of an understanding of group polarization. A decision to divide government among the legislative, executive, and judicial branches might be regarded as an effort to check and limit government by requiring a consensus among all three before the state can interfere with the private sphere. Private liberty is preserved because government is partially disabled. So too, a federal system might ensure that the nation and its subunits will check each other, generating a friction that enables private liberty to flourish.

4. Structural provisions of this sort limit the political power of present majorities (or minorities) and in this sense raise difficulties for those who believe that the only or principal purpose of constitutionalism is to provide a framework for democratic governance. But if structural provisions are generally seen as precommitment strategies, some of them can be enabling as well as constraining.[5] We can understand many structural provisions in this way. Like the rules of grammar, such provisions set out the rules by which political discussion will occur and in that sense free up the participants to conduct their discussions more easily.

The system of separation of powers, for example, constrains government, by making it harder for government to act; but it does far more than that. Separation of powers also helps to energize government and to make it more effective, by creating a healthy division of labor. This was a prominent argument during the framing period in America. A system in which the executive does not bear the burden of adjudication may well strengthen the executive by removing from it a task that frequently produces public disapproval. If the president does not adjudicate, he is able to pursue his tasks unencumbered by judicial burdens. Indeed, the entire framework enables rather than constrains democracy, not only by creating an energetic executive but more fundamentally by allowing the sovereign people to pursue a strategy, against their government, of divide and conquer. So long as it is understood that no branch of government is actually "the people," a system of separation of powers can allow the citizenry to monitor and constrain its inevitably imperfect agents. And a system of separated powers also proliferates the points of access to government, allowing people to succeed (for example) within the legislature even if they are blocked, or unheard, within the executive or judicial branches.

5. Constitutional provisions might facilitate democracy in quite another sense: a decision to take certain issues off the ordinary political agenda can be indispensable to the political process itself. In many small groups and even families, people decide not to resolve questions that would prove intractable or even explosive. Constitutional provisions have similar functions. For example, a nation might say that religious questions cannot be resolved by democratic processes, not only because there is a right to freedom of religious conscience but also because the democratic process works best if the fundamental and potentially explosive question of religion does not intrude into day-to-day decisions. A nation might create a right to private property, and prevent government from taking property without just compensation, so as to ensure that politics is devoted to soluble questions, not insoluble ones about when, exactly, one person's property should be taken for the benefit of others. The constitution here is protecting democracy by taking certain issues off the agenda. More narrowly and no doubt more controversially, the decision to constitutionalize the right to abortion might be justified because it minimizes the chances that this polarizing question will intrude into and thus disable the political process.

6. Yet another set of these "facilitative" precommitment strategies includes provisions that are designed to solve collective action problems, often in the form of prisoners' dilemmas—that is, situations in which the pursuit of rational self-interest by each individual actor produces outcomes that are destructive to all actors considered together, and that could be avoided if all actors agreed in advance to coercion, assuring cooperation.[6] A constitution might attempt to ensure that these situations do not arise. This idea has played a large role in the American constitutional experience. The leading example is the Full Faith and Credit Clause, which requires each state to enforce judgments rendered in other states. Without this provision, every state might have a strong incentive to refuse to enforce the judgments of other states; if Massachusetts chooses not to honor the judgment of a New York court against a Massachusetts citizen, then Massachusetts receives a short-term gain because the resources its citizen needs to satisfy any judgment remain within the borders of Massachusetts. But all states would be

better off if the law bound each of them to respect the judgments of others. The Full Faith and Credit Clause ensures precisely this outcome, effectively solving the problem.

Another illustration is the Commerce Clause. In the period between the Articles of Confederation and the Constitution, battles among the states produced mutually destructive tariffs and other protectionist measures. The adoption of each of these measures probably furthered the interest of each state considered in isolation. If New York could impose a tariff on goods from Massachusetts, it would be in the interest of New Yorkers, or at least some powerful New Yorkers, to do exactly that. But collectively, this system proved disastrous. It should be no surprise that the Court has consistently interpreted the clause as disabling the states from regulating interstate commerce.[7]

Especially in light of the strong emotional attachments that fuel perceptions of state self-interest, a system in which each state can choose whether to initiate protectionist measures might well lead many states to do so. But an agreement by all states to refrain from protectionism, and thus to waive their preexisting rights under the Articles of Confederation, was undoubtedly in the collective interest of the nation, because it would make national markets possible. The constitutional decision to remove control of interstate commerce from state authority solved the problem. In this case, as with the Full Faith and Credit Clause, a relinquishment of what appears to be state sovereignty very probably furthers the interest of all states concerned. This example illustrates both the importance of precommitment strategies in resolving collective action problems and the potential value of judicial review in a healthy constitutional system.

7. Constitutional precommitment strategies might serve to overcome myopia or weakness of will on the part of the society or to ensure that representatives follow the considered judgments of the people rather than their momentary passions. Protection of freedom of speech, or from unreasonable searches and seizures, might represent an effort by the people themselves to provide safeguards against the impulsive behavior of majorities. Here the goal is to ensure that the deliberative sense of the community will prevail over short-term judgments. Similarly, a constitution might represent a firm acknowledgement that the desires of the government, even in a well-functioning republic, do not always match those of the people. Constitutional limits, introduced by something like the people themselves, therefore respond to the problems created by a system in which government officials inevitably have interests of their own.

In all of these cases, the decision to take certain questions off the political agenda might be understood as a means not of disabling but of protecting democratic politics, by reducing the power of highly controversial questions to create factionalism, instability, impulsiveness, chaos, stalemate, collective action problems, myopia, strategic behavior, or hostilities so serious and fundamental as to endanger the governmental process itself. In this respect, the decision to use constitutionalism to remove certain issues from politics is often profoundly democratic.

8. We can also see many constitutional provisions as mechanisms for ensuring discussion and deliberation oriented toward agreement about the general good rather than factionalism and self-interested bargaining. In the United States, the states' relinquishment of their preexisting sovereign right to control the entry and exit of goods is the most prominent example. But the institutions of representation and checks and balances have frequently been designed to promote general discussion and compromise, to diminish the influence of particular segments of society, and to produce the incentives for and possibility of agreement.

## Precommitment and Secession

For the moment I will not speak to the issue of whether and when secession is desirable or just. Instead I want to ask whether a constitution ought to recognize a right to secede. I will understand a constitutional right to secede as encompassing (1) an explicit textual provision guaranteeing such a right or (2) an implicit understanding that the constitution creates that right, accompanied in either case by (3) a willingness to enforce that right by a court with the power of judicial review—that is, a court capable of granting and enforcing a subunit's request to secede despite the objections of the central government. Constitutional guarantees on paper often mean nothing without institutions available to vindicate them. The Soviet experience demonstrated this point in the context of individual rights as well as the context of secession; the experience of China under communism continues to demonstrate the same thing.

At first glance, the argument for a right to secede seems straightforward. If a subunit no longer wants to stay within the nation, why should it have to do so? This initial challenge draws strength from a number of specific arguments, spelled out below, including the need for local self-determination, the history of unjust acquisition in various nations, the claims of ethnic and cultural integrity, and the threat of abridgement of basic rights and liberties.

The issue of secession is, however, an unusually good candidate for an analysis that stresses the role of constitutionalism in protecting democratic rule. Indeed, the problem of secession closely parallels the problems solved by the Full Faith and Credit Clause and the Commerce Clause and even follows naturally from those examples. The initial point is that constitutional recognition of a right to secede might well have a range of harmful consequences for democratic politics. In the face of such a right, a threat to secede could be plausible at any given time, allowing the exit of the subunit from the nation to be a relevant factor in every important decision. It is not difficult to imagine circumstances in which it would be in a subunit's interest to issue that threat. Rather than working to achieve compromise, or to solve common problems, subunits holding a right to secede might well hold out for whatever they can get.

A right to secede would encourage strategic behavior—efforts to seek benefits or diminish burdens by making threats that are strategically useful and based on power over matters technically unrelated to the particular question at issue. Subunits with economic power might well be able to extract large gains in every decision involving the social distribution of benefits and burdens. A constitutional system that recognizes the right to secede will find its very existence at issue in every case in which a subunit's interests are seriously at stake. In practice, that threat could operate as a prohibition on any national decision adverse to the subunit's interests. A temporarily disaffected subunit could, in short, raise the stakes in ordinary political and economic decisions simply by threatening to leave. The threat would be especially credible and therefore disruptive if the subunit can or might prefer to exist on its own. The recognition of a right of exit on the part of the subunit could thus prevent fair dealing on the nation's part, by allowing the submit to veto policies that are justified on balance.

It might also lead to undue caution. The threat to secede might deter the government from taking action that offends a subunit but is on balance justified. Consider, for example, the issue of taxation. A tobacco-growing subunit equipped with the right to secede might be able to veto a decision to raise taxes on (say) cigarettes even if that decision would further the nation's long-term interest. Similar considerations apply to the decision to enter into war, to enact environmental regulation, or to increase or decrease aid to agriculture. A secession right cannot plausibly be justified on the ground that it is a necessary check on national policies designed to ensure that those policies are in the general interest; the fact that a state wants to secede is neither a necessary nor a sufficient reason to believe that the general interest is being violated.

Family law supplies a helpful analogy. In a marriage, the understanding that the unit is not divisible because of current dissatisfaction, but only in extraordinary circumstances, can serve to promote compromise, to encourage people to live together, to lower the stakes during disagreements, and to prevent any particular person from achieving an excessively strong bargaining position. A decision to stigmatize divorce or to make it available only under certain conditions—as virtually every state in the United States has done—may lead to happier as well as more stable marriages, by providing an incentive for spouses to adapt their behavior and even their desires to promote long-term harmony. I intend to make no sweeping comment here on the proper structure of divorce law; I argue only that there can be strong reasons for making exit difficult.

Recognition of a right to secede would also ensure that any subunit whose resources are at the moment indispensable, and that might be able to exist on its own, is in an extraordinary position to obtain benefits or to diminish burdens on matters formally unrelated to its comparative advantage. Moreover, the shared knowledge that the nation is terminable at the option of any subunit would promote instability.

In these circumstances, we might understand a ban on secession as a solution to a collective action problem. For each subunit, acting individually, recognition of the right might increase its authority to obtain a large share of the collective assets during any general allocation. But if the right to secede exists, each subunit will be vulnerable to threats of secession by the others. If the considerations marshaled thus far are persuasive, all or most subunits are quite plausibly better off if each of them waives its right to secede. More generally, the difficulty or impossibility of exit from the nation will encourage cooperation for the long term, providing an incentive to adapt conduct and even preferences to that goal.

Of course, the existence of a right to secede will have few such consequences if a threat to secede is not credible. Under some conditions, however, the threat will be a real one. Some subunits might well find it in their economic interest to exist on their own. If independence is economically preferable, the threat of secession will be fully plausible. Other subunits will suffer some economic loss if they secede but still find independence worthwhile because of gains in terms of cultural or geographical autonomy or capacity for self-governance. Here the threat of secession might be credible even if the seceding subunit would be an economic loser.

In the context of secession, the practical political problem goes especially deep. The right to secede is different from other potential vetoes on national legislative action precisely because it raises fundamental and often emotional issues having to do with the claims of ethnicity, territory, and history to separation and self-determination. These issues have a peculiar tendency to inflame both subunits and those who want them to remain part of the nation. They tend to raise the emotional stakes in such a way as to make the ordinary work of politics—not to mention day-to-day interactions in other spheres—extremely hard to undertake. Group polarization is obviously a serious risk here. It is predictable that professional polarizers would try to move public sentiment in their preferred directions. A waiver of the right to secede protects against inflamed or impulsive behavior.

On some occasions, the emotional stakes should be raised in precisely this way. But constitutional recognition of a right to secede accomplishes the relevant goals at great risk to the fundamental task of creating healthy, long-term constitutional structures. The large destabilizing effects of a right to secede may also disrupt expectations whose existence is indispensable both to economic prosperity and democratic self-determination. Even more fundamentally, a nation whose subunits may secede will be far less likely to engage in long-term planning. Interdependence will be both threatening and risky and thus will be discouraged.

Thus far I have argued that a waiver of the right to secede is a sensible precommitment strategy, one that is likely to remove a serious threat to democratic processes. There are at least two possible responses to this line of argument. The first is that if the existence of the nation confers mutual benefits—an assumed precondition for its continuation—then subunits will rarely threaten to secede even if constitutionally authorized to do so, and the threat will rarely be credible even if made. The costs of secession will usually be at least as large for the subunit as for the nation. On this view, recognition of a right to secede would never or rarely have the adverse effects claimed for it. A well-functioning nation simply will not face serious secession threats; subunits will invoke the right only in the most extraordinary circumstances. Indeed, in those circumstances the right is a necessary corrective to the status quo.

This rejoinder is not implausible. Under certain circumstances, recognition of a right to secede would probably make little difference. But the rejoinder is altogether too optimistic. Sometimes secession will further the economic interest of the subunit, or the threat might be credible because an economic loss would be counteracted by gains in terms of symbolism or subunit autonomy. Moreover, national politics affecting multiple subunits are subject to unpredictable and often highly emotional factors. Technocratic rationality does not characterize deliberations in which the specter of secession is involved. The mere possibility of secession may prevent calm negotiation.

It is true that under certain conditions, the right to secession would have few deleterious effects, and it might prevent serious harms. This is especially so in cases involving a weak or loose confederation without substantial interdependencies. In such cases, the risks posed by strategic behavior and inflamed ethnic and other passions will be less severe. For the European Community, for example, a right to secede may therefore be more sensible, and indeed it will provide a greater incentive to join in the first instance.

For those deciding on the contents of a constitution, the questions are which scenarios are most likely and which provide the worst case. The most that one can do here is to point to the often large emotional attachments to subunits, the possibility of financial gains from strategic behavior, the familiar frailties of human nature, the rational and irrational factors that can make subunits press secession claims, and the potentially debilitating effects of such claims on subunit and national processes of self-government.

In view of these considerations, it seems highly likely that recognition of a constitutional right to secede would create serious difficulties. Where strong nationalist passions persist and threaten to infect daily politics if given an explicit constitutional home, a right to secede would be especially damaging to the prospects for democratic government. All this suggests a strong presumption against a constitutional right to secede.


### Reasons for Secession

Even if a constitutional right to secede would create risks for democratic politics, the case against such a right has hardly been completed. It might well be that the countervailing considerations, justifying a right to secede, outweigh any such adverse effects. To explore this question, it will be useful to examine why a subunit of a country might want to secede. The reasons fall into five basic categories. Many of these arguments provide plausible grounds for secession as a matter of political morality.[8] I evaluate them here because they raise general issues about constitutional democracy, and with special attention to their relationship to a claimed constitutional right to secede.

A subunit might want to secede because its people are being oppressed. Governmental oppression might be limited to a subunit, or it might be part of a general pattern of governmental abuse. For example, the government might have limited the right to freedom of speech in only one part of the nation. Alternatively, the oppression might be quite general, and the subunit might want to secede because it sees itself as subject, like other subunits, to an intolerable regime.

In the latter case, something other than the fact of oppression must also be at work in order to justify secession as distinct from, say, civil disobedience or revolution. If the oppression is general, some independent factor—like cultural homogeneity or a claim to territorial integrity based on history—is necessary to unite one of the many subunits that are, by hypothesis, being oppressed. For this reason, I focus here on the case of a subunit that is singled out for injustice, in the form of abridgement of civil liberties or civil rights.

When oppression is pervasive, and not otherwise remediable, secession is a justified response; of course a subunit is entitled to leave a nation that is oppressing it. Standing alone, however, injustice or oppression does not provide a powerful case for creating a constitutional right to secede. A selective abridgement of the right of free speech is far more naturally countered by a restoration of that right than by permitting exit from the nation. If the central government suspends civil rights and civil liberties, the preferable response is to restore rights and liberties through the pressure of domestic or international law. The risk of abridgement of civil rights or civil liberties provides no good argument for a constitutional right to secede; it merely furnishes reasons for a constitutional order that makes abridgement unlikely.

If restoration is for some reason impossible, of course, secession might be necessary. One implication is that a constitutional right to secede may be necessary to deter the abridgement of civil rights and civil liberties. This argument has foundations in the work of Thomas Jefferson, who favored both small political units and occasional therapeutic rebellions—views that led him to endorse a right to secede. Thus Jefferson wrote in 1816, "If any State in the Union will declare that it prefers separation . . . to a continuance in union . . . I have no hesitation in saying, 'let us separate.' "[9]

We can find a parallel to this argument in the continuing debates over federalism and rights of interstate mobility. Any society that constitutes its government through a federal system necessarily creates a built-in safeguard against political or economic oppression, at least if it allows freedom of movement. A government that oppresses its citizenry will soon find itself without citizens at all. It is no surprise that under communism East Germany needed the Berlin Wall. In Eastern Europe, the denial of the right to travel was the denial of a crucial political right, one that belongs on the same plane as voting.

In a healthy federal system, states will often compete to attract citizens by offering better opportunities and prospects. The result should be a beneficial "race" to provide a mix of laws and regulations that promote both liberty and security. Indeed, the fact of interstate mobility in the United States is probably a far more powerful check against many forms of state tyranny than the existence of judicial review. Of course, there is a dark side to this process. The "race" can be harmful as well as beneficial. Consider cases in which states compete for revenue-providing industry by eliminating environmental or occupational regulation that would in fact be optimal; here the competition is destructive, and the national government must be authorized to impose uniform regulation on its subunits. But there can be no doubt that the right of exit operates as a powerful check on tyranny of various sorts. It might follow that a right to secede could be justified as a similar and quite valuable merchanism for ensuring against oppression by the national government. The fact that the method is indirect does not mean that it is not extremely effective.

In some contexts, a right to secede might well be justified on this ground. Especially when other institutions cannot protect civil rights and civil liberties, a secession right might be justifiable. But in general, it is doubtful whether the argument overcomes the competing considerations traced thus far. I have noted that there are far more direct and less dangerous means of protecting against the abridgement of civil rights and civil liberties. A good constitution will contain those means. Rights of interstate mobility and a federal structure will operate as additional safeguards. At least most of the time, a constitutional right to secede would create severe risks without at the same time conferring benefits that cannot be largely or entirely achieved through other strategies.

### Economic Self-Interest

A subunit might want to secede because economic self-interest suggests it would do better on its own. The subunit might be subsidizing other people of the nation in various ways; for example, it might have valuable natural resources that are being used by outsiders at costs lower than the subunit would like to charge. Or its members may be especially productive. Members of the subunit might come to believe that they will be financially better off if they create their own country.

It is far from clear that economic self-interest can justify secession as a matter of political morality. The answer will turn, at least in part, on whether there is a justification for the economic harms faced by the subunit. No subunit has a right to continue to enjoy whatever resources it currently has. Suppose that the nation is taking resources from rich subunits and giving resources to poor ones. If such redistribution is indeed justified, then the fact that the economic self-interest of the rich subunit has been jeopardized is not a good basis for secession. At any given time a subunit may be contributing more than what seems its fair share, and perhaps some subunits will be doing so for very long periods. But unless there is some kind of injustice, the mere fact that secession is in a subunit's self-interest does not justify secession.

### Economic Exploitation

A more serious argument for a constitutional right to secession would stress economic exploitation. By this term I mean not that a subunit is simply losing but that it can claim, with reasons, that the central government is treating it unfairly. We might hypothesize that the nation is systematically depleting the subunit's resources for the general good, thus reducing the subunit's wealth far below what it would be if the subunit stood alone; or the nation might be unfairly discriminating against the subunit in the distribution of general benefits and burdens. A claim for secession might well be based on this sort of behavior from the nation's center. Indeed, a right to secede—as in the case of abridgement of civil liberties and civil rights— might be justified as a means of deterring economic exploitation of subunits.

In some cases, economic exploitation might indeed justify secession as a matter of political morality. But does the prospect of exploitation argue for a constitutional right to secede? There are several problems here. The first is that it is hard to define the baseline against which to measure a claim of exploitation; the term "exploitation" is itself a placeholder for ideas that must be defended. No subunit has an antecedent right to a stream of welfare identical to what it would have received if it had not been a member of the nation. Moreover, it is extraordinarily difficult to calculate benefits and burdens, especially over long periods of time. In many cases the question of exploitation will be hard to assess in light of the many links by which subunits in a nation become economically interdependent.

Suppose that in some cases we can agree that a subunit is being exploited by the nation. In such cases, a good constitution will provide both structural and rights-based provisions designed to prevent discrimination against certain subunits, and these provisions will make a right to secede unnecessary. The subunit should, for example, be granted full representation in the legislature; this is a built-in, if partial, corrective. (It is only partial because other parts of the nation may unite against the subunit—hardly an unfamiliar phenomenon.) The United States Constitution achieves this goal in part through the establishment of a bicameral legislature in which all states, regardless of size, have equal representation in one house. This requirement is, in fact, the only element of the Constitution specifically protected by the document itself against amendment without the consent of the affected state. A constitution could also ban discriminatory taxation or require unanimous consent to certain measures raising a risk of exploitation. These strategies pose dangers as well. But the basic point is that a right to secede is a second-best and highly indirect remedy, one that creates a range of problems independent of economic exploitation and whose purposes might be accomplished through other means.

### History and Territory: The Injustice of the Original Acquisition

Secession might be sought by a subunit that claims that its membership in the nation originally resulted from unjustified aggression and that sees itself as having territorial integrity as a matter of history and international law, properly construed. Often an understanding of this kind plays a role in secession claims. Suppose subunit A existed as an independent entity at an earlier period. The larger unit absorbed subunit A through war or aggression. The subunit now seeks to separate from the nation as a way of undoing a historical wrong.

Arguments of this kind may well provide a sufficient moral reason for secession. Certainly if little time has passed since the original aggression, a right to secede seems self-evident, because it corrects the original injustice. But, for three reasons, it is doubtful whether the existence of historic abuses is a sufficient reason to create a constitutional right to secede.

The first is that a well-functioning system of international law is the best and most direct way to prevent and to respond to aggression. A right to secede is too general, applying in cases when there has not been aggression at all. At most the phenomenon of aggression justifies a moral right to secede in some narrowly defined class of cases in which membership in the nation was originally involuntary. Something like that right already exists as a matter of international law.[10] A generalized constitutional right to secession is unnecessary to recognize a right to exit from a union created by force.

The second problem is a practical one. A nation that takes other countries by force, and incorporates them, is unlikely to respect any right to secede that it has formally recognized. The Soviet Union was an example. In the event of incorporation by force, a right to secede is especially prone to becoming an ineffectual "parchment barrier," worth no more than the paper on which it is written.

The third problem is that the origins of many, perhaps most, nations often involve aggression and abuse at some point in the past, and it is not easy to decide which such abuses provide a sufficient basis for a right to secede. The category of cases in which secession can plausibly be justified on such grounds is simply enormous, and if secession is generally to be permitted, the result would be an intolerable disruption of established arrangements. This consideration suggests that while the injustice of the original acquisition will often provide a good basis for a secession right, a system that would allow secession in all such circumstances would be hard to defend.

In cases of subunits absorbed through aggression, then, the preferable remedy is a system of international law, including an internationally recognized right to restore original borders, at least when sufficiently little time has passed and when exercise of that right would not unduly disrupt existing arrangements. Sometimes a right to secede is in fact justified on this ground as a matter of political morality. But a domestic constitutional provision guaranteeing the right to secede is both too small and too large a way to deal with this problem.

### Cultural Integrity and Self-Determination

Often a claimed right to secede is built on an understanding that the subunit has a kind of cultural integrity that entitles it to self-determination. The subunit perceives itself as both homogeneous and substantially different in terms of basic norms and commitments. The very fact that it is governed by a broader entity appears to be a form of tyranny or an unjustifiable absorption by foreigners. Rule by outsiders eviscerates the subunit's distinct identity.

Whether a claim to cultural integrity justifies secession as a matter of political morality is a complex matter. Certainly ethnic homogeneity can make rule by outsiders impossible or oppressive—especially if group polarization is occurring among the ethnically homogeneous group. Just as certainly, productive interactions among heterogeneous groups can make for an especially successful democracy. History offers examples of both phenomena. It is therefore impossible to say, in the abstract, whether secession can be justified on this ground. Much will depend on how culturally homogenous groups are treated by the larger nation, the nature of the differences between the subunit and the nation, and the forms their homogeneity takes. For example, a cultural group that oppresses others in its region can hardly make a powerful moral claim for a right to self-governance if the larger nation prizes civil liberties.

Here, as before, any legitimate claims that underlie a right to secession might well be accommodated by narrower and less dangerous strategies— in particular, federalism and representation mechanisms. A system of federalism often guards against precisely the problem of rule by remote leaders having insufficient identification with or knowledge of subunits. In the experience of the United States, federalism was designed to ensure local self-determination while at the same time providing and thus benefiting from governance at the national level. Federal systems can allow a large degree of governance by subunits claiming cultural and territorial integrity. Indeed, the national constitution may restrict the central government to certain enumerated powers, including provision of national defense or regulation of interstate commerce, or it may expressly reserve certain powers of internal self-governance to the subunits. It may well be that through these routes, federal systems can accommodate many of the concerns that underlie claims to secession based on cultural integrity.

Systems of representation might also supply a corrective here. Seats in the national legislature might be set aside for subunit representatives to ensure that the views of subunits are expressed on an ongoing basis during the deliberative process. Such seats might provide a form of proportional or even superproportional representation. Perhaps a minority veto should be ensured on certain issues.

In some circumstances, of course, these solutions will be inadequate. Sometimes the claim for self-determination is largely an emotional one, coming from a group affronted by the very fact of national incorporation and national rule. Sometimes nationhood involves an inevitable surrender of components of sovereignty claimed by subunits. If full self-determination is the goal, the only remedy will be secession, enabling the subunit to escape entirely from the legal authority of the nation.

It may be that these points are sufficient, as a matter of political morality, to justify secession in some contexts. The claim for secession is surely strengthened if the argument from cultural integrity is accompanied by a claim to territorial integrity in the past. But it is doubtful that, standing alone, the argument from cultural integrity justifies a constitutional right to secede. In such cases, we are often dealing, by hypothesis, with subunits that voluntarily agreed to enter the nation at some earlier time. In such cases, the claim of cultural integrity will frequently be inadequate because sufficient commonalities with the nation are likely to exist, justifying the original agreement. Whether or not this is so, recognition of a right to secede, based on grounds of cultural integrity, is likely to pose dangers to national self-determination that are not counterbalanced by the advantages to the various subunits themselves. Whether or not the interest in cultural integrity provides a good moral justification for secession, it does not support a decision to place a right to secede in a founding document.

### A Qualified Right to Secede?

A possible response to the discussion thus far would be that the right to secede should indeed be constitutionalized but hedged with qualifications and limitations that minimize the risks I have discussed. There are several possibilities here. One strategy would allow secession if and only if a large majority of the subunit sought it. Another would allow secession only under specifically enumerated circumstances, as, for example, in cases of suspension of civil liberties or economic exploitation. Yet another would create a requirement of prolonged deliberation before secession would be lawful. Such a system might involve, for example, multiple popular votes, with substantial waiting periods between votes. A fourth approach would create a right to secede, either absolute or qualified, but make it unenforceable by the judiciary.

All of these routes have big advantages over an unqualified right to secede, but it is doubtful whether the advantages justify constitutionalization of even a qualified right to secede. A requirement of a supermajority would certainly limit the occasions for, and seriousness of, secession threats. But in cases in which the subunit can be energized—for reasons of economic self-interest or ethnic and territorial self-identification—the protection would be inadequate. It is true that a subunit might want to secede for good reasons, but as discussed earlier, there are better and less disruptive means of ensuring that the good motivations that sometimes underlie secession movements can be addressed. These involve, above all, federalism, checks and balances, entrenchment of civil rights and civil liberties, and judicial review. If these protections are inadequate, it is highly doubtful that a qualified right to secede will do the job.

There is something to be said in favor of a secession provision that would be limited to specified causes. Such a provision might be treated as a supplement to the nondiscrimination principles and basic protections of liberties. It would furnish a powerful and self-enforcing mechanism against violations of the relevant rights. But to accomplish these purposes, the right to secede is probably too blunt and dangerous an instrument. It is sensible to hope that the direct provisions discussed earlier will be sufficient. More fundamentally, the recognition of a right to secede on paper is unlikely to be a useful supplement if they are not. A state that violates its textual commitments to civil rights and liberties will probably not respect its textual commitment to secession.

A right to secede after an extended period of deliberation would probably be the best of the various alternatives. Through this route it would be possible to reduce some of the risks of an inflamed polity. Indeed, the very difficulty of obtaining secession would deter efforts to seek that remedy unless it seemed necessary and would diminish the possibility that any threat of secession could disrupt democratic and deliberative processes. For this reason it could not be said, a priori, that such a system would necessarily be undesirable. But in nations with a history of ethnic and religious tensions, even a secession right modified in this way would pose significant risks to self-governance. A prolonged deliberative period over the question of continued ties to the nation could create all of the threats emphasized earlier. Probably the best approach is not to create the right at all.

A final possibility would be to create a right to secede but to make it nonjusticiable—that is, to make the right one that courts will not recognize or enforce. India's constitution follows this strategy mainly with respect to certain "positive" rights, including the right to subsistence; South Africa follows the same basic plan (though in South Africa courts do have some role in the protection of social and economic guarantees). Such rights are recognized in the sense that the constitution makes them binding on the legislature, but the courts are unable to protect them. The argument for constitutional rights that are judicially unenforceable rights is simple: The existence of such rights establishes principles that government is morally and politically obliged to respect. But the judicial enforcement of such rights would create serious problems, above all the various difficulties produced when judges assume a policymaking role for which they lack training and competence. The right to subsistence is a plausible candidate for this strategy because of the vagueness of the right and, more fundamentally, the obvious problems in judicial definition and implementation of any such right. Perhaps the right to secede should be placed in this category.

The principal difficulty with this claim is that judicially unenforceable rights are usually those whose elaboration would strain judicial capacities. With respect to secession, there is no such problem. To make the right to secession unenforceable by courts would reflect not a problem of definition or implementation but instead ambivalence about the right itself. As distinguished from the right to subsistence, there is nothing vague about the right to secede. If the case for a constitutional right to secede is persuasive, then the right should be both entrenched in the text and judicially enforceable. If the case is weak, then an unenforceable right is no better than no right at all.

## What Constitutions Are For

I have suggested that constitutional protections should often be understood as an effort to facilitate rather than merely to frustrate democratic processes. Such efforts take many forms: the protection of rights central to self-government; the creation of fixed and stable arrangements by which people order their affairs; the removal of especially charged or intractable questions from the public agenda; the creation of incentives for compromise, deliberation, and agreement; and the solution of problems posed by collective action problems, myopia, and impulsiveness. Ideas of this sort suggest that a right to secede does not belong in a founding document.

In some cases, a right to secede will be fully justified as a matter of political morality. But the existence of occasionally powerful moral claims supplies insufficient reason for constitutional recognition of the right to secede. A nation that recognizes this right, and is prepared to respect it, may well find that it has thereby endangered ordinary democratic processes. A decision to allow a right of exit from the nation will divert attention from matters at hand, allow minority vetoes on important issues, encourage strategic and myopic behavior, and generally compromise the system of self-government. For this reason, a waiver of the right to secede should be seen as a natural part of constitutionalism, which frequently amounts to a pre-commitment strategy directed against problems of precisely this sort.

An understanding of the secession issue casts some general light on the relationship between democracy and constitutionalism. It shows that people may lack a constitutional right where they have a moral one. And it also brings home a central lesson of this book—that many constitutional provisions should be designed to ensure self-governance, and that both rights and refusals to grant rights can be understood in light of that goal.

# 5
# Impeaching the President

In a well-functioning democracy, impeachment of high officials is likely to be exceedingly rare even if the constitution provides for it. In the United States and England, for example, impeachment turns out to be irrelevant to almost all of constitutional life. But the questions raised by the impeachment power, or by any other provisions governing the removal of high officials from office, are nonetheless extremely important. Their importance lies partly in what they say about a system of checks and balances, or the separation of powers. Despite its infrequent use, impeachment provisions carry large lessons about the relationship between constitutionalism and democracy; and they tell us a great deal about other constitutional provisions with much greater daily importance, such as bicameralism in the legislature and the power of the president to veto legislation, subject to a two-thirds vote to override.

It should not be difficult to see that the impeachment power is a central part of a system of deliberative democracy. A primary goal of that power is to allow removal of high-level officials when circumstances warrant, but without permitting partisan passions to undermine the independence of the executive branch. In fact any effort to impeach the president is highly likely to be a case study in group polarization. If—as is common—people with one view are speaking mostly to one another, and if those with the opposing view also fortify their own convictions in this way, the contending sides might well polarize, making their own views increasingly extreme.

Indeed something of just this sort happened with the 1998 impeachment of President Bill Clinton. Early in the deliberations, Congressman Henry Hyde, the chairman of the House Judiciary Committee, made it clear that impeachment would be inappropriate unless there was bipartisan support for it. But of course this view did not ultimately prevail, and Hyde's own mind changed dramatically. The result was a situation in which the Republican members of the House of Representatives almost unanimously voted for impeachment, whereas the Democratic members almost unanimously voted against it. This sharp division of view attests to the pervasive importance of the mechanisms of group polarization—and partisan differences of this sort suggest the pervasive risk of deliberative trouble for constitutional democracies.

Might anything be done to reduce that trouble? What makes impeachment especially important is the evident interplay, in this domain, between constitutionalism and democracy and the search for constitutional solutions that can help counteract predictable problems in democratic deliberation. A democratic constitution's provisions on impeachment can ensure that if a high-level official is going to be removed, it will be because of a bipartisan consensus that this is appropriate, not because of a cascade-like process among smaller groups or even a majority. Thus understood, impeachment provisions are a central part of the system of checks and balances. They offer a revealing glimpse into a basic goal of that system: to ensure not an undemocratic check on majorities but a process of reflection and reason-giving, constraining the potentially adverse effects of group polarization.

I offer three more particular claims, designed for disputes in the United States in particular. The simplest is that with respect to the president, the principal goal of the impeachment clause of the American constitution is to allow impeachment for a *narrow category of egregious or large-scale abuses of authority that come from the exercise of distinctly presidential powers.* What is generally necessary is *an egregious abuse of power that the president has by virtue of being president.* It follows that the 1998 impeachment of President Clinton was clearly unconstitutional.

My second claim is that in the current period it is more, not less, important to insist on this particular understanding of the impeachment clause. In large part because of group polarization, and its interaction with current technologies, there are grave systemic dangers in resorting to impeachment except in the most extreme cases. The best course lies in legislative forbearance and self-restraint—a kind of mutual arms control agreement, to be entered into by both political parties, in the interest of the nation as a whole.

My third claim is that a sensible understanding of impeachment is best developed with close reference to the idea of deliberative democracy. A grave risk is that instead of devoting attention to issues actually bearing on people's well-being, the impeachment mechanism, and other responses to alleged scandals, will be used by self-interested politicians seeking to further their own agendas. If we see impeachment as a remedy of last resort—the culmination of a lengthy process of deliberation involving the worst abuses of public power—we will be on our way to focusing public attention not on possible official misdeeds but on how to ensure that government action is actually affecting people's lives.

Some people think that the meaning of the Constitution is settled by the original understanding, and debates about impeachment have had a striking and unmistakable "originalist" dimension. I do not accept the view that the Constitution means what it was originally understood to mean, partly for reasons connected with my criticism of "tradition" as a source of constitutional meaning (see chapter 3).[1] In my view, practices over the last two centuries and more are highly relevant to constitutional meaning—as is an assessment of what approach makes best sense, given the Constitution's aspiration to deliberative democracy. But of course the original understanding is part of the picture. Let us start, then, by examining the original understanding of the impeachment power. What was the impeachment power soon after ratification—in, for example, 1778?

## The Text

The text of the Constitution is the place to begin. It says that a president may be removed for "Treason, Bribery, or other high Crimes and Misdemeanors." While the text certainly does not resolve every question, it is highly suggestive. What it suggests is that to be impeachable the president must have engaged in large-scale abuses of distinctly presidential powers

The opening reference to treason and bribery, together with the word "other," seems to indicate that high crimes and misdemeanors should be understood to be of the same general kind and magnitude as treason and bribery (as in the Latin canon of construction, *ejusdem generis*). For a reader in 1788, the terms "treason" and "bribery" would be unmistakable references to misuse of office, probably through betraying the country in one way or another. Thus it would be reasonable to think that "other high crimes and misdemeanors" must amount to a kind of egregious misuse of public office. The Constitution does not say "Murder, Rape, and Other High Crimes and Misdemeanors," nor does it say "Blasphemy, Conspiracy, and Other High Crimes and Misdemeanors." The opening references to treason and bribery seem to limit the kinds of offenses for which a president may be removed from office.

Other provisions of the Constitution support this judgment; they suggest that the choice of terms was no coincidence, that the words "treason" and "bribery" were carefully chosen, and that the term "high" was intended as a serious restriction on the legitimate grounds for impeachment. The interstate extradition clause refers to persons "charged in any State With Treason, Felony, or other Crime," in striking contrast to the impeachment provision. Consider also the speech and debate clause, which refers to congressional immunity from arrest "in all Cases, except Treason, Felony, and Breach of the Peace," and the Fifth Amendment's grand jury clause, which guarantees the right to a grand jury when someone is "held to answer for a capital, or otherwise infamous crime." The different constitutional references to diverse "crimes" suggests that the impeachment provision had a special purpose. Because the phrase "other high Crimes and Misdemeanors" is a dramatic contrast from other provisions of the text, it is reasonable to think that those terms are a reference to abuses that are, in both nature and magnitude, similar to treason and bribery.

This reading does not entirely dispose of the interpretive problems. For one thing, the term "bribery" creates some ambiguity. A bribery could be the acceptance of a payment of money by the president, to induce someone to act in a way inconsistent with the republic's needs or desires, or it could be a payment of money by the president himself, to convince people to vote for him. But it could also be a payment by the president to a judge, to induce the judge to decide a case in favor of a childhood friend; or it could be a presidential payment of money to an athlete, to induce the athlete to allow an opposing team to win some competition. In light of the wide range of possible "bribes," it would be possible to suggest, with Judge Richard Posner,[2] that not every "bribe" is an abuse of office or even connected with office. And if this is so, it is not altogether clear what counts as "other" high crimes and misdemeanors.

There is another textual puzzle. The word "high" precedes "crimes" but not "misdemeanors"; does this suggest that any misdemeanor is a legitimate basis for impeachment? Perhaps a "high crime" *or* a "misdemeanor" is sufficient for impeachment. And is there not a difference between "crimes" and "misdemeanors," as the text seems to suggest? Perhaps—the open-minded textual interpreter might wonder, trying to reconstruct the audience's judgment in 1788—misdemeanors need not be crimes at all but can include forms of relatively minor misconduct. Perhaps, then, treason and bribery are obviously impeachable offenses, but the text grants future Houses of Representatives a great deal of leeway to remove presidents for crimes or misbehavior that fall short of those things. At the very least, the text might seem to leave this possibility open.

For someone in 1788, however, this would be a most unlikely judgment, and the apparent textual puzzles would dissolve fairly rapidly. If the Constitution has given authority to Congress to remove the president for the stated offenses ("Treason, Bribery, or other high Crimes and Misdemeanors"), it would be extremely bizarre, textually speaking, to say that the Constitution has given the authority to remove the president for any criminal offenses at all. It would be far more sensible, textually speaking, to understand "other high Crimes and Misdemeanors" in such a way as to conform to "treason" and bribery" and to take the relevant "misdemeanors" to have to meet a certain threshold of "highness" as well. Thus the phrase "high crimes and misdemeanors" would most naturally be read as a whole, to suggest illegal acts of a serious kind and magnitude and also acts that, whether or not technically illegal, also amounted to an egregious abuse of office.

Nor would the term "bribery" create serious puzzles. A reader in 1788 would be likely to read the word "bribery," in context, to mean taking or offering money in return for abuse of official office. Contrary to Judge Posner's suggestion, the term probably would not be taken as a reference to private acts of bribery. The text thus supports the view that impeachment is designed for abuses of public authority. But it does not answer every question, and armed with the text alone, reasonable people could understand similar cases in quite different ways. It is certainly appropriate to look elsewhere.

### The Founding

The founding of the United States Constitution of course occurred in two stages. The first involved the Constitution's actual drafting, which was done in secret; the second involved ratification, which was highly public. It is possible to question whether the secret meetings of the drafters should play a large role in constitutional interpretation; but what happened there is extremely interesting. Impeachment was no marginal issue. It was central to the framers' deliberations. And what emerges from those deliberations is an effort to cabin the impeachment power, in order to reduce the role of popular passions and to preserve the separation of powers, and also to define the grounds for impeachment in a way that would meet the framers' stated concern: the large-scale abuse of distinctly presidential powers. We should care about what was said at the Convention, not because those secret discussions are binding but because they give a good sense of what reasonable readers of the original document are likely to have thought that it meant—and because in thinking about the best way to interpret the Constitution, reasonable readings at the inception can be highly illuminating.

Meeting in Philadelphia in the summer of 1787, the framers sought to produce a form of government that would reject England's monarchical heritage in favor of a system of republican self-government. The framers agreed that a president was necessary to head the new nation; they shared a commitment to disciplining public officials through the system of checks and balances. But they sharply disagreed about the precise extent of presidential power and about how, if at all, the president should be removable from office. This question played a large role in the constitutional convention, as revealed by James Madison's detailed notes of the founding debate, which I summarize here. The extensive debates in the convention strongly suggest a sharply limited conception of impeachment, one that sees the process as a targeted response to the president's abuse of public power through manipulation of distinctly presidential authority, or through procurement of his office by corrupt means. The reason for this limited conception of impeachment was connected to my argument in chapter 1: The framers were entirely alert to the risk that groups of like-minded people, insufficiently concerned with broader issues, would act in a partisan manner and disrupt government as a result. Here there is an obvious link to the secession question.

The initial draft of the Constitution took the form of resolutions presented before the members meeting in Philadelphia on June 13, 1787. One of the key resolutions, found in the Convention's official journal, said that the president could be impeached for "malpractice, or neglect of duty."[3] On July 20, this provision provoked an extended debate. Three positions dominated the day's discussion. One extreme view, represented by Roger Sherman and attracting very little support, was that the legislature should have the power to remove the executive at its pleasure. Charles Pinckney, Rufus King, and Gouverneur Morris represented the opposing extreme view, that in the new republic, the president "ought not to be impeachable whilst in office."[4] This view did receive considerable support; it was defended partly by reference to the system of separation of powers, which would be compromised by impeachment, and partly by reference to the fact that the president, unlike a monarch, would be subject to periodic elections, a point that seemed to make impeachment less necessary. The third position, which ultimately carried the day, was that the president should be impeachable, but only for a narrow category of abuses of the public trust—by, for example, procuring office by unlawful means or using distinctly presidential authority for ends that are treasonous.

George Mason took a lead role in promoting the compromise course. Against Pinckney, he argued that it was necessary to counter the risk that the president might obtain his office by corrupting his electors. "Shall that man be above" justice, he asked, "who can commit the most extensive injustice?"[5] This question identified the risk, to which the convention was quite sensitive, that the president might turn into a near-monarch; and it led the crucial votes—above all, Morris—to agree that impeachment might be permitted for (in Morris's words) "corruption & some few other offences."[6] James Madison promptly concurred with Morris, pointing to a case in which a president "might betray his trust to foreign powers."[7] Capturing the emerging consensus of the Convention, Edmund Randolph favored impeachment on the ground that the executive "will have great opportunitys of abusing his power; particularly in time of war when the military force, and in some respects the public money will be in his hands."[8] The clear trend of the discussion was toward allowing a narrow impeachment power by which the president could be removed only for gross abuses of public authority.

But Pinckney, concerned about the separation of powers, continued to insist that a power of impeachment would eliminate the president's "independence."[9] Morris once again offered the decisive response, urging that he was convinced of the necessity of impeachments, because the president "may be bribed by a greater interest to betray his trust; and no one would say that we ought to expose ourselves to the danger of seeing the first Magistrate in foreign pay without being able to guard against it by displacing him."[10] At the same time, Morris insisted, "we should take care to provide some mode that will not make him dependent on the Legislature."[11] Led by Morris, the convention thus moved toward a compromise position, one that would continue the separation between the president and the Congress but permit the president to be removed in the most extreme cases. But the discussion ended without agreement on any particular set of terms.

The new draft of the Constitution's impeachment clause emerged two weeks later, on August 6. It would have permitted the president to be impeached, but only for treason, bribery, and corruption (apparently exemplified by the president's securing his office by unlawful means). With little additional debate, and for no clear reason, this provision was narrowed on September 4 to "treason and bribery." But in early September, the delegates took up the impeachment clause anew. Here they slightly broadened the grounds for removing the president, but in a way that stayed close to the compromise position that had appeared to carry the day in July.

The opening argument was offered by Mason, who complained that the provision was too narrow to capture his earlier concerns and that "maladministration" should be added, so as to include "attempts to subvert the Constitution" that would not count as treason or bribery.[12] Mason's strongest point was that the president should be removable if he attempted to undo the constitutional plan. But Madison insisted that the term "maladministration" was "so vague" that it would "be equivalent to a tenure during pleasure of the Senate,"[13] which is exactly what the framers had been attempting to avoid all along. Hence Mason withdrew "maladministration" and added the new, more precise terms "other high crimes and misdemeanors against the State."[14] The term "high crimes and misdemeanors" was borrowed from English law, as we shall see; but it received no independent debate in the Convention. During the debates, the only subsequent development—and it is not trivial—was that "against the State" was changed to "against the United States," in order to remove ambiguity.[15]

There is one further wrinkle. The resulting draft was submitted to the Committee on Style and Arrangement, which deleted the words "against the United States."[16] Hence there is an interpretive puzzle. Was the deletion designed to broaden the legitimate grounds for impeachment? This is extremely unlikely. As its name suggests, the Committee on Style and Arrangement lacked substantive authority (which is not to deny that it made some substantive changes), and it is far more likely that the particular change was made on grounds of redundancy. Hence the impeachment clause, in its final as well as penultimate incarnation, was targeted at high crimes and misdemeanors against the United States.

The unambiguous lesson of these debates is that in designing the provision governing impeachment, the founders were thinking, exclusively or principally, of large-scale abuses of distinctly public authority. The unanimous rejection of "maladministration" suggests that the framers sought to create an authority that was both confined and well defined. All of the alleged grounds for impeachment involved abuses of public trust through the exercise of distinctly presidential powers (or corruption in procuring those powers); there were no references to private crimes, such as murder and assault. The debates strongly suggest that the model for impeachment was the large-scale abuse of public office.

The same view is supported by discussion at the time of ratification and in the early period. Impeachment was explained and defended as a way of removing the president when he used his public authority for treasonous or corrupt purposes. Alexander Hamilton explained that the "subjects" of impeachment involve "the abuse of violation of some public trust. They are of a nature which may with peculiar propriety be denominated POLITICAL, as they relate chiefly to injuries done immediately to society itself."[17] This suggestion should be taken as an echo of the textual idea, on which the discussants were unanimous on September 8, that the relevant high crimes and misdemeanors must run "against the United States." One of the most sustained discussions came from the highly respected (and later Supreme Court justice) James Iredell, speaking in the North Carolina ratifying convention: "I suppose the only instances, in which the President would be liable to impeachment, would be where he had received a bribe, or had acted from some corrupt motive or other."[18] By way of explanation, Iredell referred to a situation in which "the President has received a bribe . . . from a foreign power, and, under the influence of that bribe, had address enough with the Senate, by artifices and misrepresentations, to seduce their consent to a pernicious treaty."[19]

James Wilson wrote similarly in his great 1791 *Lectures on Law:* "In the United States and in Pennsylvania, impeachments are confined to political characters, to political crimes and misdemeanors, and to political punishments."[20] Another early commentator went so far as to say that

> [t]he legitimate causes of impeachment . . . can have reference only to public character, and official duty. . . . In general, those offenses, which may be committed equally by a private person, as a public officer, are not the subjects of impeachment. Murder, burglary, robbery, and indeed all offenses not immediately connected with office, are left to the ordinary course of judicial proceedings.[21]

This was a contested view. But there was general agreement that the great purpose of impeachment was to remove from office those who had abused distinctly public power. In the ratification debates themselves, I have not been able to find a single example of an impeachable offense that did not involve this kind of abuse, and certainly the prominent examples all involved abuses of that sort.

As I have suggested, I do not believe that the meaning of the impeachment clause was settled in 1787, any more than that the meaning of the First Amendment was settled in 1789. But the original understanding is certainly a part of the interpretive picture. The best judgment is that the impeachment clause was generally designed for egregious or large-scale abuses of power that officials exercised by virtue of their office. There was a purpose behind this limited understanding—to ensure that public deliberations would not be harmed by ready resort to the impeachment mechanism by political losers to undermine or topple their adversaries. In this way the founders' conception of impeachment was part and parcel of their deliberative design.

## Two Centuries of Practice

What have been the historical practices? Tradition is not decisive, but the question is important. In many ways constitutional democracies develop a kind of "common law constitution"[22]—a constitutional order in which the meaning of constitutional provisions is settled less by the original understanding and more by practices and judgments that have been developed over time. In the context of impeachment, any kind of common-law constitution will reflect legislative rather than judicial practices. There are of course no judicial precedents with respect to what counts as an impeachable offense; but there is nonetheless a long line of historical practices, capturing a distinctive set of social judgments. We can see, from these practices, a set of understandings about constitutional meaning.

The most important lesson of history is that the exceptional infrequency of serious impeachment proceedings against the president—even in circumstances in which such proceedings might have appeared legitimate—suggests an agreement that impeachment is appropriate only in the most extraordinary cases of abuse of distinctly presidential authority. We should notice at the outset that there have been sixteen impeachments in the nation's entire history; that only two presidents, in that entire history, have been impeached; and that only one other president, in that history, has been subject to serious impeachment inquiry.

President Nixon was of course subject to an impeachment inquiry because of a series of alleged abuses of the public trust. Thus article 1 of the articles of impeachment against President Nixon referred to the an unlawful entry into the headquarters of the Democratic National Committee "for the purpose of securing official intelligence" and then conspiring to cover it up; article 2 referred to the allegation that he "repeatedly engaged in conduct violating the constitutional rights of citizens," including the use of the Internal Revenue Service, the Federal Bureau of Investigation, and the Secret Service; article 3 referred to repeated refusals to produce papers and materials under subpoenas specifically designed "to resolve by direct evidence fundamental, factual questions relating to Presidential direction, knowledge or approval of actions demonstrated by other evidence to be substantial grounds for impeachment of the President." In retrospect, a remarkable feature of these articles is their relative restraint—fastening on large-scale abuses of distinctly public authority. As I will soon suggest, the House of Representatives declined to proceed against President Nixon with an allegation of unlawful tax evasion, in exercise of that restraint.

Before President Clinton, the only president to have been impeached (though not convicted) was Andrew Johnson, who was subject to an extraordinarily partisan battle. The key counts involved allegations that he should be impeached for discharging his secretary of state in violation of the Tenure in Office Act, which Johnson believed (rightly, as it turned out) to be unconstitutional.[23] The impeachment of President Johnson was produced less by the violation of law—though there was a violation of law—than by Radical Republicans critical of Johnson on unambiguously political grounds.[24] History has not been kind to the impeachment effort, which weakened the presidency for a period of decades. But even in the Johnson case, when partisan fervor was at its height, the allegations involved the allegedly large-scale abuse of presidential authority, through the lawless exercise of presidential power. With respect to the president, at least, impeachment has been considered as a weapon of rare and last resort, in a way that vindicates the framers' emphasis on the safeguards of the electoral process.

## Dogs That Didn't Bark

To have a sense of American history, it is at least as important to have a sense of the cases in which impeachment did *not* occur as of cases in which it did occur. An examination of American history shows that even when impeachment might well have been contemplated, cooler heads prevailed, and both the nation and Congress insisted on an extremely high standard. Consider here simply a few cases (they could easily be multiplied) from twentieth-century history; in all of these the House has acted with great restraint. The House was correct to do so, both as a matter of constitutional law and as a matter of prudence. I list the cases not to complain about the nation's failure to pursue the impeachment route but on the contrary to suggest the solidity of the American presumption against impeachment.

- The House refused to include, as an impeachment count, legitimate allegations of income tax evasion against President Nixon. The basic ground for the refusal was that income tax evasion—though hardly excusable and indeed a major breach of every citizen's obligation—did not amount to a misuse of distinctly presidential authority.
- President Reagan was allegedly involved in unlawful misconduct in connection with the Iran-Contra controversy; at least he presided over an adminis-

tration allegedly involved in such unlawful misconduct. Indeed, the independent counsel's investigation yielded no fewer than seven guilty pleas and four convictions, including convictions of relatively high-level executive branch officials. Many people believed or feared that President Reagan was personally involved in the unlawful acts. Thus it would have been possible to commence impeachment hearings to investigate the charges. Nonetheless, impeachment was never considered as a serious option.

- Many people alleged that Vice President George Bush was involved in aspects of the Iran-Contra controversy, and some people suggested that he had personal knowledge of the unlawful activity. An impeachment investigation would not have been hard to imagine. Here too impeachment never emerged as a serious possibility.

- In World War II, the Lend-Lease Act allowed the president to build and sell arms and ammunition to other nations, most notably England. Before the passage of the Act, the sale of arms to other nations, including Britain, was prohibited by law. Nonetheless, it is generally agreed that President Franklin Delano Roosevelt was secretly and unlawfully transferring arms—including over twenty thousand airplanes, rifles, and ammunition—to England. Indeed, illegal approval of such weapons transfers were quite routine in two full months before Congress authorized it. Even President Roosevelt's secretary of state "felt troubled by the illegality and deception."[25] It is often said that Roosevelt both deceived and lied to Congress and the American people in connection with the program.

- There were widespread claims of a secret "deal" between President Gerald Ford and President Richard Nixon, culminating in the pardon by President Ford. At the time, many Americans suspected that such a "deal" had occurred. So far as I am aware, no evidence supports any such suspicion. But in view of the climate of the time, these claims might well have produced an impeachment inquiry.

- It was widely believed that President John F. Kennedy was involved in a series of illicit sexual relationships while in office, including an illicit sexual relationship with a woman simultaneously involved with a member of the Mafia. This relationship—some people have suggested—would potentially compromise the efforts of the Department of Justice. Some people have alleged that this reckless behavior, whether or not involving technical violations of law, reflected serious indifference to law enforcement efforts. Yet no one has suggested, at the time or since, that impeachment was the appropriate course.

These are simply a few random examples, and doubtless reasonable people will suggest that some or all of them involve conduct far less egregious, or less legitimately impeachable, than alleged in other actual or hypothetical cases. Other reasonable people will disagree. It should not be hard to come up with other examples. (Consider, as just one further illustration, the fact that President Lincoln suspended the writ of habeas corpus, a serious violation of civil liberties that was ruled unlawful.)[26] My basic point is to establish a lengthy historical practice of great restraint. As I have emphasized, that practice is not decisive on the question of what the impeachment provisions mean. But the practice has been both a safeguard of and an exercise in deliberative democracy; it should not be respected only because it has been the practice but also because the practice has been good for both democracy and constitutionalism, a point to which I now turn.

## Applications: President Clinton, Mutual Arms Control, and Beyond

My basic purpose thus far has been to defend a particular understanding of the impeachment power and to connect that understanding with an understanding of democratic constitutionalism. But two elements are missing from the picture. The first has to do with the 1998 impeachment of President Clinton. Did President Clinton commit a high crime and misdemeanor? I believe that he did not, and that the impeachment was unconstitutional. The second question, of far more general interest, has to do with future uses of the impeachment power. I suggest that it is important for members of opposing political views to enter into a kind of mutual arms control agreement, in which they self-consciously decide to use the impeachment weapon only in the most extreme cases, in a small but far from trivial effort to reduce the level of scandal-mongering and accusation that has undermined American democracy for the last decades. This suggestion is intended to ensure that impeachment plays its proper role in the constitutional system.

### The Unconstitutional Impeachment of President Clinton

The original understanding and historical practice, taken in light of constitutional commitments, converge on a simple principle: The point of the impeachment provision is to allow the House of Representatives to impeach the president of the United States for egregious misconduct that amounts to the abusive misuse of the authority of his office. This principle does not exclude the possibility that a president would be impeachable for an extremely heinous "private" crime, such as murder or rape; that question can be left undecided. But it suggests that outside of such extraordinary (and unprecedented and most unlikely) cases, impeachment is unacceptable.

How does all this bear on the allegations against President Clinton? The clear implication is that the relevant charges did not, even if proved, make out any legitimately impeachable offenses under the Constitution. It also follows that the charges made in the two approved articles of impeachment did not identify a legitimate basis for impeachment or conviction of a sitting president. These charges—in particular, perjury before the grand jury and obstruction of justice—did not involve egregious misuse of the powers of the office of the presidency. Perjury and obstruction of justice are extremely serious charges; but the alleged acts did not involve perjury or obstruction of justice in connection with an alleged abuse of office. There was no allegation, for example, that the president attempted to obstruct justice with respect to an investigation of his misuse of the Central Intelligence Agency, or that he perjured himself in connection with unlawful trading of arms to a nation with whom the United States has unfriendly relationships. There is no question that perjury and obstruction of justice could be legitimately impeachable offenses; but these acts fall far short of the constitutional standard if they involve an effort to conceal an illicit sexual relationship.

Under the standard I am suggesting, the closest claim involves the suggestion that the president lied to his advisers and enlisted their help in covering up his illicit relationship and his lies about it. The relevant acts involved, in some sense, the authority of the office of the president. And it should be unnecessary to say that these acts, if criminal, are extremely serious offenses. But here the House of Representatives was correct: This too falls far short of the legitimate bases for impeachment. We do not have, with that kind of misuse of authority, the level of misuse that would justify an analogy to treason (as understood at the time of the framing or since) or bribery.

Let us explore several responses to this claim. One possible view is that no matter the crime, it is simply unacceptable for a criminal to remain in the White House. If the president has in fact committed a crime—it might be said—he is legitimately removed from office. It should be clear that this view is not consistent with the Constitution as it is written. The president is palpably not removable for the commission of any crime. The question is whether he has committed a "high crime or misdemeanor." A related response would stress the possibility that by committing perjury and engaging in other unlawful acts, the president violated both his oath of office and his duty under the "take care" clause of the Constitution. But this is a weak argument too. It cannot be claimed that any violation of the oath of office, or the take care clause, is a legitimate basis for impeachment, without rereading the Constitution in a quite fundamental way. President Truman, for example, was held to have violated the take care clause by seizing the steel mills,[27] and many of the cases described earlier involved presidential violations of law. Law violations that amount to a violation of the oath of office, or the take care clause, cannot count as impeachable offenses without something more than that.

But it would be possible to respond to my basic suggestion—that President Clinton's alleged wrongdoing did not meet the constitutional standard—in two more subtle ways. First, it might be urged that the actual charges made at one time or another against President Clinton—frequent lies to the American public, false statements under oath, conspiracy to ensure that such false statements are made, perjury, interactions with his advisers designed to promote further falsehoods under oath, and perhaps above all perjury before the grand jury and obstruction of justice—were very serious indeed, in a sense uniquely serious. No other president has been charged with lying under oath. It follows that if these very serious charges are deemed a legitimate basis for impeachment, little or nothing will be done to alter the traditional conception of impeachment. Perhaps some of these possible claims, involving interactions with his advisers designed to promote lies or continued procedural objections to the underlying inquiry (not found appropriately impeachable by the House of Representations), even amount to abuse of power. In any case the acts of lying within the criminal justice system, and enlisting others in the effort to do so, are highly distinctive, different in kind from anything alleged about any other president; and it might be urged (as discussed below) that these acts are very close indeed to bribery. If the president may be impeached for bribing a judge, or bribing a witness, may he not be impeached for lying under oath, or for encouraging others to lie on his behalf? Second, it might be said that whatever history and past practice show, we should understand the Constitution's text to allow the president to be impeached, via the democratic channels, whenever a serious charge, of one sort or another, is both made and proved. I will take up these two responses in sequence.

If the first claim is that certain kinds of falsehoods under oath, perjury, conspiracy to lie, and so forth could be a legitimate basis for impeachment, there can be no objection. As I have suggested, a false statement under oath about a practice of using the Internal Revenue Service to punish political opponents would almost certainly be an impeachable offense; so too would a false statement about the acceptance of a bribe to veto legislation. Thus false statements under oath might well be a legitimate basis for impeachment. Indeed, lying to the American people might itself be an impeachable offense if, for example, the president says that a treaty should be signed because it is in the best interest of the United States when in fact he supports the treaty because its signatories have agreed to donate money to his campaign. Nor can it be denied that it is important to tell the truth under oath, no matter the subject of the discussion. But it does not diminish the universal importance of telling the truth under oath to say that whether perjury or a false statement is an impeachable offense depends on what it is a false statement about. The same is true for "obstruction of justice" or interactions with advisers designed to promote the underlying falsehood.

Of course anyone can be prosecuted for violating the criminal law, and if the president violates the criminal law, he is subject to criminal prosecution after his term ends. But it does not make much sense to say, for example, that an American president could be impeached for false statements under oath in connection with a traffic accident in which he was involved or that a false statement under oath, designed to protect a friend in a negligence action, is a legitimate basis for impeachment. Just as sensible prosecutors make decisions about which perjuries are sufficiently serious to warrant prosecution, so a constitutional provision allowing impeachment for "high crimes and misdemeanors" should not be taken to treat all perjuries as of a piece.

The best general statement is that a false statement under oath is an appropriate basis for impeachment if and only if the false statement involved conduct that by itself raises serious questions about abuse of office. A false statement about an illicit consensual sexual relationship, and a "conspiracy" to cover up that relationship, is not excusable or acceptable; but it is not a high crime or misdemeanor under the Constitution. The same is true for the other allegations made against President Clinton. It trivializes the criminal law to say that some violations of the criminal law do not matter, or matter much. But it trivializes the Constitution to say that any false statement under oath, regardless of its subject matter, provides a proper basis for impeachment.

Of course the president has a special obligation to the truth, especially in a court of law. As the nation's chief law enforcement officer, the president has a special obligation to the truth. Perhaps it could be concluded that false statements under oath, and associated misconduct, are genuinely unique and that impeachment for such statements and such misconduct would therefore fail to do damage to our historical practice of resorting to impeachment only in the most extreme cases. But this position has serious problems of its own. Even if it would be possible, in principle, for reasonable people to confine this alleged basis for impeachment, it is extremely doubtful that the line could be held in practice.

Consider, for example, the fact that reasonable people can and do find tax evasion far more serious than false statements about a consensual sexual activity, and that reasonable people can and do find an alleged unlawful arms deal more serious, from the constitutional standpoint, than either. The question is not whether those people are correct; they may or may not be. The problem is deeper than that. Whenever serious charges are made, participants in politics may well be pushed in particular directions by predictable partisan pressures. The serious risk is therefore that, contrary to the constitutional plan, impeachment will become a partisan tool, to be used with apparently legitimate arguments by those who have a great deal to gain. As we will soon see, a special risk of a ready resort to the impeachment instrument is that it would interact, in destructive ways, with existing trends in American democracy. From the standpoint of the constitutional structure, it is far better to draw a kind of line in the sand, one that has been characteristic of our constitutional practice for all of our history: a practice of invoking impeachment only for the largest cases of abuse of distinctly presidential authority.

## Impeachment Now

But should the nation adopt a lower standard for impeachment of the president? Should a constitutional democracy conclude that impeachment is legitimate for criminality not involving misuse of office or for misuse of office that is perhaps not as "high" as has traditionally been thought? We might consider, for example, the following propositions:

1. The president may be impeached for any violation of any law.
2. The president may be impeached for any crime.
3. The president may be impeached for any felony.
4. The president may be impeached for any violation of any law (civil or criminal) involving the performance of his official responsibilities at any time in public life.
5. The president may be impeached for any violation of any law (civil or criminal) involving the performance of his official responsibilities while in office.
6. The president may be impeached for any egregious abuse of his official powers.

In the abstract, it is not clear whether a nation should subscribe to one, two, or all of these propositions if it were creating a constitution from first principles. Undoubtedly a movement in the direction of propositions 1, 2, or 3 would push a nation more toward a parliamentary system, in which the head of the executive branch can be removed from office upon a vote of "no confidence." In the abstract, it is hardly obvious that an intermediate system—a presidential system in which the president can be removed not for mere lack of confidence but because he has committed some identifiable offense—would be inferior to the alternatives. Perhaps such a system would create more in the way of separation than a parliamentary system but not the degree of dependence that a parliamentary system creates; perhaps the degree of separation produced by our hypothetical intermediate system would be optimal. Surely it is possible to imagine assumptions under which this would be true. Institutional questions of this kind do not have acontextual answers.

For the United States, it is doubtful that we could create such a system, short of a constitutional amendment. But suppose that we could do so, via interpretation or amendment. Should we?

I think that the answer is that we should not. The reason has a great deal to do with the nature of both the contemporary presidency and modern American democracy, where political disagreements are often turned into allegations of scandalous behavior, asserting, all too often, an abuse of public trust, violation of law, or even criminality. This is not a claim that the allegations are usually offered in bad faith or are always without merit or that what emerges, in practice, does not sometimes amount to an abuse, a violation, or a crime. Political opponents can uncover something quite bad. My claim is instead that the focus on this kind of material has a series of unfortunate effects for American self-government and that the possible benefits (discouraging and discovering bad conduct) do not justify those unfortunate effects.

Let us briefly consider the Independent Counsel Act, now repealed, and then move to the topic of impeachment. The Act was a well-intentioned effort to promote trust in government by ensuring that independent officials would be entrusted with the authority to investigate allegations of improper behavior by high-level people in the executive branch. In practice, however, the Act created a variety of harmful incentives, for Congress, the media, and the counsel himself. Members of an opposing party had all the incentive to ask for the appointment of an independent counsel and to take any apparent wrongdoing extremely seriously, in such a way as to divert attention from the actual task of making lives better for citizens. Reporters who are concerned with audience share (which is to say almost all reporters) were under considerable pressure to give great attention to the nonappointment of an independent counsel, or the work of the counsel, in such a way as to crowd out news about more substantive matters. And armed with an unlimited budget, and a narrow focus, the independent counsel had a natural incentive toward zealotry, in such a way as to depart from the role of the ordinary criminal prosecutor, who would spend little or no time on many of the cases that have been the focus of independent counsel investigations. The result of all this was a true disaster for the American public—a diversion from serious issues, a fear that all politicians are crooks, and a deepened distrust of politicians.

Now consider impeachment in this light. Under current conditions, what is likely to happen if the grounds for impeachment were expanded? The risk is that impeachment would become a political weapon, one that is used as a kind of substitute for the tasks of running the country and making people's lives better. Of course one way to attempt to be elected, or reelected, is to say that a certain policy initiative is actually desirable and will do a great deal of good. But another way to get elected, or reelected, is to claim that members of the opposing party have actually committed crimes and are in fact criminals, to be eliminated from office because they are criminals. Thus the risk of a ready resort to the impeachment instrument is that it would interact, in destructive ways, with existing trends in American democracy.

There is a final point. The office of the president has assumed more rather than less importance since the founding, and in at least some respects, its importance has continued to grow in every twenty-year period in the twentieth century. This is true both domestically, where the president is entrusted with ensuring execution of an extraordinary range of legislation, and internationally, where the president is of course the only real spokesperson for the nation. In these circumstances, the great risk of the impeachment mechanism is that it is destabilizing, in a way that threatens to punish the nation as much as, or perhaps far more than, the president himself. Since the purpose of impeachment is not to punish officials but to protect the nation, this is a cruel irony.

## Imaginable Cases

By way of summary and review, let us now explore a set of possible cases for impeachment of the president.

1. The president has accepted a bribe from a foreign country, receiving substantial campaign contributions in return for a promise to help that country, even though the help endangers the national security of the United States. This is an easy case for impeachment. Even if it does not involve treason, it does involve a "high" crime and therefore an impeachable offense.

2. The president uses the FBI and the CIA in order to obtain incriminating evidence about, and to punish, political adversaries. This conduct may not

involve a violation of the criminal law. But it nonetheless involves an impeachable offense—an egregious abuse of the power of the office.

3. During a war, or a domestic crisis, the president fails to perform the basic tasks of office, not because he has made choices with which many people disagree but because he has essentially defaulted. The default may be a result of drunkenness, mental illness, physical problems, or sheer laziness. Here too there is no crime; but there is a misdemeanor sufficient to remove the president from office.

4. The president cheats on his taxes. In ordinary circumstances, this is not a legitimate basis for impeachment. There is no misuse of distinctly governmental authority.

5. The president smokes marijuana in the White House. Here too there is no basis for impeachment, because there is no misuse of distinctly governmental authority.

6. The president murders a political enemy. This is an easy case for impeachment. It falls within the same category as case 2.

7. The president murders someone simply because he does not like him. There is no political motivation; the dispute is entirely personal. This is a hard case under the analysis thus far. There is no clear view from history. On one view, there is no abuse of distinctly presidential powers, hence no impeachable offense. On another view, the best conclusion is that the president can be impeached for this level of private misconduct on the theory that this is undoubtedly an exceptionally serious crime and that the president is not likely to be fit to govern after committing such a crime. Surely the Constitution would make little sense if it did not permit the nation to remove murderers from the highest office in the land. It would probably be intolerable not to allow the president to be removable in such an extreme case; the key point is that this judgment should not be allowed to produce a different judgment about cases 4 and 5.

## Impeachment and Democracy

The notion of "high crimes and misdemeanors" should generally be understood to refer to large-scale abuses that involve the authority that comes from occupying a particular public office. Thus a president who accepted a bribe from a foreign nation—or who failed to attend to the public business during a war—would be legitimately subject to impeachment. Perjury, or false statements under oath, could certainly qualify as impeachable offenses if they involved (for example) lies about using the Internal Revenue Service to punish one's political opponents or about giving arms, unlawfully, to another nation. But the most ordinary predicate for impeachment is an act, by the president, that amounts to a large-scale abuse of distinctly presidential authority.

If there is ever to be impeachment outside of that category of cases, it should be exceedingly rare. In the current period, the argument for adhering to this view has been strengthened rather than weakened, partly as a result of current trends in the modern democratic system, which has seen insufficient attention to issues of substance and excessive focus on allegations of misconduct, criminal or otherwise. In such circumstances, the impeachment device, far from being a political tool, stands as a remedy of last resort, designed to make possible the removal of those presidents whose egregious official misconduct has produced a social consensus that continuation in office is no longer acceptable. In this way an understanding of impeachment can be made to mesh, not with the least fortunate tendencies of modern politics, but with the constitutional aspiration to a well-functioning system of democratic deliberation.

# 6

# Democracy and Rights:
# The Nondelegation Canons

The United States Constitution, like many others, seems to contain an interesting doctrine specifically designed to ensure democratic self-government. Article 1, section 1, of the Constitution vests "legislative power" in a "Congress of the United States" and not in anyone else. According to "the nondelegation doctrine," the national legislature is not permitted to give, or to delegate, its lawmaking powers to any other institution. One of the most important questions in contemporary constitutional law is whether, and in what sense, the nondelegation doctrine still lives.

Understood as a requirement of legislative deliberation, the nondelegation doctrine is closely connected with a central theme of this book, involving the need to ensure deliberation among people who disagree and have a wide range of views. By its very nature, the executive branch, run as it is by a single person, is unlikely to have a high degree of deliberative diversity, at least in comparison to the legislative branch. Group polarization, and a degree of "groupthink," are natural tendencies within the executive branch, and in particular the White House. (Recall the Israeli torture case, in which the Supreme Court of Israel said that the General Security Forces could not engage in torture without clear legislative authorization.) A requirement that Congress legislate with particularity is likely to ensure against some of the pathologies of deliberation limited to like-minded people. At the same time, such a requirement will promote "dual-branch lawmaking"—ensuring that if law is to be brought to bear against citizens, it must be because both the executive and the legislative branches, and neither one alone, has decided that this should be done. The nondelegation doctrine seems to be an excellent illustration of the potential fusion of democratic institutions with individual rights.

But there are more practical implications. If the nondelegation doctrine is alive in the United States, perhaps Congress is forbidden from letting administrative agencies "make law." On this view, serious constitutional questions are raised by the existence of the Environmental Protection Agency, the Federal Communications Commission, and the Occupational Safety and Health Administration—for all of these agencies, and many others, are really in the business of making law. Few questions are more important to the operation of government. If the nondelegation doctrine is really in the United States Constitution, then the Constitution is being violated every day. And if the nondelegation doctrine is not in the Constitution, then why do we think we have a system in which lawmaking is done by Congress?

Many people think that the nondelegation doctrine is dead.[1] According to the refrain, the doctrine was once used to require Congress to legislate with some clarity, so as to ensure that law is made by the national legislature rather than by the executive. But the nondelegation doctrine—the refrain continues—is now merely a bit of rhetoric, as the United States Code has become littered with provisions asking one or another administrative agency to do whatever it thinks best. While this is an overstatement, it captures an important truth: Since 1935, the Supreme Court has not struck down an act of Congress on nondelegation grounds, notwithstanding the existence of a number of plausible occasions.

Is the nondelegation doctrine really dead? To the extent that it is not flourishing, is there a way to promote its essential purposes, in a way that requires legislative deliberation on the most fundamental issues? I believe that the doctrine is actually alive and well. It has been relocated rather than abandoned. Federal courts commonly vindicate not a general nondelegation doctrine, which would raise serious problems, but a series of more specific and smaller, though quite important, nondelegation doctrines. Rather than invalidating federal legislation as excessively vague and open-ended, courts say that executive agencies may not engage in certain controversial activities unless and until Congress has expressly authorized them to do so. When fundamental rights and interests are at stake, the choices must be made legislatively. As a technical matter, the key holdings are based not on the nondelegation doctrine but on certain "canons" of construction.

What I mean to identify here are the *nondelegation canons*, not organized or recognized as such, but central to the operation of modern public law in America and many other nations, and designed to ensure clear legislative authorization for certain decisions. These are nondelegation canons for the simple reason that they forbid the executive, including administrative agencies, from making decisions on its own.

Consider a few examples. Executive agencies are not permitted to construe federal statutes in such a way as to raise serious constitutional questions. If the constitutional question is substantial, Congress must clearly assert its desire to venture into the disputed terrain.[2] This principle means that without clear congressional permission, courts will not permit the executive to intrude on liberty or equality in a way that might compromise the Constitution. Here is a clear effort to link institutional protections with individual rights. It is difficult to get specific language through Congress; a requirement of congressional specificity helps protect rights by ensuring that any interference with them must be clearly authorized and supported by both Congress and the executive.

In addition, Congress must affirmatively and specifically authorize the extraterritorial application of federal law. Agencies cannot exercise their ordinary discretion, under an ambiguous statutory provision, so as to apply national law outside of United States borders. A clear congressional statement to this effect is required. When treaties and statutes are ambiguous, they must be construed favorably to Native American tribes; the agency's own judgment, if it is an exercise of discretion, is irrelevant.[3] There are many more examples, including a recent canon forbidding agencies to impose high costs for trivial gains.

Some of my central purposes in this chapter are to show that these canons should be understood as entirely legitimate, that they should be used even more than they now are, and that they tell us a great deal about democracy's constitution. The nondelegation canons represent a salutary kind of *democracy-forcing judicial minimalism*,[4] designed to ensure that certain choices are made by an institution with a superior democratic pedigree. Indeed, the nondelegation canons turn out to be a contemporary incarnation of the founding effort to link protection of individual rights, and other important interests, with appropriate institutional design. In certain cases, Congress must decide the key questions on its own. This is the enduring function of the nondelegation doctrine, and it is endorsed, not repudiated, by current law.

### Intelligible Principles(?)

Let us begin with the conventional nondelegation doctrine. My conclusion is that, in general, courts should not understand article 1, section 1, of the Constitution to require Congress to legislate with specificity by sharply limiting the discretion of administrators. The most convincing claim on behalf of the conventional doctrine is far narrower and more modest: that certain highly sensitive decisions should be made by Congress and not by the executive under open-ended legislative instructions. Even those who are most skeptical of the conventional doctrine should be willing to embrace the nondelegation canons as a highly desirable alternative.

As the Supreme Court has long said, the conventional doctrine requires Congress to supply something like an "intelligible principle"[5] to guide and limit executive discretion.[6] According to its supporters, the nondelegation doctrine was a central part of the original constitutional plan, but fell into disuse in the aftermath of the New Deal. Indeed it is true that the Court referred to the nondelegation principle on a number of occasions in the pre–New Deal period.[7] Moreover, the Court invoked the doctrine to invalidate two acts of Congress in 1935, most famously in the *Schechter Poultry* case.[8] There the Court struck down a quite open-ended grant of authority, to the president, to develop "codes of fair competition"; a particular problem with the underlying statute was that it combined a high degree of vagueness with a grant of power, in practice, to private groups to develop such codes as they chose.[9] But it is also true that the Court has not used the doctrine to invalidate any statute since that time, notwithstanding many occasions when it might have found an absence of the requisite "intelligible principle."[10] Focusing on what they see as a plain breach of constitutional requirements, some observers have argued on behalf of a large-scale revival of the nondelegation doctrine in its conventional form.

For those who are committed to the conventional doctrine, there are a number of underlying concerns.[11] Many of those concerns are connected with deliberative democracy, but perhaps the most basic are textual and historical. The Constitution's textual grant of lawmaking power to Congress might well be taken to mean that Congress, and no one else, has lawmaking authority; a delegation of "legislative" power to anyone else seems inconsistent with the constitutional plan. In addition, the conceptual background of the system of checks and balances seems to provide historical support for this view—suggesting that the original understanding would have condemned open-ended grants of power to the executive. Even if there is no direct support in the founding era for the view that delegations are prohibited (a point to which I will return), the principle of nondelegation might seem such an inevitable implication of the division of powers that it went without saying.

Beyond the textual and historical points, support for the conventional doctrine comes from a series of claims about constitutional purpose and structure. The most important involves political accountability of the sort that I have emphasized throughout—and in particular that form of accountability that stems from the distinctive composition of Congress and the system of bicameralism. In light of the particular design of the central lawmaking institution, any delegation threatens to eliminate the special kind of accountability embodied in that institution (not incidentally including, in the Senate, the representation of states as such). It is worth underlining the role of bicameralism here. The evident obstacles to the enactment of federal law— a point of great relevance to the nondelegation canons—might be overcome if Congress could ask another institution, not subject to those obstacles, to enact law as it chooses.

Simply by requiring legislators to agree on a relatively specific form of words, the nondelegation principle also raises the burdens and costs associated with the enactment of federal law[12]—in a way that reduces the risks of a situation in which like-minded people are pressing one another toward an unjustifiable position. Those burdens and costs can be seen as an important guarantor of individual liberty, because they ensure that national governmental power may not be brought to bear against individuals without a real consensus, established by legislative agreement on relatively specific words, that this step is desirable. If the original institutional design was founded partly on the belief that the central government was a potential threat to freedom, open-ended delegations might seem to be a core violation of constitutional commitments.[13]

In various ways, the nondelegation doctrine also promotes values connected with the rule of law, above all insofar as it ensures that government power must be bounded by clear limitations laid down in advance. Indeed, the ban on open-ended delegations appears to be closely connected to the "void for vagueness" doctrine in constitutional law, requiring that certain laws be clear rather than open-ended. The two key purposes of the latter doctrine are to provide fair notice to affected citizens and also to discipline the enforcement discretion of unelected administrators and bureaucrats. By ensuring that those asked to implement the law be bound by intelligible principles, the nondelegation doctrine serves the same purposes. Quite apart from promoting accountability, the conventional doctrine thus promotes goals associated with the rule of law.

Finally, the requirement of legislative clarity might also seem to be a check on the problems of factional power and self-interested representation, two of the problems most feared by the framers of the United States Constitution.[14] Indeed, the nondelegation doctrine might be taken as a central means of reducing the risk that legislation will be a product of efforts by well-organized private groups to redistribute wealth or opportunities in their favor. The institutional design of Congress was intended to limit the power of well-organized private groups over government, and the requirement of general approval, from various legislators, seems to reduce the risk that self-interested representatives, with narrow agendas of their own, would use the lawmaking process to promote their parochial interests. These points might be summarized by linking the nondelegation principle with what I have been emphasizing throughout: the general constitutional goal of providing a deliberative democracy.

### Problems, Institutional and Otherwise

But as arguments for a large-scale revival of the conventional doctrine, these points raise many questions. The most serious problems are twofold. First, judicial enforcement of the nondelegation doctrine would create serious problems of judicial competence and would greatly magnify the role of the judiciary in overseeing the operation of modern government. Because the key questions are ones of degree, the nondelegation doctrine could not be administered in anything like a rule-bound way. The nondelegation doctrine is likely, in practice, to violate its own aspirations to discretion-free law.

Second, it is far from clear that a large-scale judicial revival of the nondelegation doctrine would do anything to improve the operation of the modern state. It might well make things worse, possibly much worse. I raise these questions not to suggest that the nondelegation doctrine is properly dead but to pave the way toward an appreciation of the nondelegation canons as a preferable alternative, promoting the same goals without creating the same risks.

### Questions about Pedigree

In United States law, does the conventional doctrine really have a good constitutional pedigree? It turns out that this question does not have a simple affirmative answer, from the standpoint of judicial practice, text, or history. (I will return shortly to the place of the nondelegation doctrine in constitutional doctrine generally.)

It is true that the Supreme Court *last* invalidated a statute on nondelegation grounds in 1935. But it is also true that the Court *first* invalidated a statute on nondelegation grounds in exactly the same year, notwithstanding a number of previous opportunities. It is therefore misleading to suggest that the nondelegation doctrine was a well-entrenched aspect of constitutional doctrine, suddenly abandoned as part of some post–New Deal capitulation by the Supreme Court to the emerging administrative state. Indeed it is more accurate, speaking purely descriptively, to see 1935 as the real anomaly. We might say that the conventional doctrine has had one good year and 212 bad ones (and counting).

Nor do the Constitution's text and history provide unambiguous support for the conventional doctrine. The Constitution does grant legislative power to Congress, but it does not in terms forbid delegations of that power, and I have been unable to find any indication, in the founding era, that such delegations were originally thought to be banned. Perhaps silence on the point can be taken to show that the ban on delegations was considered so obvious that it need not be discussed. But the practice of early congresses strongly suggests that broad grants of authority to the executive were not thought to be problematic. The first Congress granted military pensions, not pursuant to legislative guidelines, but "under such regulations as the President of the United States may direct."[15] The second Congress gave the president the authority to grant licenses to trade with the Indian tribes, not with limitations but under "such rules and regulations as the President shall prescribe."[16] There appears to be no evidence, in these or other cases, that members of Congress thought that such grants of authority violated a general nondelegation principle, notwithstanding extensive discussion of constitutional requirements within Congress in the early years of the nation.

These points do not demonstrate that the conventional nondelegation doctrine has no foundation in the original document. On the contrary, the best inference from article 1, section 1, is that some sort of nondelegation doctrine is part of the Constitution. But the text and history must be counted ambiguous rather than plain on the point, and the fact of ambiguity raises questions about any large-scale judicial enforcement of a nondelegation principle.

## Democracy and Delegation

Despite initial appearances, democratic considerations do not provide obvious support for the conventional nondelegation doctrine.[17] Executive agencies are themselves democratically accountable via the president. In addition, any delegation must itself have come from democracy, as an exercise of lawmaking authority. Congress may face electoral pressure merely by virtue of delegating broad authority to the executive; this is a perfectly legitimate issue to raise in an election, and "passing the buck" to bureaucrats is unlikely, in most circumstances, to be the most popular electoral strategy. If Congress has delegated such authority, maybe that is what voters want.

To be sure, these points are not decisive. We have seen that Congress has a distinctive form of accountability, through the mechanisms for representation and the system of bicameralism and it is that form of accountability, not accountability in the abstract, that justifies a nondelegation doctrine. But the democratic case for sharp limits on agency discretion is not clear-cut. In fact, congressional specificity often seems to produce outcomes that reflect the power of self-interested private groups—as, for example, where legislation reflects a capitulation to organizations using public-spirited rhetoric for their own parochial ends. And delegations often stem not from a desire to evade accountability but from a problem of lack of relevant information,[18] a pervasive and far from illegitimate basis for delegation in law or even life.[19] Indeed there is no evidence that from any point of view the old nondelegation doctrine would make the operation of federal law better rather than worse.

Clear statutory language, especially on details, is often a product not of some deliberative judgment by Congress but of the influence of well-organized private groups. It is hard to come up with any abstract reason why decisions by agencies under vague language would be worse, from the standpoint of promoting social well-being, than decisions by agencies under more specific language from Congress. And in practice, respect for regulatory agencies, and evidence that agencies do more good than harm, cannot easily be connected to the narrowness of statutory delegations. There is no evidence that executive agencies operating pursuant to open-ended authority do better, on any dimension, than agencies operating pursuant to statutes that sharply limit their discretion; nothing appears to link agency performance with clear statutory language.

It is also highly speculative—an unacceptably crude generalization—to suggest that social welfare is, on any view of that contested ideal, likely to be promoted by reducing the total volume of law. What precedes any new legislative enactment is always some body of law, whether legislatively or judicially created. Why is there any reason to think that the preceding law systematically promotes social welfare? Consider in this regard the conclusions of the most systematic and detailed empirical analysis of the sources of delegations of authority.[20] The authors emphasize that the idea of wholesale delegation is a myth; in many areas, "some of which, like the budget and tax policy, require considerable time and expertise—Congress takes a major role in specifying the details of policy."[21] Nor is Congress oblivious to executive performance. On the contrary, "legislators carefully adjust and readjust discretion over time and across issue areas."[22] Most important for my purposes, the authors conclude that delegation operates not as an alternative to *congressional* judgment but instead as a check on control of lawmaking processes by legislative *committees*. In those committees, well-organized groups can often dominate. Indeed, delegation is "a necessary counterbalance to the concentration of power in the hands of committees" or to the surrender of "policy to a narrow subset of" members. In these circumstances, the authors conclude that limits on delegation "would threaten the very individual liberties they purport to protect."[23]

There is a final point. Why should it be thought that any particular status quo, itself pervaded by law, embodies freedom and that the new law at issue would threaten to abridge freedom? Is a law forbidding discrimination on the basis of disability, or sex, something that threatens liberty, so that it is crucial to obtain legislative agreement about the details, lest liberty be overridden? Or might the discriminatory status quo, the one that precedes the new law, be the real threat to freedom? Questions of this kind raise serious doubts about the idea that the conventional doctrine would promote liberty, properly conceived. As we shall see, there are contexts in which requirements of legislative specificity would indeed operate as liberty-enhancing safeguards; but the conventional doctrine is too broad and crude to be defensible on this ground.


## Delegation and Courts

For the conventional doctrine, an especially serious problem stems from problems of judicial competence. Under that doctrine, the line between a permitted and a prohibited delegation is one of degree, and inevitably so. The distinction between "executive" and "legislative" power cannot depend on anything qualitative; the issue is a quantitative one. The real question is: How much executive discretion is too much to count as "executive"? No metric is easily available to answer that question.

In these circumstances, the overwhelming likelihood is that judicial enforcement of the doctrine would produce ad hoc, highly discretionary rulings, giving little guidance to lower courts or to Congress itself. The matter is even worse than that. Because the underlying issue is one of degree, decisions invalidating statutes as unduly open-ended are likely to suffer from the appearance, and perhaps the reality, of judicial hostility to the particular program at issue. For this reason, those concerned about rule-free law are especially likely to be uncomfortable with any large-scale revival of the conventional doctrine. Without much exaggeration, and with tongue only slightly in cheek, we might say that judicial enforcement of the conventional doctrine would violate the conventional doctrine—since it could not be enforced without delegating, without clear standards, a high degree of discretionary lawmaking authority to the judiciary. These points are more troubling still in light of the simple fact that judicial enforcement of the conventional doctrine would grant massive new authority to the federal judiciary—authority to second-guess legislative judgments about how much discretion is too much, without clear constitutional standards for answering that question.

I have not said that the conventional nondelegation doctrine deserves no place in federal law. In the most extreme cases, judicial invalidation is appropriate. It is also sensible for courts to construe ambiguous statutes so as to grant less, rather than more, discretionary authority to administrative agencies. But two serious problems have emerged with large-scale judicial use of the conventional doctrine. The first involves the considerable difficulty of principled judicial enforcement. The second involves the absence of reason to believe that the conventional doctrine would do more good than harm for modern democracy. As we shall now see, there are alternatives that do the good work of the old doctrine but without presenting these problems.

## Hidden Nondelegation Principles

I am going to argue that in order to protect important rights and interests, courts do not, and should not, allow the executive branch to make certain choices unless the national legislature has specifically decided that those choices are appropriate. But let us begin with a somewhat technical question, one that bears directly on the current status of the nondelegation doctrine: What is the authority of executive agencies to interpret the law?

When Congress has spoken clearly, everyone agrees that agencies are bound by what Congress has said. The disputed question has to do with the authority of agencies to act when Congress has not spoken clearly. Of course a very strong version of the conventional nondelegation doctrine would suggest that agencies can, in such cases, do nothing, because the underlying grant of power is effectively void. But short of this radical conclusion, what is the allocation of authority to agencies?

The place to start is *Chevron USA v. Natural Resources Defense Council*,[24] the decision that dominates modern administrative law. Seemingly technical and abstruse, the Court's decision in this case has had large implications for

American public—much larger, in fact, than many other cases receiving much more publicity.

In *Chevron*, the Supreme Court held that unless Congress has decided the "precise question at issue," agencies are authorized to interpret ambiguous terms as they see fit, so long as the interpretation is reasonable. *Chevron* creates a two-step inquiry. The first question is whether Congress has directly decided the precise question at issue. The second question is whether the agency interpretation is reasonable. Indeed, *Chevron* establishes a novel canon of construction: In the face of ambiguity, statutes mean what the relevant agency takes them to mean.

This is an emphatically "prodelegation" canon—indeed it is the quintessential prodelegation canon—and it is possible to argue that *Chevron* is highly objectionable precisely on nondelegation grounds, that it is objectionable precisely because it increases executive discretion. On this view, the problem is that under *Chevron*, agencies are not merely given authority that is often open-ended; they are also permitted to interpret the scope of their own authority, at least in the face of ambiguity. A system in which agencies lacked this authority would—it might be claimed—better promote nondelegation principles, for under such a regime, agencies would lack the power to construe statutory terms on their own.

The weakness of this objection stems from the fact that when statutory terms are ambiguous, there is no escaping delegation. By hypothesis Congress has not been clear—perhaps because it has been unable to resolve the issue, perhaps because it did not foresee it. The recipient of the delegation will be either agencies or courts. *Chevron* does increase the discretionary authority of agencies—this is the sense in which it creates a prodelegation canon— but only in relation to courts. With respect to the question whether the national legislature will actually legislate, it is neither here nor there.

It is plain, however, that a variety of canons of construction—what I am calling nondelegation canons—trump *Chevron* itself.[25] In other words, the agency's interpretation of law does not, under current doctrine, prevail if one of the nondelegation canons is at work. These canons impose important constraints on executive authority, for agencies are not permitted to understand ambiguous provisions to give them authority to venture in certain directions; a clear congressional statement is necessary.

The nondelegation canons fall in three principal categories. Some are inspired by the Constitution; others involve issues of sovereignty; still others have their foundations in public policy. The unifying theme is that the executive is not permitted to intrude on important rights or interests on its own. The national legislature, with its diverse membership and multiplicity of voices, must explicitly authorize any such intrusions. In this sense, the torture case in Israel is a classic case of a nondelegation canon—exemplifying how requirements of legislative clarity can trigger political safeguards in the service of individual rights.

### Constitutionally Inspired Nondelegation Canons

A number of nondelegation canons have constitutional origins; they are explicit efforts to promote democracy's constitution. They are designed to promote some goal with a constitutional foundation.

Consider the idea that executive agencies will not be permitted to construe statutes in such a way as to raise serious constitutional doubts. Notice that this principle goes well beyond the (uncontroversial) notion that agencies should not be allowed to construe statutes so as to be unconstitutional. The principle appears to say that constitutionally sensitive questions will not be permitted to arise unless the constitutionally designated lawmaker has deliberately and expressly chosen to raise them. For example, a law will not ordinarily be taken to allow the executive branch to intrude on the right to travel, compromise the right to free speech, interfere with religious liberty, or approach a taking of private property without compensation. The only limitations on the principle are that the constitutional doubts must be serious and substantial and that the statute must be fairly capable of an interpretation contrary to the agency's own.[26] So long as the statute is unclear, and the constitutional question serious, Congress must decide to raise that question via explicit statement. This idea trumps *Chevron* for that very reason. Executive interpretation of a vague statute is not enough when the purpose of the canon is to require Congress to make its instructions clear.

Belonging in the same category is the idea that the executive agencies will not be allowed to interpret ambiguous provisions so as to preempt state law.[27] The constitutional source of this principle is the constitutional commitment to a federal structure, a commitment that may not be compromised without a congressional decision to do so—an important requirement in light of the various safeguards against cavalier disregard of state interests created by the system of state representation in Congress. Notice that there is no constitutional obstacle to national preemption; Congress is entitled to preempt state law if it chooses. But there is a constitutional obstacle of a sort: the preemption decision must be made legislatively, not bureaucratically.

As a third example, consider the notion that unless Congress has spoken with clarity, agencies are not allowed to apply statutes retroactively, even if the relevant terms are quite unclear.[28] Because retroactivity is disfavored in the law, Congress will not be taken to have delegated to administrative agencies the authority to decide the question. The best way to understand this idea is as an echo of the notion that the due process clause raises doubts about retroactive application of law. Of course the constitutional constraints on retroactivity are now modest; while the ex post facto clause in the United States Constitution forbids retroactive application of the criminal law, the clause is narrowly construed, and Congress is generally permitted to impose civil legislation retroactively if it chooses.[29] But there is an institutional requirement here. Congress must make that choice explicitly and take the political heat for deciding to do so. It will not be taken to have attempted the same result via delegation, and regulatory agencies will not be taken to have the authority to choose retroactivity on their own. Perhaps part of the courts' motivation here is ambivalence about judicial refusal to apply the ex post facto clause, or the due process clause, so as to call into constitutional question some retroactive applications of civil law. The nondelegation canon is a more cautious way of promoting the relevant concerns.

Consider, finally, the *rule of lenity*, which says that in the face of ambiguity, criminal statutes will be construed favorably to criminal defendants. One function of the lenity principle is to ensure against delegations, to courts or to anyone else. Criminal law must be a product of a clear judgment on Congress's part. Where no clear judgment has been made, the statute will not apply merely because it is plausibly interpreted, by courts or enforcement authorities, to fit the case at hand. The rule of lenity is inspired by the due process constraint—central to democracy's constitution—on convicting people of crimes under open ended or vague statutes. While it is not itself a constitutional mandate, the idea is rooted in a constitutional principle and serves as a time-honored nondelegation canon.

### Sovereignty-Inspired Nondelegation Canons

The second category of nondelegation canons contains principles that lack a constitutional source but that have a foundation in widespread understandings about the nature of governmental authority—more particularly, in widespread understandings about sovereignty. Consider here the fact that the executive is not permitted to apply statutes outside of the territorial borders of the United States.[30] If statutes are to receive extraterritorial application, it must be as a result of a deliberate congressional judgment to this effect. The central notion here is that extraterritorial application calls for extremely sensitive judgments involving international relations; such judgments must be made via the ordinary lawmaking process (in which the president of course participates). The executive may not make this decision on its own. One of the evident purposes of this requirement is now familiar: to ensure deliberation among diverse people, and not merely within the executive branch, before a United States law will be applied abroad.

For broadly related reasons, agencies cannot interpret statutes and treaties unfavorably to Native Americans.[31] Where statutory provisions are ambiguous, the government will not prevail. This idea is plainly an outgrowth of the complex history of relations between the United States and Native American tribes, which have semisovereign status; it is an effort to ensure that any unfavorable outcome will be a product of an explicit judgment from the national legislature. The institutional checks created by congressional structure must be navigated before an adverse decision may be made. Consider, as a final if more controversial illustration, the fact that agencies are not permitted to waive the sovereign immunity of the United States, and indeed statutory ambiguity cannot be used by agencies as a basis for waiver, which must be explicit in legislation.[32] Sovereign immunity is a background structural understanding, one that may be overcome only on the basis of a judgment to that effect by the national legislature.

### Public Policy

The final set of nondelegation canons is designed to implement perceived public policy by, among other things, giving sense and rationality the benefit of the doubt—and by requiring Congress itself to speak if it wants to compromise policy that is perceived as generally held. The most generous understanding of these canons rests on the view that the relevant policies are not the judges' own but have a source in widely held, and properly held, social commitments.

There are many examples. Exemptions from taxation are narrowly construed.[33] If Congress wants to exempt a group from federal income tax, it must express its will clearly. Such exemptions are often the product of lobbying efforts by well-organized private groups and thus a reflection of factional influence; hence agencies may not create such exemptions on their own. At the same time, there is a general federal policy against anticompetitive practices, and agencies will not be permitted to seize on ambiguous statutory language so as to defeat the policy reflected in the antitrust laws.[34] If Congress wants to make an exception to the policy in favor of competition, it is certainly permitted to do so. But agencies may not do so without congressional instruction. So too it is presumed that statutes providing veterans' benefits will be construed generously for veterans, and agencies cannot conclude otherwise.[35] This idea is an analogue to the notion that statutes will be construed favorably to Native Americans; both require a congressional judgment if a group perceived as weak or deserving is going to be treated harshly.

In decisions of particular importance for the modern regulatory state, agencies are sometimes forbidden to require very large expenditures for trivial or de minimis gains.[36] If Congress wants to be "absolutist" about safety, in a way that might well compromise social well-being, it is permitted to do so by explicit statement.[37] But agencies will not be allowed to take ambiguous language in this direction. This is a genuinely novel nondelegation principle, a creation of the late twentieth century. It is an evident response to perceived problems in modern regulatory policy.[38]

### Barriers and Catalysts

How intrusive are the nondelegation canons? What kind of judicial role do they contemplate? Consider the view that these canons are best understood not as barriers but as catalysts, promoting democracy and allowing government to act so long as it does so through certain channels. The effort is to trigger democratic (in the sense of legislative) processes and to ensure the forms of deliberation, and bargaining, that are likely to occur in the proper arenas.

In a sense this understanding—of nondelegation canons as catalysts—is correct. So long as government is permitted to act when Congress has spoken clearly, no judicial barrier is in place.[39] In this way, the nondelegation canons are properly understood as a species of judicial minimalism, indeed democracy-forcing minimalism, designed to ensure that judgments are made by the democratically preferable institution. As compared with more rigid barriers to government action, the conventional nondelegation doctrine itself is a form of minimalism insofar as it requires Congress to speak with clarity and does not disable the government entirely. And because the nondelegation canons are narrower and more specifically targeted—requiring particular rather than general legislative clarity—they are more minimalist still.

But this understanding misses an important point. Nondelegation canons are barriers, and not merely catalysts, with respect to purely administrative (or executive) judgment on the matters in question. They erect a decisive barrier to certain discretionary decisions by the executive. In this respect, at least, the relevant institutions are blocked.

Canons of the sort I have outlined here are highly controversial. Judge Richard Posner, for example, fears that some of them create a "penumbral Constitution," authorizing judges to bend statutes in particular directions even though there may in fact be no constitutional violation.[40] But if the analysis here is correct, there is a simple answer to these concerns: The relevant canons operate as nondelegation principles, and they are designed to ensure that Congress decides certain contested questions on its own. If this idea is a core structural commitment of the Constitution, and if it ensures broad rather than narrow deliberation on sensitive issues, there is no problem with its judicial enforcement.

We can go further. As noted earlier, there are serious problems with judicial enforcement of the conventional nondelegation doctrine. Compare, along the relevant dimensions, judicial use of the nondelegation canons. Courts do not ask the hard-to-manage question whether the legislature has exceeded the permissible level of discretion but pose instead the far more manageable question whether the agency has been given the discretion to decide something that only legislatures should decide. In other words, courts ask a question about subject matter, not a question about degree.

Putting the competence of courts to one side, the nondelegation canons have the salutary function of ensuring that certain important rights and interests will not be compromised unless Congress has expressly decided to compromise them. Thus the nondelegation canons lack a central defect of the conventional doctrine: While there is no good reason to think that a reinvigorated nondelegation doctrine would improve the operation of modern regulation, it is entirely reasonable to think that for certain kinds of decisions, merely executive decisions are not enough.

If, for example, an agency is attempting on its own to apply domestic law extraterritorially, we might believe that whatever its expertise, it is inappropriate, as a matter of democratic theory and international relations, for this to happen unless Congress has decided that it should. Or courts might reasonably believe that retroactive application of regulatory law is acceptable not simply because the executive believes that an ambiguous law should be so construed but if and only if Congress has reached this conclusion. This judgment might be founded on the idea that political safeguards will ensure that Congress will so decide only if there is very good reason for that decision. For those who believe that retroactivity is constitutionally unacceptable, this may be insufficient consolation. But a requirement that Congress make the decision on its own is certainly likely to make abuses less common, if they are legitimately characterized as abuses at all.

These points have the considerable advantage of understanding the nondelegation canons as a modern incarnation of the framers' basic project of linking individual rights and interests with institutional design. The link comes from protecting certain rights and interests not through a flat judicial ban on governmental action, but through a requirement that certain controversial or unusual actions will occur only with respect for the institutional safeguards introduced through the design of Congress. There is thus a close connection between the nondelegation canons and a central aspiration of the constitutional structure.

As a class, the nondelegation canons are best defended on the ground that certain decisions are ordinarily expected to be made by the national legislature, with its various institutional safeguards, and not via the executive alone. A central goal of those safeguards is to ensure against the problems that occur when like-minded people are deliberating with one another and are failing to confront alternative views. In this way the nondelegation canons take their place as one of the most prominent domains in which protection of individual rights, and of other important interests, occurs not through blanket prohibitions on governmental action but through channeling decisions to particular governmental institutions, in this case Congress itself.

# The Anticaste Principle

*1994*

In chapter 1, we saw the importance of protecting deliberating enclaves, largely to ensure the emergence of arguments that would otherwise be squelched in general debate. I argued too that in some deliberative processes, members of low-status groups generally speak less and are given less respectful attention. If people are not heard, and if they do not speak, both democracy and deliberation are at risk. And if members of certain groups receive less respectful attention, both liberty and equality are at risk. Deliberating enclaves are a partial solution. But much more should be done.

In this chapter, I seek to defend a particular understanding of equality, one that is an understanding of liberty as well. I call this understanding the anticaste principle. Put too briefly, the anticaste principle *forbids social and legal practices from translating highly visible and morally irrelevant differences into a systemic source of social disadvantage, unless there is a very good reason for society to do so.* On this view, a special problem of inequality arises when membership in a group is turned into social disadvantage because of a difference that is both visible for all to see and irrelevant from the moral point of view. This form of inequality is likely to be unusually persistent and to extend into multiple social spheres, indeed into the interstices of everyday life. It is likely too to be associated with a kind of systematic humiliation of citizens from the lower caste.[1]

The anticaste principle has clear foundations in the democratic ideal. Under that ideal, everyone counts as a citizen, and there is no system of "caste" that would put some people or groups above others. The connection between the anticaste principle and democracy is clearest when members of some groups are actually disenfranchised, through explicit barriers to political participation or through more amorphous forms of political inequality. But even if everyone is allowed to participate in politics, there is a problem, from the democratic point of view, if a morally irrelevant and highly visible characteristic places some people systematically below others.

I do not claim that the anticaste principle is the only valid understanding of equality. The equality principle in most constitutions, including that of the United States, is plural rather than singular; there are several equality principles here, not just one. It would be obtuse to suggest that a simple conception of equality exhausts the term as it operates in legal and political discussion in the United States or elsewhere. Consider political equality; principles disallowing discrimination on the basis of religious conviction; principles disallowing discrimination on the basis of prejudice; and fair equality of opportunity. All of these conceptions of equality warrant support, and all of them have at least some grounding in constitutional understandings.

I emphasize the anticaste principle because it captures a commitment that has strong roots in legal understandings in constitutional democracies, because it has considerable independent appeal, because it is violated in many important parts of life in the United States (and elsewhere), and because it fits well with the best understandings of liberty as well. In other words, the anticaste principle is an important and (in my view) insufficiently appreciated part of the lawyer's conception of equality under constitutional law. In the United States, this insufficient appreciation has a significant cost: At too many periods in United States history, the Constitution's equal protection clause has been understood in a way that is insufficiently informed by, and is even antithetical to, the anticaste principle.

I emphasize as well that enforcement of the anticaste principle is mostly for legislative and executive officers and only secondarily for courts. At some point in the late nineteenth and early twentieth century, there was a large-scale transformation in the substance of the constitutional equality principle. This is a long and not-yet-told story. A set of amendments originally designed to eliminate lower caste status was eventually turned into a requirement that legislation be reasonably related to legitimate state interests, a requirement whose original home was the due process clause.[2] The transformation makes some sense if we think about the limited capacities of the judiciary. Taken seriously, a full-blown anticaste principle is beyond judicial competence. But if the Constitution is intended for other branches as well, it becomes possible to think that the broad commitments of the Fourteenth Amendment have a different meaning outside of the courtroom. It is possible, in short, to insist on the continuing importance of one of the great unused provisions of the Constitution, section 5 of the Fourteenth Amendment: "The Congress shall have power to enforce, by appropriate legislation, the provisions of this article."

## False Starts

In this section I discuss three understandings of the equality principle. All three have played a major role in democratic and sometimes constitutional debate. The first stresses the advantages of free markets. The second relies on respect for existing preferences. The third and most important sees the equality principle as a ban on unreasonable distinctions between social groups. The difficulties with each of these understandings help lay the ground for the anticaste principle.

*Craig.*

### Markets?

With the extraordinary recent outburst of international enthusiasm for free markets, it should not be surprising to find a resurgence in the view that all invidious discrimination on the basis of race and sex will be eliminated by laissez faire. On this view, the appropriate approach for law is to eliminate constraints on market ordering and to rely solely on property rights, voluntary arrangements, and freedom of contract.

In many ways, free markets are indeed an ally of equality on the basis of race and sex. This point is often overlooked. Legal barriers to female and black employment are a form of government intervention in the market, and they have often been an effective and severe hindrance to equality. An effective way to promote inequality is to create all-male or all-white cartels. Anti-female and anti-African-American cartels, especially when governmentally sponsored, can drive down both wages and employment for women and African Americans. In a free market, by contrast, all people should do well to the extent that they are able to carry out their assigned tasks—as employers, employees, coworkers, and customers. It is unnecessary to stress that women and African Americans often perform as well as or better than men and whites. Once discriminatory laws are eliminated, free markets may therefore accomplish a great deal in breaking down a system of inequality. In South Africa, for example, the system of apartheid could not possibly have survived under free markets. Too many employers would have found it desirable to hire African Americans; too many companies would have found it in their economic interest to serve people on a nondiscriminatory basis. In the American South, discriminatory barriers to employment were necessary to sustain Jim Crow in its historical form; without those barriers, segregation would have been far harder to sustain.

The point can be made through a simple example. Suppose that an employer prefers to hire only men. Suppose that he believes that women belong in the home. This employer will fail to make as much money as he otherwise would. In the end, he might even be driven out of the market. An employer who restricts himself to one social group will be at a serious disadvantage; it is as if he refused to hire people whose last names begin with certain letters. If the employer is sexist or racist, his "taste" for discrimination will operate as an implicit tax on the operation of his business. To say the least, self-imposed implicit taxes are self-defeating in a competitive market.

Much the same can be said for a company that prefers to serve only whites or men. Such a company will artificially restrict its business to one social group, and it will thus impair its own economic interests. An employer who hires and serves women as well as men should do much better in a competitive market.

As a complete solution, however, free markets will be inadequate as a remedy for sex and race discrimination. The first problem is that in a market system, third parties who are discriminators will be able to impose costs on people who agree to treat women equally to men, or African Americans equally to whites. Customers, coworkers, and others sometimes withdraw patronage and services from nondiscriminatory employers. In these circumstances, a law firm that hires female lawyers might find itself punished in the marketplace. A grocery store that hires African Americans might find it harder to attract customers. If this is so, market pressures do not check discrimination but instead increase the likelihood that it will continue. Ironically, it is the failure to discriminate that operates as a tax on the employer's business, rather than vice versa. A nondiscriminator could be facing a self-imposed tax by virtue of coworker or customer reactions.

The phenomenon is hardly unusual. Consider, for example, a shopkeeper whose customers do not like dealing with African Americans or women; a commercial airline whose patrons react unfavorably to female pilots; a university whose students and alumni prefer a primarily white faculty; a hospital whose patients are uncomfortable with female doctors or black nurses. In the early decades of the twentieth century, the long persistence of private segregation in major league baseball is a familiar example. It finds a modern analogue in studies of the prices of baseball cards, which show a race-based premium for white players.[3] In some athletic competitions, customers prefer white athletes in general, and these preferences play a role in some retention decisions. In cases of this kind, market pressures create rather than prevent discrimination.

Of course third parties do not have uniform preferences. Many and perhaps most whites and men are not discriminators. In any case third party preferences are sharply divided, and for this reason we should expect a wide range of diverse organizations, gaining and losing influence in different times and places. My point is only that in some important sectors, and for important lengths of time, the existence of third party discrimination can ensure that inequality persists even in free markets. The extent of the effect is of course an empirical question.

Thus far, then, we have seen that coworker and customer discrimination might lead markets to perpetuate discrimination. The second problem is that race and sex discrimination can be a successful and indeed ordinary market response to generalizations or stereotypes that, although overbroad and perhaps in one sense even invidious, provide an economically rational basis for market decisions.[4] If those generalizations are economically rational, the market will not operate against them. Stereotypes and generalizations are of course a common ingredient in market decisions. It can be hard to make distinctions within categories, and sometimes people make the category do the work of a more individualized and sometimes more costly examination into the merits of the particular employee.

Such categorical judgments are not only pervasive but usually legitimate. We all rely on them every day. Employers rely on proxies of various kinds, even though the proxies are overbroad generalizations and far from entirely accurate. For example, test scores, level of education, and prestige of college attended are all part of rational employment decisions. They are also imprecise. Despite their imprecision, such categorical judgments might well be efficient and thus persist in free markets; but they might also disserve the cause of equality on the basis of race and gender.

This is so especially in light of the fact that race and gender are so highly visible and thus so easily used as a proxy for other things. Different characteristics—for example, educational attainment—might be more accurate as proxies but less simple to use and thus less often used, partly because the costs of individualized inquiry are relatively high.

We might compare statistical generalizations of the sort I am describing with the familiar but not entirely clear category of "prejudice." Perhaps we can understand that controversial term to include a continuum of unnecessarily, obtusely, or inefficiently categorical judgments, including (1) a belief that members of a group have certain characteristics when in fact they do not; (2) a belief that many or most members of a group have certain characteristics when in fact only some or a few do; and (3) reliance on fairly accurate group-based generalizations when more accurate and reasonably cheap classifying devices are available or when (in other words) there is a more efficient classifying device. In all these cases, we might say that someone is acting on the basis of prejudice. What I am describing here—statistical discrimination—is quite different from these three ideas. It occurs when the generalization, though inaccurate, is less costly to use than any subclassifying device (even though subclassifications would be more accurate in particular cases). Under plausible assumptions, statistical discrimination will be efficient for employers to use; hence it will be used in markets, which will perpetuate discrimination.

It is often claimed that reliance on race- or sex-based generalizations is a product of prejudice. The claim is often right, but it makes things too easy. Such generalizations are sometimes no more overbroad than generalizations that are typically and unproblematically used in many areas of decision. Note that "college attended" is regularly used in the employment market, despite its considerable imprecision as a classifying device. In the area of sex discrimination, for example, an employer might discriminate against women not because he hates or devalues them but because he has found from experience that women devote more time to child-care than do men or that they are more likely to take leave for domestic duties. For this reason sex discrimination might be based on genuine facts (which may themselves be a product of discrimination elsewhere, particularly within the family). This form of statistical discrimination—judgments based on statistically reasonable stereotyping—need not be a form of prejudice.

Or consider the practice of "racial profiling" by the police, in accordance with which race is used, to a greater or lesser extent, as a proxy for criminality. In the most extreme cases, "driving while black" appears to be a basis for a stop by the police. In a society of free and equal citizens, this is obviously unacceptable; it is connected with the maintenance of a caste system, in which some people are not full citizens. But we can imagine harder problems. Suppose, for example, that police are operating in an overwhelmingly white area that has suffered from a series of crimes; suppose too that witnesses have identified a perpetrator as a young, African-American male. It could easily be imagined that a police officer would engage in a "stop" of someone fitting this description, not because of prejudice but because of a far from irrational judgment that this is the most sensible law enforcement strategy. And many cases could be envisaged in which police officers, in various communities, take race into account for "stops," not because they are prejudiced but because of statistical realities. The fact that certain forms of "racial profiling" seem to be used by African-American police officers attests to the possibility that statistics, and not prejudice, might be at work.

My point here is not to celebrate statistical discrimination, and I hardly mean to defend racial profiling. To be stopped in whole or in part because of skin color is plausibly so bad, and so humiliating, that such stops should be banned even if they are statistically reasonable. What I mean to suggest is a point about the effects of free markets, which, we now can see, will not block discrimination and can even perpetuate it. Statistical discrimination might well ensure that inequality will persist for women or African Americans. Because African Americans differ from whites and women differ from men, it is fully possible that in certain settings, race- or sex-based generalization are sufficiently accurate proxies for certain characteristics. The conclusion is that free markets will not drive out discrimination to the extent that discrimination is an efficient response to generalizations that, while inaccurate, have sufficient accuracy to persist as classificatory devices.

The point has a more general implication. There is no sharp discontinuity between affirmative action requirements and antidiscrimination requirements, at least where the discrimination that is being outlawed is a form of statistical discrimination.[5] The law's ban on statistical discrimination demonstrates that the law does not only forbid irrational bigotry or "prejudice." Instead, the simplest and least controversial antidiscrimination principle singles out one kind of economically rational stereotyping and condemns it. It singles out that form of stereotyping on the apparent theory that such stereotyping has harmful long-term consequences, by perpetuating group-based inequalities. Along this dimension, the distinction between affirmative action and antidiscrimination is thin in principle. It is thin because the law does not ban only discrimination rooted in prejudice or hostility; it bans discrimination in the form of statistical generalizations of the sort that employers, customers, and others rely on all the time. The ban on statistical discrimination is based on many of the reasons that support affirmative action. I do not contend that the two are the same thing. But there is an important commonality between them.

Thus far, then, I have urged that markets are unlikely to bring about equality on the basis of race and sex when third parties are in a position to impose costs on nondiscriminators and when statistical discrimination is at work. An additional problem is that in free markets, people who are subject to discrimination may fail to attempt to overcome their unequal status, because in reaction to existing discrimination, they may well become discouraged and will fail to invest in "human capital" (the economists' term for the production of economically valued characteristics). They may fail to do this simply because of current discriminatory practices. Suppose, for example, that there is current sex discrimination for any number of reasons—because employers themselves prefer men or because third parties impose pressures in discriminatory directions or because employers engage in statistical discrimination. In the face of any of these phenomena, there will be adverse consequences for women's decisions about education or training and indeed for their aspirations in general. As market participants, women might well invest less than men in training to be, say, doctors or technicians if these professions discriminate against women and thus reward their investment less than that of men. Such lower investments would be fully rational as a response to employers' practices.

Of course the same would be true in the racial context. If shops are less likely to hire African Americans than whites, African Americans should be less likely than whites to acquire the skills necessary to work in shops. If law firms are less likely to hire African Americans than whites, African Americans should, other things being equal, be less inclined than whites to go to law school. In every sector of the market that contains discrimination, the behavior of prospective black employees should be affected, in the sense that African Americans should scale back their investments in acquiring the requisite training and skills.

The result of these various factors can be a vicious circle or even spiral. Because of existing discrimination, members of the relevant groups will invest less in human capital. Because of this lower investment, the discrimination will persist or even increase, because its statistical rationality itself increases. Because of this effect, the discriminatory tastes of employers and customers will increase. Because of this effect, investments in human capital will decrease still further; and so on.

These points suggest that while free markets can often help further the cause of race and gender equality, they are hardly a panacea. Discrimination can persist because of the effects of third-party discriminators; because of statistical discrimination; and because of adverse effects on investment in human capital. If discrimination is to be reduced, markets are not enough; additional legal controls will be necessary. Of course empirical questions lurk in the background here, and one cannot get a full handle on the subject without knowing a great deal about the facts. In some imaginable contexts, third-party prejudice will be too weak to promote much discrimination, and in some imaginable contexts, prejudice can be a spur to further investments in human capital. What I am suggesting here is that on highly plausible assumptions, supported by recognizable phenomena in the United States, free markets can fail to undermine race and sex inequality.

### Preferences?

I turn now to an influential and related claim about the relationship among democracy, discrimination, and constitutional law. The claim is that the legal system should take preferences as a given, rather than attempt to alter them. The issue is especially important for sex equality, though it bears on race equality as well. In many different nations, and in some places in the United States, women frequently say that they are content with the sexual status quo, and legal efforts might therefore be thought to represent an unacceptable form of paternalism. If women themselves are content, on what basis can the legal system intervene? Is not legal intervention an illegitimate interference with the right to liberty or autonomy? Thus it is sometimes suggested that abortion cannot possibly raise problems of sex equality, since many women are opposed to abortion.

These questions raise some complex issues; I deal with them briefly here. The basic response is that a social or legal system that has produced preferences, and done so by limiting opportunities unjustly, can hardly justify itself by reference to existing preferences. The satisfaction of private preferences, whatever their content and origins, does not respond to a persuasive conception of liberty, welfare, or autonomy. The notion of autonomy should refer instead to decisions reached with a full and vivid awareness of available opportunities, with relevant information, and without illegitimate or excessive constraints on the process of preference formation. When there is inadequate information or opportunities, decisions and even preferences should be described as unfree or nonautonomous.

Private preferences often do adjust to limitations in current practices and opportunities. People might well adapt their conduct and even their desires to what is now available. Consider here the story of the fox and the sour grapes.[6] The fox does not want the grapes because he considers them to be sour; but his belief to this effect is based on the fact that the grapes are unavailable. It is therefore hard to justify their unavailability by reference to his preferences. Mary Wollstonecraft's *Vindication of the Rights of Women*[7] applies this basic idea to the area of discrimination on the basic of sex. Thus Wollstonecraft writes, "I will venture to affirm, that a girl, whose spirits have not been damped by inactivity, or innocence tainted by false shame, will always be a romp, and the doll will never excite attention unless confinement allows her no alternative."[8] Mill makes the same points in his work on sex equality.[9]

Amartya Sen offers an especially vivid real-world example from India. In 1944, the All-India Institute of Hygiene and Public Health surveyed widows and widowers about their health. About 48.5 percent of the widowers said that they were "ill" or in "indifferent" health, compared to 2.5 percent of widows so describing their condition. In fact the widows were in worse condition than the widowers.[10] In these circumstances it would seem odd to base health policy on subjectively held views about health conditions. Such an approach would ensure that existing discrimination would be severely aggravated.

One goal of a legal system, in short, is to ensure autonomy not merely by allowing satisfaction of preferences but also and more fundamentally in the processes of preference formation. The view that freedom requires an opportunity to choose among alternatives finds a natural supplement in the view that people should not face unjustifiable constraints on the free development of their preferences and beliefs.

To say all this is emphatically not to say that government should feel free to reject existing views of the citizenry or that such views are irrelevant to antidiscrimination policy. For purely pragmatic reasons, it is important for government to be cautious about intruding on widespread current views even if it seems clear that they are wrong. Democratic reforms that do not connect with public convictions are likely to be futile or self-defeating. Moreover, government is itself vulnerable to the same distortions that affect private preferences. There is no reason to think that the judgments that underlie government action are systematically less susceptible to distortion than the judgments that underlie private action. Finally, there is certainly some relation between private desires and individual well-being, and for this reason private desires should generally count in deciding on appropriate policy. All I suggest here is that private preferences are an unpromising foundation for antidiscrimination policy, since in that context, preferences may well be a product of unjust background conditions.

### Irrational or Unreasonable Distinctions?

Much of the constitutional law of equality has proceeded by asking whether similarly situated people have been treated differently. On this view, African Americans can be treated differently from whites only when they are different from whites; the same is true of treating women differently from men. Much of the time, legal doctrines in the area of discrimination allow differences in treatment when people really are different, and ban differences in treatment when people really are the same.[11]

It will readily appear that the notion that "the similarly situated must be treated similarly" is empty by itself, or purely formal. It tells us nothing on its own. To become workable, that notion requires some kind of account to explain what sorts of similarities and differences are relevant and should count. African Americans and whites, for example, are not similarly differently situated along many dimensions; for one thing, their skin color is different. So too for women and men. Some account is necessary by which to explain when differences will be treated as relevant. By itself the "similarly situated" test cannot supply those ideas. From this we might conclude that the problem with the test is that it is empty, not that it is wrong.

As a point about the "similarly situated" test in the abstract, this conclusion is right. But from much of the law over the last few decades, we can construct a general understanding of what the test means, and this understanding is not merely formal. African Americans must be treated the same as whites to the extent that they *are* (relevantly) the same as whites; women must be treated the same as men to the extent that they *are* (relevantly) the same as men. But these ideas also seem unhelpful; to what extent are African Americans relevantly the same as whites, and to what extent are women relevantly the same as men? The law has answered this question largely by saying that African Americans and whites will always be taken to be the same and that women will be taken to be the same as men unless there is (1) a physical difference associated with reproduction,[12] (2) a legal difference between them that is not itself being challenged,[13] or (3) a difference closely associated with past discrimination for which the law in dispute operates as a remedy or compensation.[14] In all other cases, distinctions between men and women will be struck down as irrational, as stereotypical, or as based on hostility and prejudice.[15] It follows that constitutional law now operates as a ban on "formal inequality" and therefore prohibits most explicit distinctions between men and women or African Americans and whites—as in laws that forbid women from having certain jobs or going to certain schools.

There is much to be said on behalf of invalidating formal distinctions on the basis of race and gender. In the United States, much of the work of the two great advocates of race and sex discrimination, respectively—Thurgood Marshall and Ruth Bader Ginsburg—has been an effort to rid the law of formal distinctions. This was exceedingly important. In the racial context, formal inequality is often associated with second-class citizenship for African Americans. Often this has been true for gender as well, as in the exclusion of women from the jury and from the practice of law. Many formal distinctions do help produce inequality in the form of second-class citizenship, and many of them are based on prejudice.

Of course some such distinctions seem more legitimate; consider official practices that provide women, but not men, with police protection on a campus facing sex-related violence or separate sports teams for men and for women. But even if some formal distinctions between African Americans and whites or men and women are justified, a strong presumption against them makes sense in most cases—and is also well adapted to the limited capacities of courts. Individualized inquiry into the legitimacy of formal distinctions might lead to too many errors in particular cases. To this it might be added that formal inequalities tend to encourage people to think in terms of race and gender, and a broad prohibition on laws containing such inequalities therefore has a desirable educative or expressive effect.

Similar ideas could help justify a judicial refusal to scrutinize laws that discriminate in fact, by having disproportionate effects on members of certain groups, but that do not discriminate in terms and hence do not violate the requirement of formal inequality.[16] Consider tests for college admission on which whites do better than African Americans, or height and weight requirements for certain jobs that are met disproportionately by men and failed disproportionately by women. Careful scrutiny of such practices might lead courts to face issues beyond their competence and even to rebalance issues that are best faced legislatively. Consider the extraordinary difficulties that would be raised by asking whether a veteran's preference law would be adopted in a world of sex equality or whether it is adequately justified in light of its discriminatory effects.

These considerations might help justify the current approach under American constitutional law, which is to uphold almost all laws that have discriminatory effects if those laws do not discriminate on their face or show a discriminatory motivation. But there is a problem with this project: It is not at all simple to come up with a sensible theory of equality that would map onto, or adequately account for, the existing approach. The constitutional law of Canada and South Africa is very different from that of the United States; in the former countries, laws that have discriminatory effects are carefully scrutinized and sometimes invalidated. There are two problems with the American approach.

First, some laws that draw lines in terms of race or gender might well promote equality as that term is often or best understood. Consider, for example, a decision of a local police department to furnish police protection for women who are traveling alone at night; suppose that the decision was based on a recent outbreak of sexual violence in the area. It is not at all clear that this decision should be taken to violate equality. Perhaps it promotes equality, by counteracting unequal social conditions that subject women to disproportionate risks. From this example it follows that some laws that treat women differently from men are acceptable and indeed promote the goal of equality, rightly understood. *Califano v. Webster*,[17] upholding formal sex discrimination in the benefit formula under social security law, is an explicit and unusual reflection of this point. Certainly alimony determinations should be required to consider domestic work, which is of course closely correlated with gender. A mere reference to "equality" cannot be conclusive on this question, since some laws that discriminate on the basis of sex might promote equality.

Alternatively, some laws raise equality concerns even if they do not violate formal equality. As a thought experiment, consider a law that forbids pregnant women from appearing in public. For biological reasons, no man can be similarly situated to a pregnant woman, and perhaps there is no problem, from the standpoint of formal equality, in these circumstances. But from the standpoint of sex equality, does this make any sense? Surely equality concerns should be raised by a law that penalizes a physical capacity limited to one gender, or turns such a capacity into a source of disadvantages that need not accompany it. Or suppose that the law forbids women from having an abortion or excludes pregnancy from a disability program. Under current constitutional law, there is apparently no issue of sex discrimination.[18] Men cannot get pregnant. A law that restricts abortion or excludes pregnancy therefore raises no equality problem. But this is an odd way to think about equality. If the law takes a characteristic limited to one group of citizens and turns that characteristic into a source of social disadvantage, there is a clear problem of inequality.[19]

We can go further. Sometimes equality requires the similarly situated to be treated similarly. But sometimes people who are differently situated ought to be treated differently, and precisely in the interest of equality. In the area of handicap, for example, it is readily seen that the use of stairs denies equality to people who are bound to wheelchairs, and that the use of oral communication creates a problem for people who cannot hear, and that the failure to provide closed captioning on television makes deafness into a serious disadvantage. Legislative changes have often been based on an understanding that people who are different ought to be treated differently if they are to be treated equally. Of course the expense of the adaptation is relevant to the question of what, exactly, ought to be done. But constitutional doctrine has rarely recognized that differences in people's situations might justify a claim for differential treatment, in the interest of equality.

This point helps account for the broader failure of American law to do as much as it might have about existing inequalities on the basis of both sex and race. In many areas there has been much progress; women cannot be excluded from professions, and laws that build on or ratify sex-based sterotypes are forbidden. But if we look at the basic indicators of social welfare, it is not clear whether the law has made much difference. The relative labor market status of women did not change much in the aftermath of constitutional decisions. The difference between the earnings of women and those of men was greater in 1980 than it was in 1955, even though the key Supreme Court decisions were in the 1970s. Women continue to face occupational segregation in the workforce, and the result is that women disproportionately occupy low-paying positions traditionally identified as female. Gerald Rosenberg's influential study concludes that "[c]ourt action contributed little to eliminating discrimination against women. Cases were argued and won but, litigants aside, little was accomplished."[20]

This conclusion is probably too severe. It is hard to measure the real-world effects of Supreme Court decisions, and the ban on unequal treatment by government may well have made an important difference for many women, even if it is hard to tie real-world data to judicial decisions. A degree of agnosticism makes good sense here. But it is highly revealing that the requirement of formal equality cannot be simply associated with large-scale changes in the social welfare.

Ironically, some existing inequalities may be partly a product of contemporary equality law. After divorce, women's economic welfare goes sharply down, whereas men's goes sharply up.[21] This is not the result of nature but instead of legal rules that assure this result by refusing to take account of domestic contributions or to see the husband's success in the employment market as a joint asset. The relevant rules might well be subject to legal attack. Certainly some existing inequalities stem from laws that do not violate formal equality. Consider veterans' preference laws, sex-based in effect if not in intent; such laws can have enormous effects on state employment. Perhaps more important is the existence of a social security system that was designed for and that benefits male breadwinners while helping women much less because they do not follow conventional male career paths. The failure to provide adequate protection against rape, sexual harassment, and other forms of sexual assault and abuse might also be seen to raise equality issues, as the formal equality approach does not.

Now we are in a position to make some general observations about the question of race and sex "differences." The question for decision is not whether there is a difference—often there certainly is—but whether the legal and social treatment of that difference can be adequately justified. Differences need not imply inequality, and only some differences have that implication. When differences do have that implication, it is a result of legal and social practices, not the result of differences alone. Since they are legal and social, these practices might be altered even if the differences remain.

An analogy may be helpful here. The problems faced by handicapped people are partly produced by physical conditions. The physical conditions of blindness, deafness, and inability to walk are not socially constructed, and these conditions would certainly create problems in a world without law. But the real-world disabilities of disabled people are a function not of handicap "alone" (a complex idea—what would current handicaps mean in a different world?) but instead of the interaction between physical and mental capacities on the one hand and a set of human obstacles made by and for the able-bodied on the other. It is those obstacles, rather than the capacities taken as brute facts, that create a large part of what it means to be handicapped. It would be implausible, for example, to defend the construction of a building with stairs, and without means of access for those on wheelchairs, on the ground that those who need wheelchairs are "different." The question is whether it is acceptable, or just, to construct a building that excludes people who need an unusual means of entry. That question may not be a simple one, but it cannot be answered simply by pointing to a difference.

To conclude: There are two fundamental problems with the "similarly situated" idea. The first is that the idea cannot be made operational without a theory of some kind. The second is that the implicit theory behind the current approach is hard to justify or even to describe. The best defense would suggest that the approach is adapted to a plausible understanding of equality, or several plausible understandings, while at the same time being well suited to judicial administration. This is not a ridiculous idea; but it suggests that a full understanding of the constitutional equality principle remains to be offered.

## The Anticaste Principle

### Definition

I suggest that in well-functioning deliberative democracies, an important equality principle stems from opposition to caste. In South Africa, the equality principle, growing out of the apartheid experience, is very much understood in these terms. In the United States, the anticaste principle grows out of the original rejection of the monarchical legacy from England and the explicit constitutional ban on titles of nobility. The principle was fueled by the Civil War amendments and the New Deal. The objection should be understood as an effort to eliminate, in places large and small, a caste system rooted in race, gender, and other morally irrelevant characteristics. A law is therefore objectionable on grounds of equality if it contributes to a caste system in this way. The controlling principle is that no group may be made into second-class citizens. Instead of asking: Are African Americans, women, or members of other groups similarly situated to whites or men, and if so have they been treated differently? we should ask: Does the law or practice in question contribute to the maintenance of second-class citizenship, or lower caste status, for African Americans, women, or members of other groups?

I do not suggest that the caste-like features of modern democracies are at all the same, in nature or extent, as those features of genuine caste societies. I do not suggest that dictionary definitions of "caste," or caste systems as understood in, say, India, lead to the simple conclusion that there are major caste-like characteristics to modern American society. Certainly it is true that African Americans and women have risen to most of the highest reaches of American society; certainly it is true that the most conspicuous legal barriers have fallen; and these phenomena, along with many others, suggest that we do not have anything like a true caste system. But I do mean to say that the similarities are what make the current practices a reason for collective concern.

The motivating idea behind an anticaste principle is that *differences that are both highly visible and irrelevant from the moral point of view ought not without good reason to be turned, by social and legal structures, into systematic social disadvantages.* A systematic disadvantage is one that operates along standard and predictable lines in multiple important spheres of life and that applies in realms that relate to basic participation as a citizen in a democracy. There is no algorithm by which to identify those realms. As a provisional working list, we might include education, freedom from private and public violence, wealth, political representation, longevity, health, and political influence. The anticaste principle suggests that with respect to basic human capabilities and functionings,[22] one group, defined in terms of a morally irrelevant characteristic, ought not to be systematically below another. As I will soon suggest, it would be possible to understand the Civil War amendments as an effort to counteract this form of disadvantage.

In the areas of race and sex discrimination, a large part of the problem is this sort of systemic disadvantage. A social or biological difference has the effect of systematically subordinating members of the relevant group—not because of "nature" but because of social and legal practices. It does so in multiple spheres and along multiple indices of social welfare: poverty, education, political power, employment, susceptibility to violence and crime, distribution of labor within the family, and so forth. By pointing to these variables, it should be clear that I am not stressing economic variables alone, though these are indeed important. I am instead suggesting reference to a broad and eclectic set of social indicators.

Systematic differences of this kind help produce frequent injuries to self-respect—the time-honored constitutional notion of "stigma." People should not be subject to humiliation.[23] A particular concern is that self-respect and its social bases ought not to be distributed along the lines of race and gender. When someone is a member of a group that is systematically below others and when the group characteristic is highly visible, insults to self-respect are likely to occur nearly every day. An important aspect of a system of caste is that social practices produce a range of obstacles to the development of self-respect, largely because of the presence of the highly visible but morally irrelevant characteristic that gives rise to caste-like status. Of course the law cannot provide self-respect, at least not in any simple or direct way. But group membership tends to fuel the cycle of discrimination discussed earlier, in which, for example, employers rely on statistical discrimination; group members adjust their aspirations to this reliance; statistical discrimination becomes all the more rational; and so on. That is the caste system to which the legal system is attempting to respond. It operates largely because the high visibility of the group-based characteristic. If the characteristic were not visible, the same pattern could not occur.

Ideas of this kind raise some obvious questions: Is it not equally bad to have, say, 10 percent of the population in bad conditions, as compared with having a high percentage of African Americans in such conditions? Should we not speak of individuals instead of groups? And exactly why must the morally irrelevant characteristic be highly visible? In well-functioning democracies, freedom from desperate conditions is a principle of both equality and liberty, and it is violated whether or not there are group-based disadvantages. I do not deny this point. Constitutional democracies should protect against desperate conditions, perhaps even through constitutional provisions—an obligation enforceable mostly through nonjudicial branches. Indeed this step has been taken in South Africa and in many international human rights documents. What I am suggesting is that a separate and independent problem of inequality, one with constitutional dimensions, arises when a group of people, defined in terms of a characteristic that is both highly visible and morally irrelevant, faces second-class status. The anticaste principle may be offended by second-class status even if most or all of the caste's members are living at or above a decent floor. A special problem with use of a highly visible but morally irrelevant characteristic is that each individual group member—every African American and every woman—is subject, some of the time, to a distinctive stigma by virtue of group membership. That stigma is part of what it means to be a member of a lower caste.

For constitutional purposes, at least, many of the political and moral complexities can be bracketed, and incompletely theorized agreements are the most promising way to proceed. Perhaps those involved in the legal system can build on the general understanding that race and gender are irrelevant from the moral point of view, without making complex and perhaps sectarian claims about moral relevance in general. As we have seen, a fortunate feature of legal thinking is that it often allows participants in legal disputes to bracket large-scale claims about the right and the good and to build on an incompletely theorized agreement about particulars (see chapter 2). There is general public agreement that race and sex are morally irrelevant in the sense that the distribution of social benefits and burdens ought not to depend on skin color or gender. That public agreement is founded on good reasons, since both of these are accidents of birth, since accidents of birth should not produce second-class citizenship, and since it is hard to see an account that would justify lesser benefits or greater burdens by reference to these particular accidents.[24]

Nor, for those thinking about the meaning of most constitutions, is the notion of moral irrelevance a new one. In most constitutional democracies the anticaste principle has distinctive historical roots. Recall that the United States Constitution forbids titles of nobility and that an important part of the founding creed involved the rejection of the monarchical heritage, largely on the ground that monarchy made caste-like distinctions among fundamentally equal human beings. The Civil War amendments were rooted in a judgment about the moral irrelevance of race, formerly taken to be relevant because of "nature." Thus in the aftermath of the American Civil War, it was expressly urged, "God himself has set His seal of distinctive difference between the two races, and no human legislation can overrule the Divine decree."[25] In the same period, antidiscrimination law was challenged squarely on the ground that it put the two races in "*unnatural* relation to each other."[26]

The post–Civil War amendments were based on a wholesale rejection of the supposed naturalness of racial hierarchy. The hierarchy was thought to be a function not of natural difference but of law, most notably the law of slavery and the various measures that grew up in the aftermath of abolition. An important purpose of the Civil War amendments was the attack on racial caste. Thus Senator Jaius Howard explained that the purpose of the Fourteenth Amendment was to "abolish[] all class legislation in the States and [do] away with the injustice of subjecting one caste of persons to a code not applicable to another."[27] The defining case of the Black Codes, placing special disabilities on the freedmen's legal capacities, exemplified the concern with caste legislation. Thus Justice John Harlan, dissenting in *Plessy v. Ferguson*,[28] wrote one of the greatest sentences in American law: "There is no caste here." Contemporary understandings of sex discrimination build on this basic idea.

Perhaps lawyers can build on social consensus and on history; but an adequate account of the subject of caste and moral irrelevance could not rest content with social agreement and with the past. I cannot offer that account here, but a few observations may be helpful. If the notion of moral irrelevance involves a lack of connection to either entitlement or desert, we might think that a wide range of differences among people are indeed morally arbitrary, in the sense that such differences do not by themselves justify more resources or greater welfare. In a market economy, those morally irrelevant differences are quite frequently translated into social disadvantages. Consider educational background; intelligence; physical strength; existing supply and demand curves for various products and services. Certainly someone does not deserve more goods and services merely by virtue of the fact many people want what he is able to provide; consider an especially fast runner from one end of a basketball court to another or an author of books about murder that are especially entertaining to read. For good instrumental reasons, we may well want to reward people who can provide widely valued goods; but the relationship between that talent and desert or entitlement is obscure.

In a market economy, many factors—strength, intelligence, and educational background—affect resources and welfare, and most or perhaps all of these factors are arbitrary from the moral point of view. Is someone really entitled to more money because he was born into a family that stressed education, or because of his intelligence, or because he happened to produce a commodity that many people like?

It seems clear that markets do reward qualities that are irrelevant from a moral point of view. But it would be difficult indeed to justify a principle that would attempt, through law, to counteract all or most of the factors that markets make relevant. The reason is that in general, the recognition of such factors is inseparable from the operation of a market economy. By and large, a market economy is a source of many important human goods, including individual freedom, economic growth and hence prosperity, and respect for different conceptions of the good. Any legal solutions that call for major intrusions on markets must be evaluated in light of the effects on various possible human goods that those alleged solutions will compromise. If legal remedies produce more unemployment, greater poverty, or higher prices for food and other basic necessities, they are, to that extent, a bad idea.

The implementation and reach of any anticaste principle should be defined by reference to considerations of this kind. The point is not that human equality should be "traded off" against the seemingly sterile and abstract notion of market efficiency. I do not claim that otherwise unjustified equality can be supported by some intrinsic good called "efficiency." Efficiency is an instrumental good, to be evaluated in terms of what it does for people, though no less important for that. I argue only that intrusions on markets may defeat valuable human goals and that this is important to keep in mind.

To be more precise: The use of the factors that ordinarily underlie markets is at least sometimes, though certainly not always, in the interest of the most disadvantaged, certainly in the sense that lower prices and higher employment are especially valuable to the poor. When this is so, any government initiative that would bar use of those factors—intelligence, production of socially valued goods, and so forth—would be perverse. Moreover, a principle that would override all morally irrelevant factors would impose extraordinary costs on society, both in its implementation and administrative expense and in its infliction of losses on a wide range of people. The anticaste principle seems to have greatest appeal in discrete contexts in which gains from current practice to the least well-off are hard to imagine; in which second-class citizenship is systemic and occurs in multiple spheres and along easily identifiable and sharply defined lines; in which the morally irrelevant characteristic is highly visible; in which there will be no major threat to a market economy; and in which the costs of implementation are most unlikely to be terribly high.

Ideas of this sort do not justify a judgment that poor people constitute a lower caste. For one thing, poor people are not so easily identifiable as such; this is a broad, amorphous, and to some degree shifting group. When people are poor, we cannot say that social and legal practices turn a highly visible and morally irrelevant characteristic into a systemic source of social disadvantage. Of course human deprivation creates a significant problem of justice, and a constitutional understanding, recognizable in many democracies, tries to provide all people with freedom from desperate conditions. I mean here to identify a separate understanding—one that supports a legal assault on the caste-like features of the status quo with respect to race, sex, and probably disability. It is relevant here that the benefits of antidiscrimination law do seem substantial and that the negative effects on the economy appear minor.

*Judges and legislators.*   In constitutional democracies, who should enforce the anticaste principle? Originally the Fourteenth Amendment to the United States Constitution was understood as an effort to eliminate racial caste— emphatically not as a ban on distinctions on the basis of race. A prohibition on racial caste is of course different from a prohibition on racial distinctions.

A ban on racial distinctions would excise all use of race in decision-making. By contrast, a ban on caste might well throw some measures having discriminatory effects into question, and it would certainly allow affirmative action programs. *yes*

Originally it was also understood that Congress, not the courts, would be the principal institution for implementing the Fourteenth Amendment. The basic idea was that Congress would transform the status of the newly freed slaves, engaging in a wide range of remedial measures. It was not at all anticipated that federal judges—responsible for the then recent and highly visible *Dred Scott*[29] decision, establishing slavery as a constitutional right— would be enforcing the amendment. Indeed, the notion that judges would play a major role in helping to bring about equality under law was entirely foreign to the Civil War amendments.

At some stage in the twentieth century, there was an extremely dramatic change in the legal culture's understanding of the notion of constitutional equality under the Constitution. The anticaste principle was transformed into an antidifferentiation principle.[30] No longer was the issue the elimination of second-class citizenship. Instead it was the entirely different question whether people who were similarly situated had been treated similarly. This was a fundamental shift. Its occurrence remains one of the great untold stories of United States constitutional history.

So long as the courts were to be the institution entrusted with enforcing the equal protection clause, the shift was fully intelligible, notwithstanding its problematic relationship with the original understanding of the Fourteenth Amendment and with the best understanding of what race and sex inequality really are. An anticaste principle is simply beyond the capacities of the judiciary, which lacks the necessary tools. The transformation in the conception of equality is therefore understandable in light of what came to be, under the Fourteenth Amendment, the astonishing institutional importance of courts and the equally astonishing institutional insignificance of Congress. But the transformation of an anticaste principle into a prohibition on differentiation has inadequately served the constitutional commitment to equal protection of the laws. It has meant that too little will be done about the second-class citizenship of African Americans and women (and the handicapped as well).

If the legal culture is to return to the roots of the constitutional commitment, and to a better understanding of equality, it is necessary to emphasize the legislature rather than the courts. It is clear that the anticaste principle, if taken seriously, would call for significant restructuring of social practices. For this reason it must be stressed that the principle is better set out and implemented by legislative and administrative bodies, with their superior democratic pedigree and fact-finding capacities, than by courts.

*Suspect classes.*   What is the relationship between the anticaste principle that I am describing and the familiar idea that some classifications are "suspect," in the sense that the courts will be hostile to discrimination against certain groups? I can start by observing that the Supreme Court has granted "heightened scrutiny" to laws that discriminate against certain identifiable groups thought likely to be at particular risk in the ordinary political process.[31] When the Court grants heightened scrutiny, it is highly skeptical of legislation, and the burden of every doubt operates on behalf of groups challenging the relevant laws.[32]

The difference between the two ideas can be described in the following way: The notion of "suspect classifications" is based on a fear that illegitimate considerations are likely to lie behind legislation, whereas the anticaste principle is designed to ensure against second-class status for certain social groups. The two ideas overlap, since lower castes may well be subject to legislation grounded on illegitimate considerations. But the two ideas are nonetheless distinct, since illegitimate considerations may lie behind legislation discriminating against groups that do not count as lower castes and since the anticaste principle imposes duties on government that go well beyond a ban on illegitimately motivated legislation.

In deciding whether to grant heightened scrutiny, the Court has not been altogether clear about its underlying rationale. The Court appears to have looked at a set of factors—above all, at the relevance of the group characteristic to legitimate governmental ends, the likelihood that the group in question will be subject to prejudice, the immutability of the relevant characteristic, the existence of past and present discrimination, and the group's lack of political power.[33] In this way, it has moved well beyond the defining case of discrimination against African Americans to include discrimination against women, illegitimates, and sometimes aliens. But most of these factors have yet to be fully analyzed. They purport to involve a quasi-factual investigation into history and data, but they depend instead on controversial and usually unidentified normative judgments. We cannot know whether a characteristic is "relevant" just by looking at facts. Often race and sex are relevant to employment decisions, in the sense that profits depend on them. We cannot know whether a group is subject to discrimination without knowing whether unequal treatment is justified; discrimination is a value-laden category.

Similarly, a major problem with the key issue of "political powerlessness" is that any judgments here are based not simply on facts about political influence. They also depend on some controversial and usually unarticulated claims about how much political power is *appropriate* for the group in question, and about the legitimacy of usual bases for legislative judgments on matters affecting the group. The claim that a group is politically weak in the constitutional sense is thus a product of some controversial evaluative claims, and these are almost never brought to the surface.

For example, it might be thought that African Americans have a good deal of political power, for they can influence elections, even elections of the president. The same is true of women, who of course can affect elections a great deal. The potentially large electoral influence of both groups does not exclude them from the category of groups entitled to particular protection against discrimination. The reason is that even if they can wield political influence, prejudice in the constitutionally relevant sense is likely to operate against both African Americans and women in the political process. African Americans may be subject to hatred or devaluation; women may be subject to stereotypes about appropriate roles that affect their political power and even their own aspirations. The conclusion is that the category of political powerlessness looks like an inquiry into political science; but it really depends on some claims about the illegitimacy of the usual grounds for government action classifying on the basis of race and sex. The real question is whether legislation disadvantaging the relevant group is peculiarly likely to rest on illegitimate grounds. Heightened scrutiny is a way of testing whether it does.

What has been said so far should be enough to show that other features of the Court's analysis— the history of discrimination, the category of prejudice, the inquiry into whether the relevant characteristic is "immutable"— can be analyzed in the same way. These ideas are designed to help determine if illegitimate considerations typically underlie legislation. As noted, a judgment that there has been a history of discrimination depends on a theory of appropriate distribution, at least of a general sort. We rarely say that criminals have suffered a history of discrimination, and if we do say this, it is not because they are punished for criminal conduct. To say that there has been prejudice is to say that the usual grounds for discrimination are impermissible, even though those grounds may represent good-faith moral convictions. Consider the widely held view that women and men should occupy different social roles, a view that may not be used to support legislation despite its popularity. Immutability is neither a necessary nor a sufficient condition for "suspect class" status. Blind people are not entitled to heightened scrutiny, even though the condition of being blind is usually immutable. And if new drugs or technology allowed African Americans to become whites, or vice versa, and made sex-change operations feasible and cheap, would courts abandon their careful scrutiny of race and sex discrimination? Surely not.

My major point here is that the anticaste principle is quite different from the antidiscrimination principle. We might therefore think that discrimination against (for example) Asian Americans and Jews should be presumed invalid, without also thinking that Asian Americans and Jews count as castes. The inquiry into suspect classification is therefore quite different from the inquiry into caste, though the two ideas do overlap. I will return to these questions in some detail in chapter 8.

*Discrimination without caste? Caste without discrimination?* It follows from what has been said thus far that many groups that are frequently subject to discrimination do not qualify as "lower castes" in the way I have understood that term. Asian Americans suffer from discrimination and prejudice; but they cannot qualify as a lower caste, since they do not appear to be systematically below other groups in terms of the basic indicators of social well-being. The same is true for many other groups subject to discrimination, including, for example, homosexuals and Jews. Homosexuals are not a lower caste in the sense that they do not do worse in terms of many of the usual indicators of social welfare. They cannot show second-class citizenship in this sense. But they are also subject to pervasive discrimination and prejudice, with possibly corrosive effects on self-respect, and in that sense discriminating on grounds of sexual orientation is connected to the issues of caste that I have been discussing.

Nothing I have said here is meant to legitimate discrimination against groups that have suffered and continue to suffer from private and public prejudice. For example, there is indeed an equality norm that is offended by discrimination on the basis of religion. But the anticaste principle does not cover groups simply by virtue of the fact that they are often subject to illegitimate discrimination. The anticaste principle has special meanings and uses. It is not exhaustive of the several constitutional principles of equality.

## The Future

*From discrimination to anticaste.* In the United States, equality law has had two principal stages. The first was concerned with preventing explicit discrimination, public or private, against African Americans and women. This was the attack on American apartheid, led by Thurgood Marshall and culminating in *Brown v. Board of Education*, and also the attack on explicit sex discrimination, led by Ruth Bader Ginsburg. The legal assault on public discrimination was eventually matched by the attack on private discrimination. The second stage consisted of challenges to public and private practices that did not involve explicit discrimination but that stemmed from prejudice or that otherwise had large and not adequately justified discriminatory effects. This second stage built on the first.

Both of these movements for reform had substantial success, certainly in eliminating the most conspicuously unsupportable public and private practices. Neither has entirely run its course. Both were connected with anticaste goals and also were plausibly well adapted to the limited institutional capacities of the judiciary. On the other hand, the successes, important as they have been, have had ambiguous effects on the inequalities discussed earlier. From what has been said thus far, it should be clear that if the elimination of second-class citizenship is an important social goal, it would be valuable to start in new directions, some of which have not typically been associated with civil rights at all.

If opposition to caste is a basic goal, civil rights policy should concern itself first and foremost with such problems as lack of opportunities for education, training, and employment; inadequate housing, food, and health care; vulnerability to crime, both public and private; incentives to participate in crime; disproportionate subjection to environmental hazards; and teenage pregnancy and single-parent families. It need not be emphasized that policies of this kind suggest a major shift in direction from the more narrowly focused antidiscrimination policies of the past.

This discussion is hardly a place for a full program for legislative reform. But in resolving current problems, most of the traditional claims of civil rights law provide incomplete help. The problem is not rooted in explicitly racial or sex-based classification, nor does it lie in prejudice, at least not in any simple sense. It lies instead in policies and programs that contribute to second-class status, often in extremely complex ways, involving interactions between past practices and a wide array of current policies.

In proposing reforms, we might look quite eclectically at a range of protections against the sorts of disparities discussed earlier. It appears, for example, that policies promoting economic growth are an important part of equality law insofar as growth is associated with employment and the reduction of poverty. But since the association is imperfect, many other steps are necessary. I simply note a few possibilities here; of course a range of details would be required in order to assess any of them.

Promising models are provided by targeted educational policies, including efforts to promote literacy and Head Start programs. Significant improvements have resulted from parental leave and "flexi-time" policies. Certainly employment-related policies are important insofar as job increases are closely connected with the reduction of poverty. The earned income tax credit, providing incentives to work and also substantial wage subsidies, has been a terrific success, removing from poverty over four million Americans, many of them female, African American, or both. Consider as well recent initiatives designed to reduce violence generally and violence against women in particular—through education, additional government resources for crime prevention and punishment, and new legal remedies for victims of sex-related violence. There is much that law can do to help.

*Against race consciousness.*   On the account I have offered, there should be no constitutional objection to genuinely remedial race- and sex-conscious policies, at least as a general rule. If a basic goal is opposition to caste, affirmative action policies are generally permissible as a matter of constitutional law (a conclusion that is largely uncontroversial in South Africa, Canada, and India, though against the tide in the United States). Partly this is a lesson of the history of the Civil War amendments; if history is relevant, it is hard to support the view that affirmative action programs are invalid. But partly it is a lesson of logic. We have seen that in an important way the antidiscrimination principle is continuous with the affirmative action principle. Insofar as statistical discrimination is outlawed, the government has singled out one form of rational categorization and subjected it to special disability. At least along this dimension, the antidiscrimination principle partakes of an affirmative action principle.

To be sure, it may be possible to generalize from the Civil War amendments a broad form of opposition to the use of skin color as a basis for the distribution of social benefits and burdens. Perhaps we should say that government ought never or rarely to consider skin color in its official decisions, because use of skin color has bad educational and expressive effects and because it legitimates the view that people should see each other, and themselves, in racial terms. But this is historically adventurous, and it would also involve an exceptionally intrusive role for the courts, one that would be highly undemocratic. Race-conscious programs occupy an exceptionally wide range. They can be found in education, employment, licensing, and elsewhere. They have been accepted at local, state, and federal levels by courts, administrators, presidents, and legislatures; they have come from people with sharply divergent views, including conservatives and liberals alike; both Democrats and Republicans have supported them. In these circumstances, judges should be extremely reluctant to impose anything like a flat ban on race-conscious programs.

One might conclude from what has been said thus far that race- and sex-conscious remedial policies are not only unobjectionable but mandatory under an anticaste principle. Perhaps such policies are necessary in order to counteract second-class status; certainly many people have so thought. But it must be acknowledged that many such policies have been a mixed success and in some places and ways a conspicuous failure. Some platitudes are worth repeating: In some places, race-conscious judgments have stigmatized their purported beneficiaries, by making people think that African Americans are present because of their skin color. In some places, such judgments have fueled hostility and increased feelings of second-class citizenship. Some people who would do extremely well in some good institutions—schools or jobs—are placed, by affirmative action programs, in positions in which they perform far less well, with harmful consequences for their self-respect. Ironically, affirmative action programs can aggravate problems of caste, by increasing the social perception that a highly visible feature like skin color is associated with undesirable characteristics.

Perhaps this is partly a product of the unfortunate rhetoric of affirmative action. But partly it is a result of a deep-seated resistance to "racialism" as productive of frequent unfairness in individual cases and as destructive to widespread convictions about the relationship between individual achievement and social reward. Elaborate arguments might be and have been offered to try to undermine this resistance and these convictions. But it is at least revealing that sometimes these arguments seem too elaborate and complicated to persuade many of the people toward whom they are aimed.

To say this is not to say that all or most affirmative action programs should be abolished. There is too much variety to allow for sensible global judgments. But we know enough to know that such programs have often failed and that it is often better to try race-neutral alternatives.

All this suggests both a presumption in favor of race- and gender-neutral policies and the need to develop legal reforms that are not gender or race conscious—that do not give rise to widespread fears that government is playing favorites or subject to the lobbying pressure of well-organized private groups. And it would be possible to administer an anticaste principle in race- and gender-neutral terms. One can think of many examples. These include wage supplements for the working poor; broad-based anticrime and antidrug measures; literacy and educational programs; policies designed to protect children from poor health and from poverty, including neonatal care and childhood immunizations; and programs designed to discourage teen pregnancy and single-headed families. Policies of this kind could easily be designed in race- and sex-neutral terms; and such policies would be directed against many of the important problems faced by both African Americans and women.

These are some of the directions in which equality law might move in the future. It is ironic but true that a third stage of civil rights policy, directed most self-consciously against race and gender caste, might also be self-consciously designed—for reasons of policy and principle—so as to avoid race and gender specificity.

# Homosexuality and the Constitution
## 1994

> Decisions of individuals relating to homosexual conduct have been
> subject to state intervention throughout the history of Western civi-
> lization. Condemnation of those practices is firmly rooted in Judeo-
> Christian moral and ethical standards.... Blackstone described
> "the infamous crime against nature" as an offense of "deeper ma-
> lignity" than rape.
> —*Chief Justice Warren Burger*, Bowers v. Hardwick (1986)

> I'm going to make you my girlfriend.
> —*Mike Tyson to his challenger Razor Ruddock (1991)*

How does a democratic constitution deal with discrimination on the basis of
sexual orientation? Gays and lesbians face discrimination in multiple domains. Are they therefore members of a lower caste?

This is far from clear. For one thing, sexual orientation is not highly
visible; it can be readily concealed. For another, gays and lesbians, as a group,
do not rank systematically below heterosexuals along multiple dimensions of
social welfare. It cannot be said, for example, that gays and lesbians are
poorer, less employed, and more subject to criminal violence than heterosexuals (though hate crimes against homosexuals are not uncommon). On
the other hand, homosexuals do face discrimination in many arenas, and
they are often subject to humiliation, in a way that produces damage to self-
respect and is also associated with barriers to political influence. The most
sensible conclusion is that even though gays and lesbians do not entirely
qualify as a lower caste, the anticaste principle raises serious questions about
discrimination on the basis of sexual orientation.

I will urge here that such discrimination usually cannot be defended in
deliberative terms and also that those concerned with preventing second-class

citizenship should presume that this form of discrimination is illegitimate. To understand these points, it will be useful to begin with a story.

In 1993, Jamie Gorelick, general counsel of the Department of Defense, testified before a subcommittee of the House Armed Services Committee. Defending President Clinton's new "Don't ask, don't tell" policy, Gorelick was asked to explain how someone alleged to be homosexual could establish that she was not, in fact, homosexual.

Gorelick answered with an example: "In one instance a woman was alleged to have said that she was a lesbian. She came in and said essentially that the statement had been misunderstood. And actually, she introduced evidence—she brought in boyfriends who testified essentially that she was heterosexual—and the conclusion was reached that she would be retained." Gorelick offered this illustration to show how accused members could prove their heterosexuality and defend themselves against losing their job.

At that moment in the House hearings, you might suppose that the ban on homosexuals in the military would be in serious trouble. Is it really possible to imagine a trial in which a member of the American military has to defend herself against a charge of lesbianism by asking former boyfriends to testify on her behalf? What would the boyfriends be expected to say? Would they be subject to cross-examination? If the issue is whether the defendant is really homosexual, what particular questions might be asked, by way of resolving that contested issue? Surely—you might suppose—Gorelick's commendably candid response would raise doubts about the legitimacy of the policy she was attempting to defend. Yet there was no visible reaction to Gorelick's anecdote. It was as if the proceeding that she described was perfectly acceptable, a matter of common sense, entirely routine.

Since that hearing, and quite unexpectedly, discrimination on the basis of sexual orientation has become one of the most important equality issues of our time. In American law, the development is unexpected because *Bowers v. Hardwick,*[1] the Georgia sodomy case, had been thought to resolve most of the issues as a matter of constitutional law. But suppose that homosexuals are excluded from federal employment, whether in the military or elsewhere. Or suppose that federal law recognizes heterosexual marriages but not homosexual marriages or "civil unions." Does *Bowers* resolve the issue? This is most unclear, for *Bowers* was decided under the due process clause, not the equal protection clause, and did not involve discrimination at all. Perhaps most discrimination on the basis of sexual orientation is constitutionally unacceptable.

My goal in this chapter is to describe the appropriate role of constitutional law in cases involving this form of discrimination. I focus throughout on American law, because the issue has been litigated very little elsewhere. Much of the discussion will, however, bear on the inevitable future constitutional disputes on these issues in other nations. Consider, for example, the remarkable ruling in South Africa invalidating laws forbidding sodomy on the ground that such laws produce impermissible discrimination between heterosexuals and homosexuals.[2] As far as I am aware, South Africa's constitution is the only founding document in the world that expressly bans discrimination on the basis of sexual orientation. But almost all constitutions contain general protections of both liberty and equality, and many disputes will arise on this issue in the future. It is noteworthy too that many democracies, responding to concerns about both equality and dignity, have eliminated prohibitions on same-sex relations, with decriminalization of sodomy occurring in the United Kingdom, Ireland, Australia (with the exception of Tasmania), New Zealand, Canada, and most of western Europe.

My basic claim here is that discrimination on the basis of sexual orientation is generally unconstitutional in a deliberative democracy, in part because it can rarely be defended in deliberative terms. Usually such discrimination is really an effort to stigmatize and humiliate fellow citizens, an effort that raises concerns associated with the anticaste principle and that cannot be defended by reference to constitutionally legitimate reasons. It follows that the equal protection clause, aimed at unacceptable discrimination, is the best route for future constitutional developments. This is in part because the equal protection clause is a self-conscious attack on traditional practices, whereas the due process clause is more preservative, building on traditional practices. I devote special attention to what seems to me to be the most interesting and powerful if somewhat exotic argument: that discrimination on the basis of sexual orientation is a form of discrimination on the basis of sex. If the anticaste principle bans most forms of sex discrimination, it also bans most forms of sexual orientation discrimination, because the latter is a subset of the former. I also suggest that courts should play a catalytic role in this domain, proceeding incrementally, and in an incompletely theorized way, to the extent that this is possible.

Nice
Tie
?

## Constitutional Possibilities

In applying the Constitution to issues involving homosexuality, there are many options.

*Privacy*

It is perhaps most tempting to apply the right of privacy—a form of "substantive due process"—to sexual autonomy in homosexual relations. As a practical matter, however, this route has been foreclosed by *Bowers v. Hardwick,* upholding Georgia's sodomy law against constitutional law. *Bowers* has been rightly maligned, and we should not be at all unhappy if the Court overrules it. A free society does not ban consensual relations of this kind. But for at least two reasons, the outcome in that case has at least a degree of plausibility.

First, any form of substantive due process has controversial foundations as a matter of text and history.[3] It is unclear, to some reasonable people, that substantive due process deserves much life as a basis for invalidating legislation, except perhaps in the most egregious cases. Second, any constitutional "privacy" rights usually are rooted in Anglo-American traditions, which often have refused to recognize the legitimacy of homosexuality. In chapter 3, I questioned the idea that tradition should be used as the foundation for constitutional rights. But if the due process clause creates substantive rights largely because of tradition—and this is the prevailing understanding—the privacy claim in *Bowers* was vulnerable.

Maybe these are largely technical difficulties. Substantive due process is well established in a number of privacy cases, and perhaps the relevant tradition should be read at a sufficient level of abstraction to include consensual relations between homosexuals. If a state is going to forbid people from engaging in consensual sexual activity, it should certainly have to come up with a good reason for the ban. In the case of people who are under age, it can point to the absence of real consent. In the case of incest among adults, it can point to psychological harms and to risks to the children who might result. In the case of adultery, it can perhaps refer to the need to protect the marital relationship. It is hard to find a similar justification for bans on consensual sodomy among adults. In these circumstances, a decision to overrule *Bowers v. Hardwick* should be counted as a cause for celebration.

But there are other difficulties. The fundamental problem for homosexuals is not adequately described as a simple absence of privacy. Homosexuals can disguise their sexual orientation. The "closet" can furnish a degree of privacy. But the possibility of disguise is hardly a full solution to current problems. Indeed, the possibility of disguise can perpetuate stigma and inequality by making people think that their sexual orientation is abhorrent, a kind of dark secret, something to be withheld from public view. The result is likely to be a form of humiliation and serious injury to self-respect, in a way that is associated with the maintenance of a caste system. For this reason the emphasis on privacy rights seems to misconceive the basic issue. The lack of privacy against public and private intrusion is certainly one problem, but it is a problem primarily because of deeper problems of discrimination. As suggested by a South African scholar, in words quoted (though not entirely with approval) by the South African Constitutional Court,

> the privacy argument has detrimental effects on the search for a society which is truly non-stigmatizing as far as sexual orientation is concerned. . . . [T]he privacy argument suggests that discrimination against gays and lesbians is confined to prohibiting conduct between adults in the privacy of the bedroom. This is manifestly not so. . . . Privacy as a rationale for constitutional protection therefore goes insufficiently far, and has appreciable drawbacks even on its own terms.[4]

### Equality in General

What about equality? Does discrimination on the basis of sexual orientation offend the Constitution's equality principle?

Begin with a technical issue. Many people have argued that because the Supreme Court held that the due process clause does not forbid states from outlawing consensual sodomy, the equal protection clause is unavailable as a basis for challenging discrimination against gays and lesbians. If the Constitution permits states to criminalize homosexual conduct, surely—it might be urged—the same Constitution cannot say that states cannot discriminate against homosexuals.

But this argument is much too glib. It ignores central differences between the equal protection clause and the due process clause. Because the equal protection clause was designed as an attack on traditions, it is a far more promising source of new constitutional doctrine than the right to privacy. Most generally, the due process clause is associated with the protection of traditionally respected rights from novel or short-term change. It is largely backward looking. By contrast, the equal protection clause is self-consciously directed against traditional practices. It was designed to counteract practices that were time-honored and expected to endure. It is based on a norm of equality that operates as a critique of past practices. Under the equal protection clause, the fact that a practice is long-standing is neither here nor there; the clause was designed as an attack on practices that were well entrenched. Because opposition to homosexuality has deep historical roots, the equal protection clause is the more sensible source of constitutional doctrine.

Recall here the distinction, noted in chapter 3, between preservative and transformative constitutions. In American constitutional law, the due process clause has generally operated as a preservative provision, while the equal protection clause has been transformative. If this is so, the latter provision is available to test discrimination on the basis of sexual orientation even if the due process clause has little to say on the subject.

## Equality and Rationality

Under the equal protection clause, the Supreme Court has invalidated certain forms of discrimination on the ground that they are irrational or unconnected with any legitimate public purpose.[5] This idea is connected with an idea about democracy, indeed reflecting the core of the deliberative approach: The distribution of benefits or the imposition of burdens must reflect a conception of the public good. Benefits and burdens may not be based solely on political power or on a naked preference for one group over another.

The Court has also disqualified, as justifications of legislation, certain ideas on the ground that they reflect "prejudice," "animus," or "hostility." A statute based on "prejudice" cannot qualify as rational.[6] It is under this line of argument that the Supreme Court invalidated a discriminatory law in _Romer v. Evans_, contending that the discrimination was explicable only by reference to "animus" against homosexuals and that "animus" could not count as legitimate under the equal protection clause. And _Romer_ is only one example; in several important cases, lower federal courts have said that discrimination on the basis of sexual orientation can indeed be irrational because it is a simple product of prejudice or irrational fear.

Thus, for example, some courts have said that the exclusion from the military of people with homosexual "orientation"—unaccompanied by homosexual acts—is irrational and therefore unconstitutional under the equal protection clause.[7] In the important ruling in _Steffan v. Aspin_,[8] the Court of Appeals for the District of Columbia Circuit held that it was irrational to exclude from military service people of homosexual orientation, short of a demonstration of homosexual conduct. In the court's view, homosexual orientation alone was not a legitimate basis for discharge because it was unconnected with any plausible government interest. The court did not address the question whether homosexual conduct could be a basis for discharge. Two district courts reached the same conclusion, finding exclusion from the military to be unconnected with any legitimate public goal.[9]

In part because of its modesty, I believe that the use of rationality review is quite promising and rightly leads to invalidation in most cases of discrimination against homosexuals. Typically governments defend discrimination against homosexuals on the ground that tangible harms are at stake, such as adverse effects on morale, or abuse of children. Thus in *Romer*, the state claimed that it was forbidding localities from protecting homosexuals through antidiscrimination legislation, not because it disliked homosexuals but because it sought to protect religious groups from interference with religious practices and to ensure that local resources would not be diverted from cases involving race and sex discrimination. But in *Romer* itself, it was hard to see how the discrimination would be a good way of preventing those harms. If the state wants to protect religious groups, it should not allow discrimination against homosexuals but say more straightforwardly that any ban on discrimination cannot be applied to those groups. If the state wants to allocate resources mostly to race and sex discrimination, enforcement officers can do that in any case.

Of course the idea of irrationality, or "animus," really depends on a judgment that the grounds that lie behind legislation are objectionable or invidious. For example, the underlying judgment in *Romer* must be that at least for purposes of the equal protection clause, it is no longer legitimate to discriminate against homosexuals simply because the state wants to discourage homosexuality. Discrimination must be justified on some other, public-regarding ground. The underlying concern must be that a measure discriminating against homosexuals, like a measure discriminating against the mentally retarded, is likely to reflect irrational hatred and fear, directed at who people are as much as what they do. Here we can find a desire to fence off and seal off members of a despised group whose characteristics are thought to be in some sense contaminating, corrosive, or contagious. It is here that discrimination on the basis of sexual orientation has caste-like features. Of course there are widespread religious objections to homosexuality. But in a pluralistic democracy, those objections are a legitimate basis for moral suasion, not for the use of law.

### Don't Ask, Don't Tell

To be sure, any judgment that discrimination is "irrational" requires a close encounter with the particular government action at issue. Different forms of discrimination might be treated differently. Consider, for example, a ban on grade-school teaching by homosexuals. The ban should be struck down as irrational. Harder questions are raised by bans on military service by homosexuals or by "known" homosexuals, as in the military policy of "Don't ask, don't tell." As a test case for rationality review, the military policy deserves detailed discussion, especially in light of the courts' usual, and entirely appropriate, posture of extreme deference to the military.

Why does the military discriminate against homosexuals? Some people have urged that sexual impositions in the military context are unacceptable; that the admission of people known to be homosexual would have adverse effects on military morale; that it would undermine recruitment; that the interest in privacy is substantial, and that young soldiers should be protected from serving in such close quarters with people of the same sex who might have a sexual interest in them. To be sure, it is not easy to separate these interests from prejudice or hostility, and in the military context, many of the grounds for discrimination are disturbingly close to those that have justified race segregation and the exclusion of women. But courts should undoubtedly be cautious in the military setting in light of the high stakes, the possibility (even if slight) of disaster, and the complexity of the underlying factual issues, which are not well suited to judicial resolution. To assess this issue, it is necessary to explore the underlying justifications in more detail.

The first basis for "Don't ask, don't tell" is that sexual relationships and sexual impositions—above all, involving superiors—are intolerable in the military setting. A prime concern is sexual harassment. To be sure, there is an irony in seeing the law of sexual harassment invoked by people not normally so enthusiastic about that law. Some defenders of the policy seem to fear that homosexual men will frequently treat heterosexual men the same way that heterosexual men sometimes treat women, and they are eager to protect heterosexual men against that kind of treatment. Undoubtedly many people do believe—and here they are entirely right—that all steps should be taken to ensure that sexual harassment does not occur in the military setting. If sexual impositions create the difficulty, however, then the natural solution is to ban sexual impositions of any kind, not to forbid gays and lesbians from serving their country.

Perhaps the problem is not sexual harassment but sexual relations. Perhaps the military setting is incompatible with even voluntary sexual relations among members of the service, at least when they must work together in close quarters. But if this is so—and it certainly seems reasonable to think that it is so—then the solution is to ban the relevant relations. Indeed, current policy imposes restrictions on "fraternization," and any such restrictions could be applied to homosexual relationships.

Perhaps the strongest argument against abolition of the discriminatory policy—and what really seems to underlie the idea of "unit cohesion"—is that even without sexual harassment and sexual relations, it would be very hard for many young men and women to know that they are serving with open gays and lesbians. Of course there is, in the military, a degree of segregation between young men and young women, partly to prevent the kinds of entanglements, tensions, and misunderstandings that might genuinely undermine military preparation and effectiveness. The ban on open homosexuality might be defended as preventing the same sorts of difficulties. And if the lifting of that ban really would hurt morale and recruitment and cause serious internal problems, it would not be so easy for outsiders to dismiss the military's underlying concern. When Colin Powell and other members of the Joint Chiefs of Staff resisted President Clinton's initiative in 1993, this was their fundamental objection. And there is a genuine interest in sexual privacy as well, raised most vividly, perhaps, in the context of communal barracks and showers.

Yet this argument is not without its own problems. If some young people find it hard to work in close quarters with homosexuals, this is often because of a form of ignorance and prejudice (and sometimes hatred) that is not ordinarily a legitimate basis for denying people employment opportunities. Giving in to these feelings tends to perpetuate and to ratify them. The argument also depends on highly speculative empirical claims about the harmful effects of a nondiscriminatory policy. It is important to remember that an exceptionally wide range of countries do not exclude homosexuals from the armed services. There are no bans, no analogues to "Don't ask, don't tell," and apparently no problems for "unit cohesion" in Denmark, Norway, Finland, Belgium, Spain, the Netherlands, France, Canada, Germany, Switzerland, Sweden, and Israel. Nor must we look abroad for similar evidence. Gays and lesbians fought for their country in World War II, the Korean War, and the Vietnam War, and their military records show that they served the nation as well, on average, as heterosexuals. Sexual privacy is a legitimate interest, and perhaps a nondiscriminatory policy would require special efforts to protect privacy. But if military commanders were genuinely committed to make nondiscrimination work, it is hard to imagine that such a policy would create serious problems.

Does this mean, then, that courts should strike down "Don't ask, don't tell" as unconstitutional? When the military is involved, courts should be extremely cautious about rejecting the considered judgments of the elected branches of government. But it is one thing to adopt a general posture of deference; it is quite another for courts to permit the government to exclude, to stigmatize, and to humiliate a class of citizens whose members have long served the nation with distinction. In the aftermath of a large number of documented abuses under "Don't ask, don't tell," the Defense Department has been embarking on an effort to ensure against harassment, violence, and witch hunts—to provide antiharassment training and to require investigations to be launched only on the basis of solid evidence. But even if the reforms make things better, there is something farcical and bizarre, and more than slightly Orwellian, about this earnest and highly publicized effort to ensure that people will be investigated as acknowledged or practicing homosexuals only if there is actual evidence that they are, in fact, acknowledged or practicing homosexuals. The most fundamental problem with the policy is not the occasional abuses, egregious as some have been, but its very core.

The best solution would be for Congress, which has an independent obligation to the Constitution, to reject the "Don't ask, don't tell" policy on equal protection grounds and to work with the military to accommodate its concerns. But this is one of the exceedingly rare cases, I believe, in which courts would be justified in invalidating a military practice as irrational under the equal protection clause of the Constitution.

## Same-Sex Marriages

Does the Constitution require states to recognize same-sex marriages? Does a democratic constitution require nations to allow people of the same sex to marry one another? For most of the history of the world, the answer would be obvious: Of course "marriage" can be reserved to male-female unions. Now the answer is not so obvious. The reason is that the ban on same-sex unions is not easy to explain in deliberative terms. I will suggest that this is an area where courts should fear to tread and should give democracy ample time to deliberate; but on the question of constitutional principle, the ban runs into serious difficulties.

Perhaps the ban could be justified as a means of restricting the benefits of marriage to relations that involve children. But this justification is quite crude, to say the least. Homosexuals can adopt children if the law permits, and, if the law permits, homosexuals might even have children with a biological connection to one parent. In any case, many heterosexual marriages do not involve children, because the couple cannot or does not want to have children. Moreover, the state does not prevent marriage by infertile couples, by fertile couples who choose not to have children, or by people too old to have children. It is entirely implausible to defend the ban on same-sex marriages by urging that marriage should be restricted to situations involving the potential to have biological offspring.

The state might say that it does not want to "advertise" that same-sex relations can be happy, healthy, and successful, and the grant of a marriage license would be an endorsement of a practice deserving at best neutrality

and not approval. But this argument is fragile as well. Whether same-sex
relations are less happy and healthy than heterosexual relations—indepen- ⟩ Nice
dent of public and private discrimination—is most unclear. Much the same
might be said about interracial relations, where there is also a risk of unhap-
piness, and the possibility of less happiness in that context is not a reason
for discrimination.

A final argument would rely on the widespread moral disapproval of
same-sex relations. This argument was found sufficient in *Bowers v. Hardwick*,[10] and perhaps it is enough here too. But the crucial distinction is that
we are supposing here that the ban on same-sex marriage is being challenged  *Essentially*
under the equal protection clause, not the due process clause; and the former,  *Soundly*
unlike the latter, is an attack on widespread social convictions, not an endorsement of them. Of course widely held moral convictions are usually a
legitimate basis for law. But such convictions are not *always* legitimate; consider the bans on miscegenation or discrimination against the mentally retarded. The question is what underlies the moral conviction and whether it
can be defended in deliberative terms. This is an exceedingly complex issue,
one that judges, in search of incompletely theorized agreements, ought to try
to bracket if they can. It seems reasonable to start by suggesting that when
moral disapproval is a legitimate ground for law in a heterogeneous society,
it is usually because the behavior being regulated is a source of what diverse
people could see as either harm to others (the easiest case) or harm to self
(less easy, but paternalism is not constitutionally banned). With this starting
point, it is difficult to see the constitutionally legitimate basis for the moral
disapproval here. At the very least, it is hard to see why the state should deny
members of same-sex relationships the same benefits and privileges that they
would have if only they were permitted to marry.

Despite these points, I believe that at the national level and in the short
term, the Supreme Court should be extremely reluctant to require states to
recognize same-sex marriages. It is far better for these developments to occur
at the state level, usually through legislatures but sometimes through courts,
as in the case of the Vermont Supreme Court concluding, in 1999, that gay
couples must be provided the same civic benefits as heterosexual couples.[11]
The Supreme Court of the United States should proceed more incrementally.
I will return to these questions shortly.


### Equality and Suspect Classes

It might be argued that discrimination on the basis of sexual orientation is
analogous to discrimination on the basis of race or sex and therefore should

be invalidated except in the rarest of circumstances. This is a highly plausible contention. Though the Supreme Court has not come close to endorsing the argument, it has attracted some favorable attention from lower courts. In *Jantz v. Muci*,[12] a district court held that discrimination on the basis of sexual orientation "is inherently suspect," and a panel of the Court of Appeals for the Ninth Circuit agreed, though its opinion was subsequently vacated.[13]

In chapter 7 we saw that the Supreme Court has granted "heightened scrutiny" to laws that discriminate against certain identifiable groups likely to be at particular risk in the ordinary political process. When the Court grants heightened scrutiny, it is highly skeptical of legislation, and the burden of every doubt therefore operates on behalf of groups challenging the relevant laws. Discrimination on the basis of sexual orientation is especially likely to reflect prejudice or "animus." When government disadvantages homosexuals, it will often do so because of an unreasoned or visceral belief in their sickness or inferiority or because of sheer ignorance of relevant facts. In this way, discrimination on the basis of sexual orientation is closely akin to discrimination on the basis of race and sex. In all of these settings, prejudice—understood as stereotypical thinking based on factual falsehoods and often rooted in simple hostility—is likely to account for discrimination.

It is clear too that homosexuals have been and continue to be subject to public and private discrimination. If homosexuals do not count in all respects as members of a lower caste, at least it is clear that in many domains, they have not been treated as first-class citizens. For most of American history, disclosure of homosexual orientation was grounds for inflicting serious social harms. Even today, homosexuals must often keep their orientation secret in order to be free from discrimination and even violence. In many sectors of the economy, homosexuals cannot easily obtain jobs if their sexual orientation is disclosed. Homosexuals may well be politically powerless in the constitutionally relevant sense. They often have difficulty in making alliances with other groups by virtue of the existence of widespread prejudice and hostility directed against them. Precisely because they are often anonymous (that is, not known to be homosexual) and diffuse (that is, not tightly organized), they face large barriers to exerting adequate political influence. The ability to conceal can actually make things worse from the standpoint of exercising political power. This problem, severe in itself, is heightened by the fact that people who challenge discrimination on the basis of sexual orientation are often "accused" of being homosexual themselves, which may have harmful consequences for their reputations.[14] The existence of widespread hostility against homosexuals can thus make it difficult for homosexuals and heterosexuals alike to speak out against this form of discrimination.

But there are some real complexities here. One problem with the issue of "political powerlessness" is that the key judgment—that a group does or does not have political power—is inevitably based not simply on facts about political influence but also on some controversial and usually unarticulated claims about how much political power is appropriate for the group in question—and about the legitimacy of the usual bases for legislative judgments on matters affecting the group. Do women have political power? In one sense they obviously do; but discrimination against them is nonetheless subject to special judicial scrutiny under the equal protection clause. It might be thought that homosexuals have a good deal of political power, for they can influence elections, even elections of the president. But the same is true not only for women but also for African Americans, who obviously influence elections a great deal. The potentially large electoral influence of both of these groups does not exclude them from the category of groups entitled to particular protection against discrimination.

The reason is that even if political influence can be wielded, prejudice in the constitutionally relevant sense is likely to operate in the political process against both blacks and women. The category of political powerlessness looks like an inquiry into some issues in political science, but it really depends on some judgments about the legitimacy of the usual grounds for government action. To say that homosexuals are politically powerless, it is necessary to say that the usual grounds for discrimination are impermissible. This is not a claim about political power alone. The usual grounds may indeed be impermissible; in fact I believe that they are. My point here is only that this claim cannot be separated from the claim of insufficient political power.

The Supreme Court has sometimes said that it disfavors discrimination based on "immutable" characteristics, but this is a confusing claim. In fact the emphasis on immutability has much obscured analysis. Homosexuality may or may not be immutable in the relevant sense; this is a sharply disputed issue as a simple matter of fact. Mutability, however, is not the decisive factor. In fact mutability is neither a necessary nor a sufficient condition for special judicial protection under the equal protection clause. For one thing, immutable characteristics are not an illegitimate basis for adverse governmental action. Blind people can be told not to drive, and deaf people can be deprived of the job of answering the telephone, and courts do not give special scrutiny to these forms of discrimination. Even if there were a biological predisposition toward certain criminal behavior, we could surely punish that behavior so as to deter and stigmatize it. If homosexual conduct can legitimately be punished, it ought not to matter if it can be shown that homosexual orientation is produced by biology or early childhood experiences.

These points show that an immutable characteristic is not a sufficient condition for special judicial protection. Government discriminates against immutable characteristics all the time, and most of the time there is no constitutional difficulty. Nor is an immutable characteristic a necessary condition for special judicial protection against discrimination. Suppose, for example, that skin color or gender could be changed through new technology. Would this change the constitutional analysis? It is clear that it would not. Discrimination on the basis of race would not become acceptable if scientists developed a serum through which blacks could become white.

The real question is whether legislation disadvantaging the relevant group is peculiarly likely to rest on illegitimate grounds; careful judicial scrutiny is a way of testing whether it does. On this count, discrimination against homosexuals is just as objectionable as discrimination against blacks and women is. In the vast bulk of cases, discrimination on the basis of sexual orientation is indeed rooted in "animus"—in unjustified stereotypes and even hatred. Courts should therefore require government to defend any such discrimination in exceedingly persuasive terms. It is also possible to build on existing law, with an argument that, while seemingly exotic, seems to me to capture much of what is at stake.

### Equality, Sex Discrimination, and Homosexuality

Is discrimination on the basis of sexual orientation a form of discrimination on the basis of sex? I believe that it is.

To approach this issue, consider Chief Justice Burger's striking concurrence in *Bowers*. There, the chief justice quoted, with approval, Blackstone's suggestion that sodomy is "an offense of 'deeper malignity than rape,' a heinous act, 'the very mention of which is a disgrace to human nature,' and 'a crime not fit to be named.' "[15] It is worthwhile to linger for a moment over the suggestion that consensual sexual relations among men are of "deeper malignity than rape." How could this possibly be so? Why did both Blackstone and the chief justice think it worthwhile to compare the two crimes, and to assert the comparatively greater malignity of consensual sodomy?

I think that the answer closely links the problem of discrimination on the basis of sex with that of discrimination on the basis of sexual orientation. Rape has often seemed far less violative of human nature than sodomy, and this says a good deal about the character of sex discrimination and sex differences. Let me turn more generally, then, to the equality principle of the Fourteenth Amendment.


## The Anticaste Principle Revisited

In chapter 7 we saw that at the origin, the central target of the Fourteenth Amendment was not irrational distinctions on the basis of race but the system of racial caste. Those who framed and ratified these amendments were aware that the system of racial hierarchy had often been attributed to nature. The Civil War amendments were based on a wholesale rejection of the supposed naturalness of racial hierarchy. The hierarchy was thought to be a function not of natural difference but of law, most notably the law of slavery and the various measures that grew up in the aftermath of abolition.

We should similarly understand the problem of sex discrimination, to the extent that it is troublesome, as amounting to the creation of something like a system of caste, based on gender and often operating through law. That system, like the racial caste system and others as well, is often attributed to "nature" and "natural differences." Consider here John Stuart Mill's remarks: "But was there any domination which did not appear natural to those who have it? . . . So true is it that unnatural generally means only uncustomary, and that everything which is usual appears natural. The subjection of women to men being a universal custom, any departure from it quite naturally appears unnatural."[16] Building on the racial analogue, the appropriate equality principle in the area of sex equality is an opposition to caste. The controlling principle to be vindicated through law is not that women must be treated "the same" as men but that women must not be second-class citizens.

It is often said that women and men are different and that the differences help both to explain and to justify existing social and legal inequality. It is often claimed, for example, that women are different from men and that different treatment in law is therefore perfectly appropriate. Indeed, in many legal systems, including that in America, the basic social and legal question is: Are women different from men? If not, have they been treated similarly? However widespread, this approach will not do. The question for decision is not whether there is a difference—often there certainly is—but whether the legal and social treatment of that difference can be adequately justified. When differences do produce inequality, it is a result of legal and social practices, not the result of differences alone. Since they are legal and social, these practices might be altered even if the differences remain. In any case, inequality is not justified by the brute fact of difference.

We can go further. Differences between men and women—especially those involving sexuality and reproduction—are often said to explain sex inequality, indeed to be the origin of inequality. But it might be better to think that at least some such differences are an outcome of inequality or its product. Certainly some and perhaps many of the relevant "real differences" between men and women exist only because of sex inequality. Differences in physical strength, for example, would certainly exist without inequality, but such differences as there now are undoubtedly have a good deal to do with differences in expectations, nutrition, and training. These differences cannot solely be attributed to women's sexual and reproductive capacities. Indeed, the degree of difference between men and women is notoriously variable across time and space. These variations are sufficient to show that what society attributes to nature is often a social product.

Even differences in desires, preferences, aspirations, and values are in significant part a function of society and even law—in particular of what these institutions do with sexuality and reproduction. Preferences are often adaptive to the status quo, and a status quo containing caste-like features based on sex will predictably affect the preferences of men and women in different ways. It will lead to distinctive processes of preference formation, inclining men and women in different directions in both the public and private spheres.

## On Sex Difference and Sexual Orientation

I turn now to the relationship between sex discrimination and discrimination on the basis of sexual orientation. The ban on same-sex marriages is not now thought to raise a problem of sex inequality under the United States Constitution. But might the legal ban (and the social taboo) not be a product of a desire to maintain a system of gender hierarchy, a system that same-sex marriages tends to undermine by complicating traditional and still influential ideas about the "natural difference" between men and women?

As Andrew Koppelman has urged in an important essay, bans on same-sex marriage have very much the same connection to gender caste as bans on racial intermarriage have to racial caste.[17] The best analogy here is *Loving v. Virginia*, in which the Court invalidated a ban on interracial marriage. I am speaking here of the real-world motivations for these bans, and I am assuming, as does current law, that impermissible motivations are fatal to legislation. To say this is not to say that the ban on same-sex marriages is necessarily unacceptable in all theoretically possible worlds. But here, the ban is like a literacy test motivated by a discriminatory purpose or a veteran's preference law designed to exclude women from employment. In making this argument here, I owe a great debt throughout to Koppelman's argument, though I add some concerns here about inequality and caste.

### Love and Marriage

In 1958, Richard Loving, a white man, and Mildred Jeter, a black woman, were married in the District of Columbia. Soon thereafter, they returned to their home in Virginia and were promptly indicted. Their crime was to have married in violation of Virginia's prohibition on interracial marriage. They pleaded guilty to the charge and were sentenced to a year in jail. The trial judge suspended the sentence on the condition that the Lovings leave Virginia and not return for twenty-five years. The judge said: "Almighty God creates the races white, black, yellow, malay and red, and he placed them on separate continents. And but for the interference with his arrangement there would be no cause for such marriages. The fact that he separated the races shows that he did not intend for the races to mix."[18] The Lovings challenged the antimiscegenation law on constitutional grounds, claiming that the law deprived them of the "equal protection of the laws." Thus was born the most aptly titled case in the entire history of American law, *Loving v Virginia*.

The legal issues before the United States Supreme Court in *Loving* were relatively straightforward. In 1954, the Court had decided *Brown v. Board of Education*.[19] There, the Court emphasized that racial discrimination is constitutionally unacceptable and that "separate but equal" is not equal.[20] The *Brown* Court held that under the Constitution, the government could not discriminate against blacks. This was the issue in *Loving:* Was the ban on racial intermarriage a form of discrimination in the relevant sense? On this question, there was sharp dispute. Virginia thought that the answer was "Clearly not."

Virginia's lawyers argued that antimiscegenation laws punished whites and blacks equally. They claimed that there was no discrimination against blacks. The only relevant discrimination was against people who sought to participate in mixed marriages, and such people were racially diverse. Unlike in *Brown*, where racial separation marked racial inequality, here separation was truly equal. Discrimination against people who seek to participate in mixed marriages is not "racial discrimination" at all. It does not draw a line between blacks and whites. It is a form of discrimination to be sure—but not the form that justifies special judicial skepticism under the Constitution. Because blacks and whites were treated exactly alike, that kind of skepticism was unwarranted.

From the standpoint of the 1990s, the argument may seem odd, even otherworldly. But if we linger over it, we will see that its logic is straightforward and even plausible. It is true that in an important way, laws forbidding interracial marriages treat blacks and whites alike. How did the Supreme Court respond? The key sentence in *Loving* says that "the racial classifications [at issue] must stand on their own justification, as measures designed to maintain White Supremacy."[21] This striking reference to white supremacy—by a unanimous Court, capitalizing both words and speaking in these terms for the only time in the nation's history—was designed to get at the core of Virginia's argument that discrimination on the basis of participation in mixed marriages was not discrimination on the basis of race.

The Supreme Court appeared to be making the following argument. Even though the ban on racial marriage treats blacks and whites alike—even though there is formal equality—the ban is transparently an effort to keep the races separate and, by so doing, to maintain the form and the conception of racial difference that are indispensable to white supremacy. Viewed in context—in light of its actual motivations and its actual effects—the ban was thus part of a system of racial caste. Virginia really objected to racial inter-mixing because it would confound racial boundaries, thus defeating what the district judge saw as "natural" differences produced by God's plan. In a world with miscegenation, natural differences between blacks and whites would become unintelligible; the very word "miscegenation" would lose its meaning.

Indeed, in a world with racial mixing, it would be unclear who was really black and who was really white. The categories themselves would be unsettled—revealed to be a matter of convention rather than nature. In such a world, white supremacy could not maintain itself. Because this was the assumption behind Virginia's law, the law stood revealed as an unacceptable violation of the equal protection principle.

Now let us imagine another case. Two women seek to marry. They are prevented from doing so by a law forbidding same-sex marriage. They argue that the relevant law violates their right to be free from sex discrimination. They might try to establish this argument by saying what seems clearly true, that if one of them were a man, there would be no barrier to the marriage. The law therefore seems to contain explicit discrimination on the basis of sex. It treats one person differently from another simply because of gender. It is therefore a form of sex discrimination.

Laws forbidding same-sex relations do involve an explicit gender classification. Under current law, however, it is not clear how successful the argument would be. The prohibition on same-sex marriage, it is sometimes said, discriminates on the basis of sexual orientation rather than on the basis of sex. There is no sex discrimination because women and men are treated exactly the same. If a man wants to marry a man, he is barred; a woman seeking to marry a woman is barred in precisely the same way. For this reason, women and men are not treated differently. From this we see that the complaint in our hypothetical case is really about discrimination on the basis of sexual orientation, not about discrimination on the basis of sex.

This indeed seems to be the answer offered by current constitutional law. Thus concluded the Supreme Court of Missouri as against an argument of this kind. According to the court:

> The State concedes that the statute prohibits men from doing what
> women may do, namely, engage in sexual activity with men. However, the
> State argues that it likewise prohibits women from doing something
> which men can do: engage in sexual activity with women. We believe it
> applies equally to men and women because it prohibits both classes from
> engaging in sexual activity with members of their own sex. Thus, there is
> no denial of equal protection on that basis.[22]

As Koppelman has shown, it is readily apparent that this response is the same answer offered by the State of Virginia in the *Loving* case—an answer that was rejected on the ground that the ban on racial intermarriage was connected with the unacceptable institution of white supremacy. But for participants in the current legal system, it is much harder to say that bans on same-sex relations are connected to a similarly unacceptable social institution. Exactly how is the prohibition on same-sex marriage an effort to promote sex inequality or even male supremacy? How can one have anything to do with the other? Racial intermarriage was objectionable because of its effects on racial differences that were deemed natural and desirable but that were thought (by the 1960s) to have social consequences only because of social institutions that produced a caste-like system based on race. Surely, it might be suggested, the question of same-sex relations raises no analogous issues.

I believe that it is puzzlement about such matters that accounts for the failure to see that *Loving* is a relevant or even decisive precedent for the view that the prohibition on same-sex relations is impermissible sex discrimination. In the end, however, *Loving* is the crucial precedent for protecting same-sex marriages or unions. Very briefly: A ban on racial intermarriage is part of an effort to insist that with respect to race there are just "two kinds." The separation of humanity into two rigidly defined kinds, white and black, is part of what white supremacy means. Even though some people have darker skin color than others and even though genes do diverge, this separation is, in important respects, a social artifact. People's genetic composition is very complex; most so-called blacks have many white ancestors; the division of humanity into "blacks" and "whites" is hardly determined by genetics. To say that there are just "two kinds" of people, black and white, is not a simple report on the facts; it is instead the construction of a distinctive and unnecessary way of thinking about human beings. That distinctive way of thinking about human beings, to the extent that it is converted into action based on law, raises serious problems under the equal protection clause.

It is tempting to think that the same cannot be said for the separation of humanity into two other kinds, women and men. Perhaps that separation is genuinely ordained by nature; perhaps it is not a social artifact at all, at least not in the same way. Certainly there are women and men, and certainly this fact, at least, is determined by genetics. Who would deny that the distinction between men and women is fundamental in this sense?

But this argument goes by too quickly. It is indeed true that some people are black, in the sense that they have African American ancestors, and others are white, in the sense that they do not. Very plausibly, this is no less true, or less "factual," than the division of humanity into men and women. The question is what society does with these facts. It is reasonable to think that the prohibition on same-sex marriages, as part of the social and legal insistence on "two kinds," is as deeply connected with male supremacy as the prohibition on racial intermarriage is connected with white supremacy. Same-sex marriages are banned partly because of what they do to—because of how they unsettle—gender categories. Same-sex marriages are banned partly because they complicate traditional gender thinking, showing that the division of human beings into two simple kinds is part of sex-role stereotyping, however true it is that women and men are "different."

As Koppelman has demonstrated, this is not merely a philosophical or sociological observation. It is highly relevant to the legal argument. It suggests that, like the ban on racial intermarriage, the ban on same-sex marriages may well be doomed by a constitutionally illegitimate purpose. The ban has everything to do with constitutionally unacceptable stereotypes about the appropriate roles of men and women. Moreover, the ban may well have constitutionally unacceptable effects. It is part of a system of sex-role stereotyping that is damaging to men and women, heterosexual and homosexual alike, though in quite different ways. Indeed, one of the most interesting issues has to do with the distinctive ways in which the ban differentially harms heterosexual men, gay men, heterosexual women, and lesbians.

Certainly this thesis is not belied by the fact that some "macho" cultures do not stigmatize male homosexuality as much as (say) the United States. Even in such cultures, a sharp distinction is drawn between passivity and activity in sexual relations, and cultural understandings of passive and active operate in gendered terms. The passive role is both stigmatized and identified with femininity, whereas the active role is socially respectable and identified with masculinity. In such cultures, sex-role distinctions have somewhat different manifestations, but sex discrimination is fully operative in thinking both about men and women and about sexuality.

There are important distinctions here between the reasons that underlie the stigmatization of, or the prohibition on, male homosexual relations on the one hand and those that account for bans on female homosexual relations on the other. The evidence suggests that the social opprobrium against male homosexuality comes largely from the perceived unnaturalness of male passivity in sex. The male heterosexual opposition to male homosexuality stems largely from the desire to stigmatize male sexual passivity. We might speculate that subjection to sexual aggression of this kind is especially troublesome because, in a way, it turns men into women, and in this way complicates ordinary views about the sex difference. Thus, it is a familiar part of violent male encounters that the victim will be feminized, as in the boxer Mike Tyson's remark to challenger Donovan "Razor" Ruddock quoted in the epigraph: "I'm going to make you my girlfriend." I suggest that far from being an oddity, this comment says something deeply revealing about the relationship between same-sex relations and the system of caste based on gender.

The ban on lesbian relations appears to stem from quite different concerns.[23] Part of the purpose of such bans may be to ensure that women are sexually available to men;[24] lesbianism has been problematic partly for this reason. Another part of the concern may be the fact that lesbianism also complicates gender difference by creating a sexually active role for women,[25] one that also undermines existing conceptions of natural difference. It is for this reason familiar to see that socially active women are stigmatized as lesbians. Indeed, a charge of lesbianism is a standard delegitimating device operating against women who have assumed stereotypically male social roles. There is thus a close connection between sex inequality and the prohibition on lesbianism.

Considerations of this sort help to maintain the legal and social taboo on homosexuality, in a way that might well be damaging to both men and women, heterosexual and homosexual alike, though of course in very different ways and to quite different degrees. The distinction between the rigid categories "male" and "female," with the accompanying social and sexual traits "active" and "passive," has especially conspicuous harmful effects for gay men and lesbians. But for all of us, the categories and the traits are much too crude to account for social and sexual life when both of these are going well. For heterosexual women as well, the distinction can be highly damaging because it is rigidly confining and untrue to the complexity of their experience, even when their sexual attraction is directed to men. The damage is closely connected to the caste-like features of the current system of gender relations. For heterosexual men, very much the same is true, since a degree of passivity in society and in sexual relations is both an inevitable and a desirable part of life and since it is such an unnecessary burden to be embarrassed by or ashamed of this.

Whether or not judges should accept an argument of this kind today, it should ultimately be concluded, outside if not inside the courtroom, that the prohibition on same-sex relations is a form of discrimination on the basis of sex, just as the prohibition on miscegenation was a form of discrimination on the basis of race. Both prohibitions are invalid under the equal protection clause.

## Prudence and Constitutionalism:
## The Example of Abraham Lincoln

Abraham Lincoln always insisted that slavery was wrong. On the basic principle, Lincoln allowed no compromises. No justification was available for chattel slavery. But on the question of means, Lincoln was quite equivocal—flexible, strategic, open to compromise, aware of doubt. The fact that slavery was wrong did not mean that it had to be eliminated immediately or that blacks and whites had to be placed immediately on a plane of equality. In Lincoln's view, the feeling of "the great mass of white people" would not permit this result.[26] In his most striking formulation, he declared: "Whether this feeling accords with justice and sound judgment, is not the sole question, if indeed, it is any part of it. A universal feeling, whether well or ill-founded, can not be safely disregarded."[27]

In Lincoln's view, efforts to create immediate social change in this especially sensitive area could have unintended consequences or backfire, even if those efforts were founded on entirely sound principle. It was necessary first to educate people about the reasons for the change. Passions had to be cooled. Important interests had to be accommodated or persuaded to join the cause. Issues of timing were crucial. Critics had to be heard and respected. For Lincoln, rigidity about the principle would be combined with caution about introducing the means by which the just outcome would be achieved. For this reason, it is a mistake to see Lincoln's caution about abolition as indicating uncertainty about the underlying principle. But it is equally mistaken to think that Lincoln's certainty about the principle entailed immediate implementation of racial equality.

As Alexander Bickel has emphasized, the point is highly relevant to constitutional law, especially in the area of social reform.[28] As it operates in the courts, constitutional law is a peculiar mixture of substantive theory and institutional constraint. The best substantive thinking might call, for example, for a vigorous and immediately vindicated anticaste principle, combating race and sex inequality far more aggressively than has the Supreme Court. But because of institutional constraints, courts might be reluctant to vindicate that right or to enforce that principle. Constitutional rights might therefore be systematically underenforced by the judiciary.[29] The reasons have to do with the courts' limited fact-finding capacity, their weak democratic pedigree, their limited legitimacy, and their probable futility as frequent instigators of social reform. There is therefore some space or gap between what courts are (properly) willing to require and what the Constitution is (properly) interpreted to mean.

In the area of welfare rights, the point seems readily visible. Let us suppose (to be sure, very controversially) that the Constitution should be interpreted to create such rights in the form of minimum guarantees of subsistence, on the theory that the equal protection of the laws so requires. Judicial enforcement of welfare rights might call for a difficult managerial role. Courts would have to oversee complex institutions in order to ensure vindication of the relevant rights. Because of the distinctive nature of the welfare problem, the creation of subsistence rights might have adverse effects on other programs with equally compelling claims to public monies. To say the least, courts are not well positioned to see those adverse effects. The managerial role is one for which they are ill suited. This point applies in many areas of social reform.

In the area of sex discrimination, such managerial issues are rarely present. If the ban on same-sex marriage is challenged on equal protection grounds, continuing judicial supervision of complex institutions is not really an issue. Nonetheless, there is reason for great caution on the part of the courts. An immediate judicial vindication of the principle could well jeopardize important interests. It could galvanize opposition. It could weaken the antidiscrimination movement itself. It could provoke more hostility and even violence against gays and lesbians. It could jeopardize the authority of the judiciary. It could well produce calls for a constitutional amendment to overturn the Supreme Court's decision. At a minimum, courts should generally use their discretion over their dockets in order to limit the nature and the timing of relevant intrusions into the political process. Courts should also be reluctant to vindicate even good principles when the vindication would clearly compromise other important interests, including ultimately the principles themselves.

In the area of homosexuality, we might make some distinctions. Certain imaginable rulings would minimally stretch judicial capacities and authority; other imaginable rulings would pose problems of judicial prudence in their most severe form. For example, the argument I have explored here—for the proposition that same-sex relations and even same-sex marriages may not be banned consistently with the equal protection clause—is, to say the least, quite adventurous. If the Supreme Court of the United States accepted the argument in the near future, it might cause a constitutional crisis, a weakening of the legitimacy of the Court, an intensifying of homophobia, a constitutional amendment overturning the Court's decision, and much more. Any Court, even one committed to the basic principle, should hesitate in the face of such prospects. It would be far better for the Court to start cautiously and to proceed incrementally.

The Supreme Court might, for example, accept the most narrow arguments, and reject or (better) avoid resolving the more general and intrusive ones. The Supreme Court might emphasize—as it seems to have done in *Romer v. Evans*—that government cannot discriminate against people of homosexual orientation without showing that those people have engaged in acts that harm a legitimate government interest. Courts could recognize that discrimination on the basis of orientation alone has the basic characteristics of a "status offense" disfavored in United States law.[30] Narrow rulings of this sort would allow room for public discussion and debate before obtaining a centralized national ruling that preempts ordinary political process over a moral issue about which society is in a state of evolution.

We can go further. Constitutional law is not only for the courts; it is for all public officials. The original understanding was that deliberation about the Constitution's meaning would be part of the function of the president and legislators as well. There was not supposed to be a judicial monopoly on that process. The post–Warren Court identification of the Constitution *then sorta not.*

*Same people who impeach Clinton but not Reagan*

with the decisions of the Supreme Court has badly disserved the traditional American commitment to deliberative democracy. In that system, all officials, not only the judges, have a duty of fidelity to the founding document. And in that system, elected officials will have a degree of interpretive independence from the judiciary. They will sometimes fill the institutional gap created by the courts' lack of fact-finding ability and policy-making competence. For this reason, they may conclude that practices are unconstitutional even if the Court would uphold them or that practices are valid even if the Court would invalidate them. Lincoln is an important example here as well. Often he invoked constitutional principles to challenge chattel slavery, even though the Supreme Court had rejected that reading of the Constitution.

Whatever the Supreme Court may say or do, it is therefore crucial for elected officials and even ordinary citizens to contend that discrimination on the basis of sexual orientation is incompatible with constitutional ideals. For example, the president has far more room to reach such conclusions than does the Court. But even a president determined to end such discrimination would not fare well if he insisted on immediate vindication of the principle. Instead, the president should be pragmatic and strategic. Following Lincoln's example, a president might insist, in all contexts, that this form of discrimination is wrong because it violates the most basic ideals of the Constitution. Indeed, it is both right and good for the president to show the connection between discrimination on the basis of sexual orientation and other forms of discrimination, most notably discrimination on the basis of sex.

In implementing the relevant principles, however, there is room for caution and care. Like the Supreme Court, the president and other officials can be selective about putting relevant issues on the agenda. Public officials might use especially egregious cases—involving, for example, discharge of qualified soldiers from the military or discrimination against people with AIDS to give weight to the principle in contexts in which it seems most acceptable. They can start slowly with the easiest areas. One of their major goals should be education. A relatively radical attack on the prohibition of same-sex marriages might come many years down the road, when the basic principle has been vindicated in many other less controversial contexts. But even if the principle is held firmly in view, and even if it is seen as part of a constitutional mandate, its vindication in American law and life need not be immediate—largely because an immediate insistence on principle would compromise so many other social goals, including those that underlie the principle itself.

Before long, I believe, discrimination on the basis of sexual orientation will be seen as difficult to defend in deliberative terms, as contributing to the maintenance of a system with caste-like features, as a product of unthinking prejudice and hostility, much like discrimination on the basis of race and gender. This appears to be an emerging view all around the world.[31] Courts should play a part in this process, requiring tangible justifications for the infliction of social harm, fortifying the process of democratic deliberation, and requiring genuine reason-giving in all cases of discrimination. But the judicial role is secondary. If discrimination against homosexuals is eventually to be seen—as I think that it should—to be inconsistent with constitutional principles, it will be the result of an extended process of deliberation among heterogeneous citizens, in which courts play a catalytic role.

# Sex Equality versus Religion

What is the relationship between religious liberty and the anticaste principle? Consider the following potential conflicts between sex equality and freedom of religion, conflicts that arise in one or another form in many nations:

1. Certain Jewish synagogues educate boys separately from girls, and certain Jewish schools refuse to admit girls. Some Jewish girls and their parents contend that this is a form of sex discrimination that contributes to sex-role stereotyping, in a way that produces second-class citizenship for women. They object in particular to the fact that such stereotyping is taken for granted in much of their community.

2. A Catholic university refuses to tenure several women teachers in its canon law department. A disappointed faculty member complains that this is a form of employment discrimination.[1] The university responds that courts cannot intervene in a religious matter of this kind.

3. A young man trains and studies for ordination to the priesthood of the Society of Jesus. He is repeatedly subjected to sexual harassment by two ordained priests. The harassment takes the form of unwanted sexual comments, propositions, and pornographic mailings. He brings suit for employment discrimination.[2] The defendants contend that courts cannot interfere with internal religious affairs.

4. Mormon employers engage in various practices of sex discrimination in employment. They refuse to hire women for certain jobs; they claim that being male is a good faith occupational qualification for certain positions. These practices are undertaken in the private sector, in institutions that both have and do not have explicitly religious functions.

5. A Western nation allows immigrant men to bring multiple wives into the nation. It recognizes their polygamous marriages and various discriminatory practices (including "assigning" teenage girls to older men for marriage) that accompany certain religious convictions.

Conflicts between sex equality and religious institutions create severe tensions in a constitutional democracy. Such conflicts raise the obvious question: Is government permitted to control discriminatory behavior by or within religious institutions?[3]

The question assumes particular dimensions in light of some of the topics discussed here. Religious institutions sometimes consist of like-minded people—or if they are not entirely like-minded, their members tend to agree on certain key questions, and the answers to those questions are rarely contested. By their very nature, religious institutions often operate as deliberating enclaves, with the large virtues and vices of such organizations. Group polarization is extremely likely here. Of course a constitutional democracy protects religious institutions, as a central way of protecting liberty and also as a principal part of the general protection of deliberating enclaves. But if sex discrimination is troublesome because it offends the anticaste principle, then discrimination by religious institutions might be particularly troublesome, especially because such institutions sometimes inculcate the values and norms that create a caste system in the first instance. What are the limits of protection for religious institutions, especially when equality, and even the anticaste principle, are at stake?

In addressing this question, I focus on an insufficiently explored puzzle. In the United States and in many other nations, it is generally agreed that most ordinary law, both civil and criminal, is legitimately applied to religious organizations. Thus, for example, a constitutional democracy may prohibit members of a religious institution from engaging in murder, kidnapping, or assault, even if those acts are part of religious ceremony and guided by religious precepts. At the same time, it is generally agreed that there are important limits on the extent to which the law of sex discrimination is legitimately applied to religious organizations. The state does not, for example, require the Catholic Church to ordain women as priests, and religious institutions are plainly permitted to engage in acts that would be unacceptable discrimination if carried out by a secular entity.[4] Interference with religious autonomy is usually prohibited if sex discrimination is the ground for the interference.

An important commonplace of democratic theory and practice might therefore be deemed the *asymmetry thesis*. According to this thesis, it is unproblematic to apply ordinary civil and criminal law to religious institutions, but problematic to apply the law forbidding sex discrimination to those institutions. Thus it is acceptable to prevent priests from beating up women (or anyone else) as part of a religious ceremony, or to ban Orthodox Jews from assaulting Reform women rabbis, even if they are sincerely motivated by a religiously founded idea of male rabbinate. But it is often thought unacceptable to ban sex segregation in education or to prohibit religious groups from excluding women from certain domains.

What is the source of this asymmetry? Can it be defended?


## Puzzles and Conflicts

Freedom of religion has a privileged place in constitutional democracies, and in the United States, as elsewhere, the law forbidding sex discrimination contains important exemptions for religious institutions. The law itself permits "bona fide occupational qualifications" based on sex, and courts have said that the free exercise clause of the Constitution requires courts to refrain from adjudicating sex discrimination suits by ministers against the church or religious institution employing them—even though ministers could certainly complain of assault or rape.[5] This principle has been read quite broadly to apply to lay employees of institutions (including high schools and universities) whose primary duties consist of spreading the faith or supervising religious rituals.[6]

As I have suggested, the resulting doctrine is a puzzle in light of the fact that almost no one believes that in general such organizations should be exempted from most of the law forbidding civil and criminal wrongs. The puzzle is not only obvious but also important, for there is good reason to believe that some of the most pernicious forms of sex discrimination are a result of the practices of religious institutions, which can produce internalized norms of subordination. These internalized norms help produce a caste system founded on sex. Both boys and girls learn a great deal about proper roles from what religion teaches them. Of course many religious institutions are committed to sex equality, but this is hardly a universal commitment. In the extreme case, suppose that members of a religious community believe that men and women naturally occupy different social roles, with men as primarily breadwinners and women as primarily mothers. We have seen that if members of the community are speaking mostly with one another, the view is likely not merely to be perpetuated but to be fortified, very possibly ending up in an extreme version of what people originally thought. The fortification, through internal discussion, is closely associated with the creation of second-class citizenship for women and with the creation of a caste system based on gender.

For those who object to discriminatory views and practices, the remedy of "exit"—the right of women to leave a religious order—is crucial. But the right to leave will not be enough when young girls have been taught in such a way as to be unable to scrutinize the practices with which they have grown up. People's preferences and beliefs do not reflect freedom when they are an outgrowth of unjust background conditions; in such circumstances it is not even clear whether the relevant preferences are authentically "theirs."

There is a further problem. Seemingly isolated decisions of individual women may help establish and reproduce norms of inequality that are injurious to other women. Women interested in sex equality therefore face a collective action problem; rational acts by individual women can help sustain discriminatory norms.[7] To say the least, it is not obvious how a constitutional democracy should respond to this problem. But some measures prohibiting sex discrimination, including discrimination by religious institutions, might make things better.

### The Smith Principle: Generality and Administrability

To answer the underlying question, and to understand the asymmetry principle, it is necessary to step back a bit and offer some more general words about the relationship between constitutional law and religious institutions. In the United States, there is a sharp and continuing debate about whether a state may apply "facially neutral" laws to religious institutions.[8] A law is facially neutral if it does not specifically aim at religious practices or belief. A law banning the burning of animals or the use of peyote is facially neutral, whereas a law banning the Lord's Prayer, or the Ten Commandments, is facially discriminatory.

Under current law in the United States, any facially neutral law is presumed to be constitutionally acceptable.[9] This means that a law that requires everyone to pay taxes, or to close business on Sunday, or to refrain from using certain drugs is unobjectionable, even if such a law intrudes directly on the religious practices of certain groups. The presumed validity of all facially neutral laws might be deemed the "*Smith* principle," after the highly controversial Supreme Court decision that established it. Congress attempted to "overrule" *Smith* with the Religious Freedom Restoration Act, but the Court struck down the Act as beyond legislative power.[10]

The *Smith* principle seems to be undergirded by two distinct ideas. The first involves a claim about how liberty can be protected by the political safeguards that accompany democratic processes. On this view, a secular law that is neutral on its face is highly unlikely to interfere with religious liberty, properly conceived. The reason is that the democratic process is likely to be a sufficient safeguard against laws that are facially neutral but genuinely oppressive. The very neutrality (hence generality) of such laws is a guarantee against oppressiveness: When a number of people and groups are subject to a law, they are likely to mobilize against that law and to prevent its enactment (unless there are very good reasons for it). When a law speaks in general terms, and thus applies to everyone, it is unlikely to be enacted if it is truly oppressive. But when particular groups are specifically targeted, the political process will not protect them. In suggesting that facially neutral laws will generally be valid, *Smith* is connected with a long-standing theme in constitutional democracies to the effect that generality is a check on unjustified interferences with liberty.

The second basis for the *Smith* principle involves judicial *administrability:* Even if some facially neutral laws raise serious problems for religious liberty in principle, it is very hard for courts to administer a test for constitutionality (or political legitimacy) that would require a kind of balancing of the opposing interests. Suppose that a particular law bans peyote use, or animal sacrifice or the payment of taxes, in a way that appears to infringe on some religious practices. How can courts possibly know how to strike the right balance? By virtue of its simplicity—upholding facially neutral laws—the *Smith* principle makes it unnecessary for courts to worry over these issues. Because courts have limited time and capacities, and because they are prone to error, the *Smith* principle might be acceptable simply because it makes the law much easier to apply.

The best defense of the *Smith* principle, and of current constitutional law in the United States, is that even if it protects religious liberty too little, It comes close to protecting religious liberty enough—and it does so with the only principle that real-world institutions can apply fairly and easily. This is not to say that *Smith* is obviously correct. There is a formidable challenge to American law on this point. Many facially neutral laws do impose substantial burdens on religion; some of these lack sufficiently strong justifications. Perhaps real-world institutions, including judicial institutions, are perfectly capable of drawing the appropriate lines.

## Constitutional Possibilities

With this background, I now turn to the reasons why a state might be permitted to apply the ordinary civil and criminal law to religious institutions but be proscribed from applying the law of sex discrimination to such institutions.

1. The first possibility is that a state should be allowed to interfere with religious practices only when it has an especially strong reason for doing so (sometimes described as a "compelling interest"). The ordinary criminal and civil law provides that reason; the law that forbids sex discrimination does not. On this view, it is one thing for a state to prohibit murder or assault; here the state's justification is obviously sufficient. It is quite another thing for a state to forbid discriminatory practices; here the state's justification is far weaker.

There can be no doubt that an intuition of this kind helps explain current practice. Indeed, I believe that it plays a large role in establishing the conventional wisdom and the asymmetry thesis itself. And the idea would have some force if the ordinary criminal and civil law always directed itself against extremely serious harms. But it does not. The ordinary law prohibits torts that are often relatively trivial (intentional infliction of emotional distress, little libels, minor assaults even without physical contact). And the state is not forbidden from applying the tort law when the underlying torts fall in this category. Under the *Smith* principle, there is no weighing of the state's interest to assess its magnitude. Thus, for example, state law that prohibits the intentional infliction of emotional distress is entirely applicable to religious institutions. Like everyone else, priests and rabbis are not permitted to tell people falsely that their children have just been run over by trucks, even if those people are religious enemies.

In short, religious organizations are fully subject to civil and criminal law even if the state has no large interest at stake. And it is not easy to explain why the interest in being free from sex discrimination is, in principle, so modest as to be weaker than the interests that underlie various aspects of the ordinary civil and criminal law. Often the interest in eliminating sex discrimination is far stronger than the particular interest involved in ordinary law. In fact general prohibitions on sex discrimination are also neutral on their face. If they apply to every institution, including religious institutions, they should be acceptable under *Smith*. But in United States constitutional law, it continues to be assumed that there is a special problem with applying the ban on sex discrimination to religious institutions.

Now perhaps it will be responded that the *Smith* principle is wrong and that religious institutions should not be subject to ordinary civil and criminal law when the state lacks an especially strong reason for invoking that ordinary law. This idea lay behind the 1996 Religious Freedom Restoration Act, which was designed to require the state to offer a "compelling" justification for any intrusion on religious practices. As I have noted, that Act was invalidated by the Supreme Court in 1997 as beyond Congress's power, but it does exemplify a widely shared view about the nature of religious liberty. For my purposes what is important is that even if we reject the *Smith* principle, and require "compelling" justification for any interference with religious practices, we will not approve of the asymmetry between the law banning sex discrimination and ordinary law. If the *Smith* principle is wrong, some ordinary law cannot legitimately be applied to religious institutions; whether the law of sex discrimination can be so applied depends on the nature of the relevant "balancing," an issue to which I will shortly turn.

2. It might be argued that the real issue involves freedom of association—the right of group members to associate with whomever they choose. In the highly publicized *Boy Scouts* case,[11] a closely divided Supreme Court ruled that the Boy Scouts have a constitutional right not to be subject to laws forbidding discrimination on the basis of sexual orientation. The Court said that the Boy Scouts have political goals and that these would be compromised by laws that prohibited the Scouts from discriminating. If the Boy Scouts have an associational right that would exempt them from the antidiscrimination laws, it might be asked, surely the same is true of religious organizations?

There is much to be said on behalf of the general principle invoked in the *Boy Scouts* case. Under a democratic constitution, people do have freedom to associate, and this right carries with it a general right of exclusion—a right to create deliberating enclaves of like-minded people. If, for example, the state forced a small group of deliberating people to admit people who fundamentally disagreed with them, the Constitution would be violated. If the state required a religious group to employ people who did not share the group's religious conviction, there would be a clear constitutional problem. Almost certainly a small group of religious people could not be forced to admit women if this was inconsistent with the group's religious convictions. Perhaps it can be generalized, from this example, that the state lacks power to force a religious organization not to discriminate, against women or anyone else.

But this rationale is not really an argument for the asymmetry thesis. It is no more than a restatement of the thesis. The underlying question is whether religious groups have an associational right that would permit them to discriminate, if they are not permitted to violate the ordinary civil and criminal law. A reference to associational liberty cannot resolve that puzzle. To be sure, the ordinary civil and criminal law do not ordinarily interfere with associational liberty. But the question is why the associational interest, when it exists in even diluted forms, should "trump" the state's countervailing interest in promoting sex equality. That question remains unanswered.

3. It might be thought that a prohibition on sex discrimination would impose a substantial burden on religious beliefs and practices, or even strike at their heart, whereas the ordinary civil and criminal law does not. In fact I believe that an idea of this sort lies behind the freedom of association argument just made. The concern is that a general law that forbids religious groups from discriminating imposes a large burden on those groups, a burden that cannot be adequately justified. If the *Boy Scouts* case is to be extended to the religious setting, it is because religious groups would be substantially burdened by any restriction on their associational liberty and because the government is unable to justify the imposition of that burden.

On this view, the *Smith* principle is wrong; some exemptions from facially neutral laws are necessary.[12] But the reason for any religious exemptions is respect for religious autonomy—respect that can coexist with ordinary civil and criminal law but not with the law forbidding sex discrimination. For some religious institutions, a secular mandate of sex equality would be intolerable, whereas application of ordinary law fits comfortably, in general, with their own beliefs and practices. The asymmetry thesis might be defended on this ground.

The argument is not implausible. Sometimes ordinary civil or criminal law is entirely consistent with the norms of religious institutions; indeed, such law often grows directly or indirectly out of religious norms. And it is also possible to imagine requirements of sex equality that would strike at the heart of religious convictions. But as a defense of the asymmetry thesis, the argument is quite weak. Some aspects of ordinary civil and criminal law do indeed strike against practices and beliefs that are central to some religions. Consider, for example, the laws forbidding animal sacrifice or the use of drugs or even laws forbidding certain kinds of assault and imprisonment. And some aspects of the law of sex discrimination interfere not at all with some religious beliefs and practices.

Now it is possible that as a class, ordinary civil laws coexist easily with most religious practices and beliefs, whereas the law of sex discrimination does not. But to the extent that this is so, it is a contingent, time-bound, highly empirical fact, one that bears little on the question of principle from the point of view of a democratic constitution. If, for example, it were thought that the state could interfere with religious practices only when the interference was not serious, we could not justify a sharp asymmetry between ordinary law and the law of sex discrimination. We would have to proceed in a more fine-grained way; we would not endorse the asymmetry thesis.

4. It might be possible to defend the asymmetry thesis with the suggestion that an appropriate test depends on both the strength and nature of the state's interest and on the extent of the adverse effect on religion. A weak interest (in preventing, let us suppose, merely technical libels) might be insufficient to justify any intrusion at all; an illegitimate interest (in, say, preventing the strengthening of a religion that is perceived hostile to the political status quo) would be ruled entirely off limits to government; an "overriding" interest (in, for example, preventing murder) would justify any intrusion no matter how severe; a strong or "compelling" interest would justify most intrusions. Most cases would therefore be easy. The hardest problems would arise where a strong or "compelling" interest, on the part of the state, were matched by a plausible claim, on the part of the religion, that the interference would seriously jeopardize the continuing functioning of the relevant religion.

In principle, I believe that it would be best for constitutional democracies to reject the *Smith* principle and to adopt a standard that looks at the strength and the legitimacy of the state's reason for interfering with religious practices. To be sure, to adopt such a standard, we would have to have a high degree of confidence in those who would administer it. Such a standard would require courts (or other institutions) to decide which aspects of the civil and criminal law were sufficiently justified. Thus we could imagine reasonable judgments in favor of a legal ban on killing and torturing animals but against a legal ban on peyote, on the ground that the former created a risk to third parties. The legitimacy of applying principles against sex discrimination to religious institutions would depend on an assessment of the strength of the interest in those principles and the extent of the interference with religious institutions.

Doubtless different outcomes would be imaginable in different contexts, and I do not mean to sort out all of the conceivable dilemmas. My basic point is that the asymmetry between most civil and criminal law and the law banning sex discrimination could not be sustained. Under the standard I am proposing, some ordinary law would not legitimately be applied to religious institutions, and some of the law banning sex discrimination could be so applied. The legal standard would force a candid assessment of the nature of the intrusion and the strength of the underlying interest, and not rest content with homilies (by no means followed with most civil and criminal law) about the legitimate autonomy of religious institutions.

*[handwritten margin note: As if such matters could even be decided objectively outside the contest]*

## Balancing and Blocks

I offer these conclusions:

1. Constitutional democracies protect religious liberty; this is one of their highest priorities. But they generally apply ordinary civil and criminal law to those institutions, at least if those forms of law are neutral on their face. Political safeguards tend to guard against oppressive law.

2. Deliberation within religious enclaves is likely to fortify the commitments of members and possibly push them in an extreme direction. A constitutional democrat should take no position against this effect as such. In fact a constitutional democrat will welcome the polarization effect insofar as it increases the level of social diversity. But to the extent that the commitments that are being fortified threaten the freedom and equality of citizens, there is reason for genuine concern. If within-group deliberation promotes second-class citizenship for some, or contributes to the maintainence of a system with caste-like features, there should be no constitutional obstacle to reasonable efforts to supply correctives. Hence measures that attempt to promote sex equality by prohibiting discrimination within religion institutions should not be ruled entirely off limits.

3. There is a plausible rationale for the view that a liberal social order should accept all laws that do not discriminate "on their face" against religious institutions and practices. This principle would authorize the application to those institutions of most civil and criminal law and and also of law forbidding sex discrimination. Though plausible, this principle is not in the end acceptable, because it would allow the state to subject religious institutions to laws that substantially burden those institutions, or even strike at their heart, without at the same time serving a sufficiently important governmental purpose.

4. It is not only plausible but also correct to say that a liberal social order should disallow facially neutral laws if they (1) interfere in a significant way with religious practices or impose a substantial burden on religious institutions and (2) are not supported by a legitimate and sufficiently strong justification. But this idea does not support a categorical distinction between ordinary civil and criminal law and laws forbidding sex discrimination. In many cases, the idea would allow religious institutions to immunize themselves from ordinary law but forbid them from immunizing themselves from the law prohibiting discrimination on the basis of sex.

5. There is no plausible rationale for the view, embodied in the practice of many liberal cultures, that it is unproblematic to apply ordinary civil and

criminal law to religious institutions but that it is problematic to apply to those institutions laws forbidding sex discrimination.

These conclusions mean that there is no *general* barrier to applying such laws to religious institutions. Whether it is legitimate to do so depends on the extent of the interference with religious convictions and the strength of the state's justification. Reasonable people can reach different conclusions about particular cases; but it would follow that in at least some of the cases traced in at the beginning of this chapter, the religious practice would have to yield. This is a domain in which many constitutional democracies have yet to live up to their promise. They immunize religious institutions from antidiscrimination law without making an adequate inquiry into the problems that can be caused, for freedom and equality alike, by religious practices that inculcate principles of inequality on the basis of sex.

# 10
## Social and Economic Rights?
## Lessons from South Africa

*Must turn to S.Af. because to practice "anti caste", gov't must be compelled to enforce economic rights, as in S. Africa. Case!*

I have argued that the anticaste principle captures an important part of a democratic constitution's commitment to equality; but I have also said that the principle does not exhaust the meaning of equality as a constitutional ideal. Should a democratic constitution also try to ensure that people will not live in desperate conditions? Should it create rights against starvation or homelessness?

The answers to these questions point toward what might well be the most striking difference between constitutional rights in the late eighteenth and early nineteenth centuries and constitutional rights in the current period. Before the twentieth century, democratic constitutions made no mention of rights to food, shelter, and health care. In more recent times, rights of this kind are usually protected in the most explicit terms. A remarkable feature of international opinion—indeed a near consensus—is that socioeconomic rights deserve constitutional protection. The principal exception to the consensus is the United States, where most people think that such rights do not belong in a constitution.

My aim in this chapter is to shed light on the underlying questions, largely by discussing an extraordinary decision by the Constitutional Court of South Africa,[1] one that carries some significant lessons for the future. In that decision, the Court set out a novel and exceedingly promising approach to judicial protection of socioeconomic rights. This approach requires close attention to the human interests at stake, and sensible priority-setting, but without mandating protection for each person whose socioeconomic needs are at risk. The virtue of the Court's approach is that it is respectful of democratic prerogatives and of the limited nature of public resources, while also requiring special deliberative attention to those whose minimal needs are not being met. The approach of the Constitutional Court stands as a powerful rejoinder to those who have contended that socioeconomic rights do not belong in a constitution. It suggests that such rights can serve not to preempt democratic deliberation but to ensure democratic attention to important interests that might otherwise be neglected in ordinary debate. It also illuminates the idea, emphasized by the Court itself, that all rights, including the most conventional and uncontroversial, impose costs that must be borne by taxpayers.

To be sure, it is far too early to say whether the Court's approach can accommodate the concerns of those who object to judicial protection of socioeconomic rights. But for the first time in the history of the world, a constitutional court has initiated a process that might well succeed in the endeavor of ensuring that protection without placing courts in an unacceptable managerial role. This point has large implications for how we think about citizenship, democracy, and minimal social and economic needs.

## A Debate and a Resolution

*In general.* For many years, there has been a debate about whether social and economic rights, sometimes known as socioeconomic rights, belong in a constitution. The debate has occurred with special intensity in both eastern Europe and South Africa. Of course the United States Constitution, and most constitutions before the twentieth century, protected rights of free speech, religious liberty, and sanctity of the home, without creating rights to minimally decent conditions of life. But in the late twentieth and early twenty-first centuries, the trend is otherwise, with international documents, and most constitutions, creating rights to food, shelter, and more.

Some skeptics have doubted whether such rights make sense from the standpoint of constitutional design. On one view, a constitution should protect "negative" rights, not "positive" rights. Constitutional rights should be seen as individual protections *against* the aggressive state, not as private entitlements *to* protection by the state. A constitution that protects socioeconomic rights might, on this view, jeopardize constitutional rights altogether, by weakening the central function against preventing the abusive or oppressive exercise of government power.

But there are many problems with this view. Even conventional individual rights, like the right to free speech and private property, require governmental action. Private property cannot exist without a governmental apparatus, ready and able to secure people's holdings as such. So-called negative rights are emphatically positive rights. In fact all rights, even the most conventional, have costs.[2] Rights of property and contract, as well as rights of free speech and religious liberty, need significant taxpayer support. In any case we might well think that the abusive or oppressive exercise of government power consists not only in locking people up against their will, or in stopping them from speaking, but also in producing a situation in which people's minimal needs are not met.

If the central concerns are citizenship and democracy, the line between negative rights and positive rights is hard to maintain. The right to constitutional protection of private property has a strong democratic justification: If people's holdings are subject to ongoing governmental adjustment, people cannot have the security and independence that the status of citizenship requires. The right to private property should not be seen as an effort to protect wealthy people; it helps ensure deliberative democracy itself. But the same things can be said for minimal protections against starvation, homelessness, and other extreme deprivation. For people to be able to act as citizens, and to be able to count themselves as such, they must have the kind of independence that such minimal protections ensure.

On the other hand, a democratic constitution does not protect every right and interest that should be protected in a decent or just society. Perhaps ordinary politics can be trusted; if so, there is no need for constitutional protection. The basic reason for constitutional guarantees is to respond to problems faced in ordinary political life (see chapter 4). If minimal socioeconomic rights will be protected democratically, why involve the Constitution? The best answer is that such rights are indeed at systematic risk, perhaps because those who would benefit from them lack political power. It is not clear if this is true in every nation. But certainly it is true in many places.

Perhaps more interestingly, critics of socioeconomic rights have made a point about political institutions. In particular, they have argued that socioeconomic rights are beyond judicial capacities.[3] On this view, courts lack the tools to enforce such guarantees. If they attempt to do so, they will find themselves in an impossible managerial position, one that might discredit the constitutional enterprise as a whole. How can courts possibly oversee budget-setting priorities? If a state provides too little help to those who seek housing, maybe it is because the state is concentrating on the provision of employment or on public health programs or on educating children. Is a court supposed to oversee the full range of government programs, to ensure that the state is placing emphasis on the right areas? How can a court possibly acquire the knowledge, or make the value judgments, that would enable it to do that? A judicial effort to protect socioeconomic rights might seem to compromise, or to preempt, democratic deliberation on crucial issues.

It would be possible to respond to these institutional concerns in various ways. Perhaps constitutions should not include socioeconomic rights at all. Perhaps such rights should be included but on the explicit understanding that the legislature, and not the courts, will be entrusted with enforcement. The Constitution of India expressly follows this route, attempting to encourage legislative attention to these rights without involving the judiciary. The advantage of this approach is that it ensures that courts will not be entangled with administration of social programs. The disadvantage is that without judicial enforcement, there is a risk that the constitutional guarantees will be mere "parchment barriers," meaningless or empty in the real world.

*The case of South Africa.*　The appropriate approach to socioeconomic rights was intensely debated before ratification of the South African Constitution.[4] The idea of including socioeconomic rights was greatly spurred by international law, above all by the International Covenant on Economic, Social and Cultural Rights, to which I will return. Much of the debate involved the appropriate role of the judiciary. In part this was a relatively abstract debate, posing a concrete real-world issue but founded on the set of theoretical considerations just sketched, involving judicial capacities and the proper place, if any, of socioeconomic rights in a democratic constitution. But aside from these points, the debate was greatly influenced by the particular legacy of apartheid and by claims about what to do about that legacy at the constitutional level. In the view of many of those involved in constitutional design, the apartheid system could not plausibly be separated from the problem of persistent social and economic deprivation. In the end the argument for socioeconomic rights was irresistible, in large part because such guarantees seemed an indispensable way of expressing a commitment to overcome the legacy of apartheid—the overriding goal of the new constitution.

Recall here that some constitutions are *preservative*; they seek to maintain existing practices. But other constitutions are *transformative*; they set out certain aspirations that are emphatically understood as a challenge to long-standing practices; they are defined in opposition to those practices. The South African constitution is the world's leading example of a transformative constitution. A great deal of the document is an effort to eliminate apartheid "root and branch." Constitutions are often described as precommitment strategies, designed to ensure against myopic or mistaken decisions in ordinary politics.[5] If is it apt to describe the South African Constitution in these terms, this is because the document is designed to ensure that future governments do not fall prey to anything like the evils of the apartheid era. The creation of socioeconomic rights is best understood in this light.


## A Continuing Debate

But what, in particular, is the relationship among socioeconomic rights, courts, and legislatures? The South African Constitution hardly speaks unambiguously on this topic. The rights in question typically take the following form, an evident acknowledgement of limited resources:

1. Everyone has the right to [the relevant good].
2. The state must take reasonable legislative and other measures, within its available resources, to achieve the progressive realisation of this right.

This is the basic form of constitutional rights to "an environment that is not harmful to their health or well-being" (section 24); housing (section 26); and health, food, water, and social security (section 27).

A provision of this kind does not clearly create or disable judicial enforcement. On the basis of the text alone, it would be easy to imagine a judicial ruling to the effect that enforcement is reserved to nonjudicial actors within "the state." On this view, the South African constitution is, with respect to judicial enforcement, closely akin to the Indian constitution. But it would also be easy to imagine a ruling to the effect that courts are required to police the relevant rights, by ensuring that the state has, in fact, taken "reasonable legislative and other measures, within its available resources, to achieve progressive realisation of this right." If, for example, the state has done little to provide people with decent food and health care, and if the state is financially able to do much more, it would seem that the state has violated the constitutional guarantee.

In certifying the Constitution, the South African Constitutional Court resolved this question in just this way, concluding that socioeconomic rights are indeed subject to judicial enforcement.[6] The Court said that such rights "are, at least to some extent, justiciable." The fact that resources would have to be expended on them was hardly decisive, for this was true of "many of the civil and political rights entrenched" in the Constitution. The Court correctly said that many rights, including so-called negative rights, "will give rise to similar budgetary implications without compromising their justiciability." But in a final sentence, the Court added new ambiguity by suggesting that at "the very minimum, socio-economic rights can be protected negatively from improper invasion." This last sentence added considerable ambiguity because it did not say whether and when courts could go beyond the "minimum" to protect rights "positively"; nor did it make entirely clear what it would mean to invade socioeconomic rights "negatively." Perhaps the Court's suggestion was that when the state, or someone else, actually deprived someone of (for example) shelter, say by evicting him from the only available source of housing, judicial enforcement would be appropriate. But if this is all that the Court meant, the socioeconomic rights would be hardly justiciable at all; this would be an exceedingly narrow use of judicial authority in overseeing the relevant rights.

The ultimate outcome of the debate over judicial protection of socioeconomic rights carries both particular and general interest. It is of particular interest in South Africa, where a substantial percentage of the population lives in desperate poverty. Does the Constitution do anything to help them? For example, might the judiciary play a role in ensuring that governmental priorities are set in the way that the Constitution apparently envisages? Or might judicial involvement in protecting socioeconomic rights actually impair reasonable legislature efforts to set sensible priorities? The outcome has general interest because it should tell us a great deal about the social and democratic consequences, both good and bad, of constitutional provisions creating socioeconomic rights. Thus far discussion of this issue has been both highly speculative and uninformed by actual practice.[7] The South African experience will inevitably provide a great deal of information.

The Constitutional Court has now rendered its first major decision involving these rights, in a case involving the right to shelter.[8] It is to that case that I now turn.

## The Background

### The Housing Shortage and the Apartheid Legacy

It is impossible to understand the South African dispute over the right to shelter, or the proceedings in the Constitutional Court, without reference to the effects of apartheid. The central point is that in the view of most observers, the system of apartheid is directly responsible for the acute housing shortage in many areas of the nation.

One of the central components of apartheid was a system of "influx control" that sharply limited African occupation of urban areas. In the Western Cape, the government attempted to exclude all African people and to give preference to the colored community. The result was to freeze the provision of housing for African people on the Cape Peninsula in 1962. None-theless, African people continued to move into the area in search of jobs. Lacking formal housing, large numbers of them moved into "informal set-tlements," consisting of shacks and the like, throughout the Peninsula. The inevitable result of the combination of large African movements into urban areas and inadequate provision of housing was to produce shortages, amount-ing to over one hundred thousand units by the mid-1990s. Since that time, governments at national and local levels have enacted a great deal of legis-lation to try to handle the problem. Nonetheless, many thousands of people lack decent housing. At the same time, the South African government has limited sources and a large variety of needs, stemming from the AIDS crisis, pervasive unemployment (about 40 percent), and persistent, pervasive pov-erty.

### Grootboom and Wallacedene

The *Grootboom* case was brought by nine hundred plaintiffs, of whom 510 were children. For a long period, the plaintiffs lived in an informal squatter settlement named Wallacedene. Most of the people there were desperately poor. All of them lived in shacks, without water, sewage, or refuse removal services. Only 5 percent of the shacks had electricity. The named plaintiff, Irene Grootboom, lived with her family and that of her sister in a shack of about twenty square meters.

Many of those at the Wallacedene settlement had applied for low-cost housing from the municipality. They were placed on the waiting list, where they remained for a number of years. In late 1998, they became frustrated by the intolerable conditions at Wallacedene. They moved out and put up shacks and shelters on vacant land that was privately owned and earmarked for formal low-cost housing. A few months later, the owner obtained an eject-ment order against them. But Grootboom and others refused to leave, con-tending that their former sites were now occupied and that there was nowhere else to go. Eventually they were forcibly evicted and their homes burned and bulldozed. Their possessions were destroyed. At this point they found shelter on a sports field in Wallacedene, under temporary structures consisting of plastic sheets. It was at this stage that they contended that their constitutional rights had been violated. It is worthwhile to pause over the nature of human existence for those at Wallacedene. For them, insecurity was a fact of daily life. It should not be controversial to say that the status of citizenship is badly compromised for people in such conditions.

# The Constitution

Two provisions were of central importance to the plaintiffs' claim. The first is section 26, which provides:

(1) Everyone has the right to have access to adequate housing.

(2) The State must take reasonable legislative and other measures, within its available resources, to achieve the progressive realisation of this right.

(3) No one may be evicted from their home, or have their home demolished, without an order of court made after considering all the relevant circumstances. No legislation may permit arbitrary evictions.

The second was section 28(1)(c), limited to children. That section reads:

Every child has the right . . . to family care or parental care, or to appropriate alternative care when removed from the family environment [and]. . . . to basic nutrition, shelter, basic health care services and social services.

At the outset several points should be made about these sections. First, section 26(3) imposes a duty on the private sector, not only on government. Under this section, it is unconstitutional for a private person to evict another private person, or to demolish a home, without judicial permission. From the constitutional point of view, this is a striking innovation, for constitutions do not typically impose obligations on private landlords. From the standpoint of economic policy, it also raises several interesting questions. Obviously the goal of section 26(3) is to ensure that poor people continue to have housing; but the creation of a kind of property right in continued occupancy is likely to have some unintended bad consequences. If it is difficult to evict people, landlords will have a decreased incentive to provide housing in the first instance. The result might be a diminished stock of private housing. Another result might be extensive private screening of prospective tenants, since landlords will be entirely aware that once a tenancy is allowed, it will be very difficult to terminate it. The extent of these effects is of course an empirical question.

For purposes of constitutional interpretation, the largest puzzle has to do with the relationship between sections 26 and 28. It would be possible to read section 28 as giving children unqualified rights to various goods—ensuring that children have those goods even if resources are scarce. On this view, the government has an absolute obligation to ensure that children eat, are housed, and have health care and social services. Under this interpretation, section 26 creates as qualified right for everyone ("progressive realisation") whereas section 28 requires an unqualified right for children in particular. Whether or not it is correct, this is a textually plausible reading.

The lower court proceeded in exactly this way, holding that section 28 creates a freestanding, absolute right, on the part of children, to the protections thus mentioned. On this interpretation, the rights are not qualified by "available resources" or by the "progressive realisation" clause. Perhaps children are given, by that clause, two sets of rights: first to the care of adults, preferably parents; second to state support of basic needs.

### Grootboom in the Constitutional Court

In *Grootboom*, the Constitutional Court rejected this interpretation of section 28. At the same time, it held that section 26 imposes a judicially enforceable duty on government; that "reasonableness" is required; and that the plaintiffs' constitutional rights had been violated, because of the absence of a program to provide "temporary relief" for those without shelter. In short, the Court held that the Constitution required not only a long-term plan to provide low-income shelter but also a system to ensure short-term help for people who had no place to live. I believe that this is the first time that the high court of any nation has issued a ruling to this effect. What is most striking about that ruling is the distinctive and novel approach to socioeconomic rights, requiring not shelter for everyone but sensible priority-setting, with particular attention to the plight of those who are neediest. I will say more by way of evaluation below; let us begin by tracing the Court's explanation of its decision.

### Section 26: Rights and Resources

*A note from international law.*    The movement for socioeconomic rights cannot be understood without reference to international law, which firmly recognizes such rights and which seems to put the weight of international opinion behind them. Hence the Court began by emphasizing the significant background provided by the International Covenant on Economic, Social, and Cultural Rights (a covenant signed but not yet ratified by South Africa).

Section 11.1 of the Covenant provides that the parties "recognize the right of everyone to an adequate standard of living for himself and his family, including adequate food, clothing and housing, and to the continuous improvement of living conditions." Hence the "parties will take appropriate steps to ensure the realization of this right." A more general provision of the Covenant, applicable to all relevant rights, makes a promise "to take steps

... to the maximum of its available resources, with a view to achieving progressively the full realisation of the rights recognized in the Covenant by all appropriate means, including particularly the adoption of legislative measures."[9]

But what does this mean? The United Nations Committee on Economic, Social, and Cultural Rights is entrusted with monitoring the performance of states under the Covenant. In its interpretive comments, the Committee urges that states face a "minimum core obligation," consisting of a duty to "ensure the satisfaction of, at the very least, minimum essential levels of each of the rights." The Constitutional Court referred to this idea with some interest, suggesting the possibility of "minimum core obligations" imposed by section 28. But in the Court's view, that idea had many problems, because judicial enforcement would require a great deal of information to be placed before the court, in order to "determine the minimum core in any given context." In this case, sufficient information was lacking, and in any event the Court thought that it would not be necessary to define the minimum core in order to assess Grootboom's complaint.

*Text and context.* The Court's more specific analysis of section 26 began with an emphasis on the fact that all people have a right not to shelter regardless of financial constraints but to legislative and other measures designed to achieve "the progressive realization of this right." At the same time, the state, and "all other entities and persons," are constitutionally required "to desist from preventing or impairing the right of access to adequate housing." By itself this idea is quite ambiguous; what counts as prevention or impairment?

The Court explained that to implement the right, the state faced two kinds of duties. With respect to "those who can afford to pay for adequate housing," the state's duty is to "unlock the system, providing access to housing stock and a legislative framework to facilitate self-built houses through planning laws and access to finance." What is most striking here is the Court's emphasis on the "unlocking" role of the Constitution. On one interpretation, at least, the state is under a duty to ban a system of monopoly in housing—to create markets sufficiently flexible to provide housing to those who can pay for it. It is not clear that this is all, or even most, of what the Court had in mind. The idea of "planning laws" and "access to finance" might be taken to mean something other than, or in addition to, a competitive housing market. But it is certainly worth noticing that the analysis of a duty for "those who can afford to pay" operates along its own separate track, requiring a kind of open housing market for those with the resources to participate.

For poor people, of course, the state's obligation is different. Here the constitutional duty might be discharged through "programmes to provide adequate social assistance to those who are otherwise unable to support themselves and their dependents." In this case, the central issue was whether the government had created "reasonable" measures to ensure progressive realization of the right. The Court concluded that it had not, notwithstanding the extensive public apparatus to facilitate access to housing. The reason for this conclusion was simple: "[T]here is no express provision to facilitate access to temporary relief for people who have no access to land, no roof over their heads, for people who are living in intolerable conditions and for people who are in crisis because of natural disasters such as floods or fires, or because their homes are under threat of demolition."

The Court acknowledged that it would be acceptable not to have a provision for those in desperate need "if the nationwide housing programme would result in affordable houses for most people within a reasonably short time." Note that "most people" does not mean all people; hence the clear implication is that a deprivation of housing, for some, would not necessarily be unreasonable or inconsistent with the constitutional plan. In this respect, the constitutional right involved the creation of a *system* of a certain kind rather than the creation of fully individual protections. But under the existing governmental program at the national level, it could not be said that "most people" would have "affordable houses" within a reasonably short time. Hence the nation's housing program is constitutionally unacceptable insofar as "it fails to recognize that the state must provide for relief for those in desperate need. . . . It is essential that a reasonable part of the national housing budget be devoted to this, but the precise allocation is for the national government to decide in the first instance."

The Court also acknowledged that the constitutional obligation might be adequately carried out at the local level and that the local government, Cape Metro, had put in place its own land program specifically to deal with desperate needs. But that program had not been implemented, in large part because of an absence of adequate budgetary support from the national government. "Recognition of such needs in the nationwide housing programme requires" the national government "to plan, budget and monitor the fulfilment of immediate needs and the management of crises. This shall ensure that a significant number of desperate people in need are afforded relief, though not all of them need receive it immediately."

In the Court's view, the Constitution did not create a right to "shelter or housing immediately upon demand." But it did create a right to a "coherent, co-ordinated programme designed to meet" constitutional obligations. The obligation of the state was therefore to create such a program, including reasonable measures specifically designed "to provide relief for people who have no access to land, no roof over their heads, and who are living in intolerable conditions or crisis situations." It is here that we can find a novel, distinctive, and promising approach to a democratic constitution's socioeconomic rights, an issue I take up in more detail below.

### Section 28: Special Rights for Children?

So much for Section 26. What of Section 28, which, it might be recalled, was understood by the lower court to create an absolute right to shelter for children? In brief, the Court refused to interpret article 28 in this way. Instead it understood section 28 to add little to the basic requirements of section 26. In the Court's view, section 28 creates no independent socioeconomic rights. This was an exceedingly narrow reading of section 28, evidently a product of pragmatic considerations. The Court's responsiveness to those pragmatic considerations is itself noteworthy, especially insofar as it suggests judicial reluctance to intrude excessively into priority-setting at the democratic level.

The Court's central holding was that with respect to children, the obligation to provide shelter and the like "is imposed primarily on parents and family, and only alternatively on the state." What this means is that when children are removed from their parents, the state must protect the specified rights by, for example, ensuring that children are housed and fed. But section 26 "does not create any primary state obligation to provide shelter on demand to parents and their children if children are being cared for by their parents or families."

To be sure, the state has some constitutional duty to children under the care of their parents and families. The state "must provide the legal and administrative infrastructure necessary to ensure" compliance with section 28, through, for example, "passing laws and creating enforcement mechanisms for the maintenance of children, their protection from maltreatment, abuse, neglect or degradation." The state is also obliged to comply with the various independent protections of socioeconomic rights. But section 28 created no freestanding obligation for the state to shelter children within the care of their parents. Since the children in *Grootboom* were being cared for by their parents, the state was not obliged to shelter them "in terms of section 28(1)."

At first glance, this is a puzzling reading of section 28, hardly foreordained by the text of the provision. Apparently the Court was led to that reading by what it saw as the "anomalous result" of giving those with children "a direct and enforceable right to housing" under that section, while depriving those "who have none or whose children are adult." This would be anomalous because it would allow parents to have special access to shelter if and because they had children. In any case a holding to this effect would make children into "stepping stones to housing for their parents." But would this really be so anomalous? It might seem to make sense to say that children should have a particular priority here—that their right should be more absolute—hence that adults with children would have a preferred position. Why would that view be especially peculiar?

The Court also expressed a stronger concern. If children were taken to have an absolute right to shelter, the document's limitations on socioeconomic rights would be quite undone. The "carefully constructed constitutional scheme for progressive realisation of socioeconomic rights would make little sense if it could be trumped in every case by the rights of children." Here, I think, is the heart of the Court's skepticism about the idea that section 26 should be taken to create absolute rights. If section 26 were so understood, it would trump even reasonable priority-setting, thus disallowing the state from deciding that in view of sharply limited resources, certain needs were even more pressing.

### Citizenship, Courts, and Decent Lives

What I will urge here is that the approach of the South African Constitutional Court answers a number of questions about the proper relationship among socioeconomic rights, constitutional law, and democratic deliberation. There should be little question that people who live in desperate conditions cannot live good lives. People who live in such conditions are also unable to enjoy the status of citizenship.

On the other hand, legislatures in poor nations, and perhaps in less poor ones, cannot easily ensure that everyone lives in decent conditions. An especially plausible concern with socioeconomic rights is the difficulty, for courts, of steering a middle course between two straightforward positions: (1) that socioeconomic rights are nonjusticiable and (2) that socioeconomic rights create an absolute duty, on government's part, to ensure protection for everyone who needs them. The second position is of course the standard approach to most constitutional rights. If the government has violated someone's right to free speech, or to freedom of religion, it does not matter that it has respected the rights of most people, or almost everyone else.

As I have emphasized, all rights have costs.[10] The right to free speech will not be protected unless taxpayers are willing to fund a judicial system willing and able to protect that right. In fact a system committed to free speech is also likely to require taxpayer resources to be devoted to keeping open certain arenas where speech can occur, such as streets and parks. In protecting the most conventional rights, the government must engage in some form of priority-setting. But when cases go to court, conventional rights are and can be fully protected at the individual level, and not merely through the creation of some kind of "reasonable" overall system for protection. The existence of a reasonable overall system for protecting free speech rights is no defense to a claim that, in a particular case, a right to free speech has been violated.

By their very nature, socioeconomic rights are different on this count, certainly in the light of the "progressive realisation" clause. No one thinks that every individual has an enforceable right to full protection of the interests at stake. In these circumstances it is difficult indeed to find an approach that avoids creation of individual rights and that avoids a conclusion of nonjusticiability. The only alternative to these extremes is an approach to public law that is generally unfamiliar in constitutional law but that is the ordinary material of administrative law, governing judicial control of administrative agencies: a requirement of reasoned judgment, including reasonable priority-setting.

In a typical administrative law case, an agency is faced with a burden of explanation. It must show why it has adopted the program it has chosen; it must account for its failure to adopt a program of a different sort. For courts, a special attraction of this position is that it protects against arbitrariness while it also recognizes the democratic pedigree of the agency and the simple fact of limited resources. If an agency has allocated resources in a rational way, it has acted lawfully.

What the South African Constitutional Court has basically done is to adopt an *administrative law model of socioeconomic rights*. Courts using that model are hardly unwilling to invalidate an agency's choices as arbitrary. That, in effect, is what the Constitutional Court did in *Grootboom*. The Court required government to develop, and fund, a program by which a large number of poor people are given access to emergency housing. What the Court called for is some sort of reasonable plan, designed to ensure that relief will be forthcoming to a significant percentage of poor people. On this view, the Constitution constrains government not by ensuring that everyone receives shelter but by requiring government to devote more resources than it otherwise would to the problem of insufficient housing for the poor. More particularly, the Court requires government to maintain a plan for emergency relief for those who need it. This is the particular gap found unacceptable in *Grootboom*.

But there is a twist here. For those whose socioeconomic rights are violated, the real problem is one of government *inaction*—a failure to implement a program of the sort that, in the view of some, the Constitution requires. The plaintiffs in *Grootboom* were seeking government action that had not, to that point, been forthcoming, in the particular form of a right to emergency relief. Hence the *Grootboom* Court's approach is most closely connected to a subset of administrative law principles, involving judicial review of inaction by government agencies. In cases of this kind, everyone knows that the agency faces a resource constraint and that in the face of a limited budget, any reasonable priority-setting will be valid and perhaps even free from judicial review. At the same time, there is a duty of reasonableness in priority-setting, and an agency decision that rejects a statutory judgment, or that does not take statutory goals sufficiently seriously, will be held invalid. This is what the South African Court ruled in *Grootboom*.

The broader point here is that a constitutional right to shelter, or to food, can strengthen the hand of those who might be unable to make much progress in the political arena, perhaps because they are unsympathetic figures, perhaps because they are disorganized and lack political power. A socioeconomic guarantee can have an enduring function. It can do so in part by promoting a certain kind of deliberation, not by preempting it, as a result of directing political attention to interests that would otherwise be disregarded in ordinary political life.

### Larger Lessons

Should constitutions protect social and economic rights? It is certainly relevant that if basic needs are not met, people cannot really enjoy the status of citizens. A right to minimal social and economic guarantees can be justified, not only on the ground that people in desperate conditions will not have good lives but also on the ground that democracy requires a certain independence and security for everyone. But there are many complexities here. A government might attempt to meet people's needs in multiple ways, perhaps by creating incentives to ensure that people will help themselves rather than by looking to government. Perhaps there is no special need for constitutional safeguards here; perhaps this is an issue that can be settled democratically. In any case social and economic guarantees threaten to put courts in a role for which they are quite ill suited. While modern constitutions tend to protect those guarantees, we can understand the judgment that, in some nations, they would create more trouble than they are worth.

In *Grootboom,* the Constitutional Court of South Africa was confronted, for the first time, with the question of how, exactly, courts should protect socioeconomic rights. The Court's approach suggests, also for the first time, the possibility of providing that protection in a way that is respectful of democratic prerogatives and the simple fact of limited budgets.

In making clear that the socioeconomic rights are not given to individuals as such, the Court was at pains to say that the right to housing is not absolute. This suggestion underlies the narrow interpretation of the provision involving children and also the Court's unambiguous suggestion that the state need not provide housing for everyone who needs it. What the constitutional right requires is not housing on demand but a reasonable program for ensuring access to housing for poor people, including some kind of program for ensuring emergency relief. This approach ensures respect for sensible priority-setting, and close attention to particular needs, without displacing democratic judgments about how to set priorities. This is now the prevailing approach to the constitutional law of socioeconomic rights in South Africa.

Of course the approach leaves many issues unresolved. Suppose that the government ensured a certain level of funding for a program of emergency relief; suppose too that the specified level is challenged as insufficient. The Court's decision suggests that whatever amount allocated must be shown to be "reasonable"; but what are the standards for resolving a dispute about that issue? The deeper problem is that any allocations of resources for providing shelter will prevent resources from going elsewhere—for example, for AIDS treatment and prevention, for unemployment compensation, for food, for basic income support. Undoubtedly the Constitutional Court will listen carefully to government claims that resources not devoted to housing are being used elsewhere. Undoubtedly those claims will be stronger if they suggest that some or all of the resources are being used to protect socioeconomic rights of a different sort.

What is most important, however, is the Constitutional Court's adoption of a novel and highly promising approach to judicial protection of socioeconomic rights. The ultimate effects of the approach remain to be seen. But by requiring reasonable programs, with careful attention to limited budgets, the Court has suggested the possibility of assessing claims of constitutional violations without at the same time requiring more than existing resources will allow. And in so doing, the Court has provided the most convincing rebuttal yet to those who have claimed, in the abstract quite plausibly, that judicial protection of socioeconomic rights could not possibly be a good idea. We now have reason to believe that a democratic constitution, even in a poor nation, is able to give some protection to those rights, and to do so without placing an undue strain on judicial capacities.

# Conclusion: Democracy's Constitution

In modern nations, political disagreement is the source of both the gravest danger and the greatest security. The people of such nations diverge on many questions, ranging from the most fundamental to the most insistently practical. Is equality prior to liberty? What do these terms mean? How should government regulate the Internet? Should welfare programs be expanded? What form should environmental programs take?

A deliberative democracy, operating under a good constitution, responds to political disagreements not simply by majority rule but also by attempting to create institutions that will ensure reflection and reason-giving. Some disagreements can be dispelled by getting clear on the facts. Others can be handled by delegating decisions to people who are especially trusted, perhaps because they are specialists in the topic at hand. Sometimes deliberation will show that one or another view really cannot be sustained, and people will change their minds accordingly. One of the points of constitutional arrangements is to protect the processes of reason-giving, ensuring something like a "republic of reasons."

In this light, constitutional institutions, such as a system of checks and balances, are best understood not as a way of reducing accountability to the public but as a guarantee of deliberation. Deliberative democracies do not respond mechanically to what a majority currently thinks. They do not take snapshots of public opinion. A deliberative democracy requires the exercise of governmental power, and the distribution of benefits and burdens, to be justified not by the fact that a majority is in favor of it but on the basis of reasons that can be seen, by all or almost all citizens, as public-regarding.

In all democracies, however, there is a constant source of deliberative trouble: Political disagreement can be heightened simply by virtue of the fact that like-minded people are talking mostly with one another. It is a simple social fact that if people tend to agree and spend some time in conversation with one another, they are likely to end up thinking a more extreme version of what they thought before. It follows that if like-minded people are talking mostly with one another, social fragmentation is highly likely. New technologies, including the Internet, increase this risk, simply because they make it so easy for like-minded people to find each other and to insulate themselves from competing views. In the worst cases, hatred and even violence are possible consequences.

A democracy's constitution can be extremely helpful here. It can increase the likelihood that government power will be unavailable to those who have not spoken with those having competing views. It can ensure that government will not act unless and until diverse people have had an opportunity to consult with one another and to listen to one another's concerns. The system of checks and balances is central here. Part of its point is to make sure that government does not act simply because one or another segment wants it to do so. And a democratic constitution can increase the likelihood that whatever their disagreements about largest or most abstract issues, people can agree on particular practices and on the low-level reasons that justify them. In a good democracy, constitutional rights protect political dissent and ensure against police invasions of the home—and people who disagree on a great deal can emphatically endorse those rights.

Democracy's constitution is not tradition's constitution. A central purpose of a constitution, and of a deliberative democracy, is to subject long-standing practices to critical scrutiny. Good constitutions have a mixture of preservative and transformative elements. They seek to entrench long-standing practices that seem, on reflection, to deserve special status. At the same time, they set out ideals and aspirations that are understood to eliminate long-standing practices and to point the way toward changes, both small and large. The constitutional commitment to reason-giving is inconsistent with respect for tradition as such. In the end traditionalism is much too timorous, and self-defeating to boot, because the traditions of constitutional democracies include criticism of traditions, not blind deference to them.

These points have many implications for the appropriate content of a democratic constitution. One of the central points of such a constitution is to solve problems that are particularly likely to arise in that nation's ordinary political life. Democratic constitutions are not mere paper but pragmatic instruments, designed to solve concrete problems and to make political life work better. Such constitutions are badly misconceived if they are understood as a place to state all general truths or to provide a full account of human rights. In a nation at risk of fragmentation, a constitutional right to secede would be a large mistake, not because there is no moral right to secede but because a constitutional right to that effect would undermine one of the projects at hand. If a nation is likely to neglect its poorest citizens, the case for social and economic guarantees, ensuring decent food and shelter, is quite strong. In a nation that might fail to take appropriate advantage of free markets, constitutional protection of free markets (including freedom of contract and private property) will make a great deal of sense.

The general lesson is that democratic constitutions operate as "precommitment strategies," in which nations, aware of problems that are likely to arise, take steps to ensure that those problems will not arise or that they will produce minimal damage if they do. A case in point: An "arms control agreement" against resort to the impeachment mechanism is best understood as a way of minimizing the danger that that mechanism will be used for partisan reasons, in a way that raises the spectre of scandal-mongering rather than deliberation about what matters most to citizens' lives. The high barrier for impeachment—generally requiring egregious misuse of official power—is simply an example of the use of institutional devices to ensure that democracy will be genuinely deliberative.

One of my principal themes has involved the creative use of judicial power, not simply to "block" democracy but to energize it and to make it more deliberative. Suppose, for example, that a court is asked to forbid the president or the Federal Communications Commission from issuing a regulation that would regulate violence in the entertainment industry, on the ground that the regulation would invade free speech. The court has several alternatives. It could strike down the regulation on free speech grounds; it could uphold the regulation; or it could say that a regulation that raises such serious constitutional problems cannot be valid unless Congress has specifically called for it. The third approach is far less intrusive than the first, because it is more respectful of democratic prerogatives. It leaves open the possibility that if the national legislature is clear on the point, the regulation might be valid. And if the national legislature is able to enact the relevant law, the argument for its validity is certainly strengthened.

I have suggested that this sort of democracy-promoting approach to constitutional law deserves a prominent place in many nations. Such an approach shows how the protection of rights can be secured, not by saying that a democratic government cannot do what it wants but by promoting the minimal degree of deliberation and accountability that must accompany any invasion of rights. A special virtue of this approach is that it is alert to the need for deliberation among diverse people and to the high risk of group polarization within bureaucracies and the executive branch. To those who say that this approach makes rights less secure, it should be responded that democratic self-government is a right too—and that when rights are clearly at risk, the Constitution should certainly play a more aggressive role, forbidding legislative action as well.

A democratic constitution has a lot to say about equality. The idea of deliberative democracy comes with its own internal morality. That internal morality ensures against second-class citizenship for anyone. A democratic constitution forbids a situation in which laws turn a morally irrelevant characteristic, especially if that characteristic is highly visible, into a systematic basis for second-class citizenship. I have urged that this anticaste principle is the central part of the equality principle of democracy's constitution.

If this is so, many practices not now thought to raise constitutional issues—including the economic disadvantages faced by African-American children and the problem of sex-related violence—should be seen in constitutional terms, even if courts should play little or no role. The anticaste principle also raises serious questions about discrimination on the basis of sexual orientation, seeing that form of discrimination as a species of discrimination on the basis of sex and as part of a fabric of arrangements designed to ensure perpetuation of the false and pernicious notion that men and women are simply "two kinds." I have also urged that the anticaste principle throws into doubt the widely held view that religious liberty always "trumps" sex equality. Sometimes religious practices not only embody but also embed sex inequality, by affecting preferences and beliefs at the most fundamental level, even for children. A democratic constitution hardly disables its citizens from responding to the situation.

In this light it should be clear that the promise of the anticaste principle has hardly been exhausted. As a central part of a democratic constitution, that principle still has a great deal of work to do. I have not argued that democratic constitutions should protect social and economic rights; that question cannot be answered in the abstract. But I have urged that people who live in desperate conditions—like people who lack property rights—cannot have the security and independence that are presupposed by the status of citizenship. In this way, the defense of rights to food and shelter is similar to the defense of the right to private property. We have seen that a modest judiciary, invoking social and economic guarantees, can spur democratic attention to urgent needs that might otherwise be neglected.

By itself, a democratic constitution does not guarantee good lives for citizens. Nor does it guarantee justice. But a democratic constitution nonetheless does a great deal. As I have emphasized, one of its principal virtues is that it responds to the pervasive threat of deliberative trouble. It does this partly by reducing the likelihood of group polarization and partly through embodying and promoting incompletely theorized agreements—making it possible for diverse people to reach agreement where agreement is necessary, and making it unnecessary for people to reach agreement when agreement is impossible. The result is a significant victory for both mutual respect and social stability.

Democracy is a distinct and limited ideal. It should not be confused with other social aspirations. But by ensuring reason-giving, by increasing exposure to diverse views, and by prohibiting second-class citizenship, a democratic constitution goes a long way toward promoting a wide range of social goals, emphatically including justice itself.

# Notes

*Introduction*

1. Association for Civil Rights in Israel v The General Security Service (1999).
2. See Kent v. Dulles, 357 U.S. 116 (1958).
3. See Amartya Sen, Poverty and Famines (Oxford: Oxford University Press, 1983).
4. There are many discussions of the subject. See, e.g., Amy Gutmann & Dennis Thompson, Democracy and Disagreement 128–64 (Cambridge: Harvard University Press, 1997); Deliberative Democracy (Jon Elster ed., Cambridge: Cambridge University Press, 1998); Jurgen Habermas, Between Facts and Norms 274–328 (Cambridge: MIT Press, 1997).


*Chapter 1*

1. See Amy Gutmann & Dennis Thompson, Democracy and Disagreement 128–64 (Cambridge: Harvard University Press, 1997); Deliberative Democracy (Jon Elster ed., Cambridge: Cambridge University Press, 1998); Jurgen Habermas, Between Facts and Norms 274–328 (Cambridge: MIT Press, 1997); Cass R. Sunstein, The Partial Constitution 133–45 (Cambridge: Harvard University Press, 1993).
2. Aristotle, Politics 123 (E. Barker trans., 1972).
3. Caryn Christenson & Ann Abbott, *Team Medical Decision Making, in* Decision Making in Health Care 267, 273–76 (Gretchen Chapman & Frank Sonnenberg eds., Cambridge: Cambridge University Press, 2000).
4. What I offer here is a highly cognitive picture of movements toward extremism. Undoubtedly this is only part of the picture. For an emphasis on different aspects of group movement, see, e.g., Sigmund Freud, Group Psychology and the Analysis of the Ego 3–30, 62–77 (New York: Bantam Books, 1960).
5. See, e.g., Dan Kahan, *Social Influence, Social Meaning, and Deterrence*, 83 Va. L. Rev. 349 (1997).
6. See Harold H. Gardner, Nathan L. Kleinman, & Richard J. Butler, *Workers' Compensation and Family and Medical Leave Act Claim Contagion*, 20 J. Risk and Uncertainty 89, 101–10 (2000).
7. See Marianne Bertrand, Erzo F. P. Luttmer, & Sendhil Millainathan, Network Effects and Welfare Cultures (Apr. 9, 1998) (unpublished manuscript).

8. See Ardith Spence, Wants for Waste (1999) (unpublished Ph.D. dissertation, University of Chicago).

9. See Stephen Coleman, *The Minnesota Income Tax Compliance Experiment State Tax Results* (Minnesota Department of Revenue, April 1996).

10. See Robert Kennedy, Strategy Fads and Competitive Convergence (1999) (unpublished manuscript).

11. See H. Wesley Perkins, *College Student Misperceptions of Alcohol and Other Drug Norms Among Peers, in Designing Alcohol and Other Drug Prevention Programs in Higher Education* 177–206 (U.S. Department of Education ed. 1997); Timur Kuran & Cass R. Sunstein, *Availability Cascades and Risk Regulation,* 51 Stan. L. Rev. 683, 767 (1999). A good outline of contagion effects can be found in Gardner, Kleinman & Butler, *supra* note 6, at 91–4.

12. See Andrew Caplin & John Leahy, *Miracle on Sixth Avenue: Information Externalities and Search,* 108 Econ. J. 60, 61 (1998).

13. See George Akerlof, *A Theory of Social Custom, of Which Unemployment May Be One Consequence,* in *An Economic Theorist's Book of Tales* 69 (Cambridge: Cambridge University Press, 1984).

14. See the overview in Solomon Asch, *Opinions and Social Pressure, in Readings About the Social Animal* 13 (Elliott Aronson ed., New York: W. H Fellman, 1995).

15. *Id.* at 15.

16. Dominic Abrams et al., *Knowing What to Think by Knowing Who You Are,* 29 Brit. J. Soc. Psych. 97, 106–8 (1990). See also the discussion of the "downside" of social ties among group members in Brooke Harrington, Cohesion, Conflict and Group Demography (2000) (unpublished manuscript), showing that when social ties are in place, dissent may be suppressed, and decisions may be worse as a result.

17. Consider the fact that the least conformity, and the greatest accuracy, was found when people who thought of themselves in a different group were speaking publicly. At the same time, the largest number of conforming, inaccurate responses came when people thought of themselves in the same group and were speaking publicly—even though the number of inaccurate *private* responses in that experimental condition was not notably higher than in other conditions. See Abrams et al., *supra* note 16, at 108.

18. See Abrams et al., *supra* note 16, at 108. By contrast, people who thought that they were members of a different group actually gave more accurate, nonconforming answers when speaking *publicly*, which creates an interesting puzzle: Why was there more accuracy in public than in private statements? The puzzle is solved if we consider the likelihood that subjects could consider it an affirmative good to disagree with people from another group (even if they secretly suspected that those people might be right). In the real world, this effect may well be heightened when people are asked whether they agree with opponents or antagonists; they might well say "no" even when the answer is "yes," simply because agreement carries costs, either to reputation or to self-conception.

19. Asch, *supra* note 14, at 21.

20. See, e.g., Sushil Biikhchandani et al., *Learning from the Behavior of Others,* J. Econ. Persp., Summer 1998, at 151; Lisa Anderson & Charles Holt, *Information Cascades in the Laboratory,* 87 Am. Econ. Rev. 847 (1997); Abhijit Banerjee, *A Simple Model of Herd Behavior,* 107 Q. J. Econ. 797 (1992); Andrew Daughety & Jennifer Reinganum, *Stampede to Judgment,* 1 Am. L. & Ec. Rev. 158, 159–65 (1999).

21. See Mark Granovetter, *Threshold Models of Collective Behavior*, 83 Am. J. Sociology 1420 (1978); for a recent popular treatment, see Malcolm Gladwell, *The Tipping Point* 5–22 (Boston: Little, Brown, 2000).

22. See Anderson & Holt, *supra* note 20, at 847.

23. See Sushil Bikhchandani et al., *A Theory of Fads, Fashion, Custom, and Cultural Change as Informational Cascades*, 100 J. Polit. Econ. 992 (1992); Kuran & Sunstein, *supra* note 11, at 715–35.

24. See Robert Shiller, *Irrational Exuberance* 151–67 (Princeton: Princeton University Press, 2000).

25. See Kennedy, *supra* note 10.

26. Several of these examples are discussed in Kuran & Sunstein, *supra* note, 11, at 725–35, and in Granovetter, *supra* note 21, at 1422–4.

27. Daughety & Reinganum, *supra* note 20, at 167–82 (discussing possibility of herd behavior by courts).

28. See Timur Kuran, *Public Lies, Private Truths* 4–20 (Cambridge: Harvard University Press, 1996).

29. I do not deal here with the general and related question whether groups amplify or eliminate various cognitive and motivational biases in individual decisions. For a general overview, finding mixed results, see Norbert Kerr, Robert MacCoun, & Gerald Kramer, *Bias in Judgment: Comparing Individuals and Groups*, 103 Psych. Rev. 687 (1996).

30. See David Isenberg, *Group Polarization: A Critical Review and Met-analysis*, 50 J. Personality and Soc. Psych. 1141 (1986).

31. Of course, when different deliberating groups polarize in different directions, the consequence can be greater variance among groups, notwithstanding small initial differences. A group whose members are initially but tentatively disposed to reject some proposal might start out very close to a group whose members are initially but tentatively disposed to approve of that proposal. If the two groups have a number of intragroup discussions, but no intergroup discussions, they may end up very far apart.

32. See Roger Brown, *Social Psychology* 222 (New York: The Free Press, 1986). These include the United States, Canada, New Zealand, India, Bangladesh, Germany, and France. See, e.g., Johannes Zuber et al., *Choice Shift and Group Polarization*, 62 J. Personality and Social Psych. 50 (1992) (Germany); Dominic Abrams et al., *Knowing What To Think by Knowing Who You Are*, 29 British J. Soc. Psych. 97, 112 (1990) (New Zealand). Of course it is possible that some cultures would show a greater or lesser tendency toward polarization; this would be an extremely interesting area for empirical study.

33. See D. G. Myers, *Discussion-Induced Attitude Polarization*, 28 Human Relations 699 (1975).

34. Brown, *supra* note 32, at 224.

35. D. G. Myers and G. D. Bishop, *The Enhancement of Dominant Attitudes in Group Discuission*, 20 J. Personality and Soc. Psych. 286 (1976).

36. See *id.*

37. See J. A. F. Stoner, A Comparison of Individual and Group Decisions Including Risk (1962) (unpublished master's thesis, School of Management, Massachusetts Institute of Technology); J. A. F. Stoner, *Risky and Cautious Shifts in Group Decisions*, 4 J. Experimental Social Psych. 442 (1968).

38. See Brown, *supra* note 32, at 208–10, for an overview.

39. Paul Cromwell et al., *Group Effects on Decision-making by Burglars*, 69 Psychological Reports 579, 586 (1991).

40. See Brown, *supra* note 32, at 207. Note, however, that one account of group polarization finds that the effect lies in conformity to the "prototypical group member," defined as such by reference to a "meta-contrast principle: the less a person differs from in-group members and the more he or she differs from out-group members, the more representative is he or she of the in-group." See Craig McGarty et al., *Group Polarization As Conformity to the Prototypical Group Member*, 21 British J. Soc. Psych. 1, 3 (1992). This position raises many questions; it seems to have the strongest fit with the data in cases in which in-groups and out-groups can readily be understood as such by subjects. See *id.*

41. Isenberg, *supra* note 30, and Brown, *supra* note 32, at 210–25, review this literature; see also John Turner et al., *Rediscovering the Social Group* 142–70, (New York: Blackwell 1986), for an overview and an attempt to generate a new synthesis.

42. A. I. Teger & D. G Pruitt, *Components of Group Risk-Taking*, 3 J. Experimental Social Psych. 189 (1967).

43. See, e.g., Mark Kelman et al., *Context Dependence in Legal Decision Making*, in *Behavioral Law and Economics* 61, 71–6 (Cass R. Sunstein ed., New York: Cambridge University Press, 2000).

44. See Brooke Harrington, The Pervasive Effects of Embeddedness in Organizations 24 (2000) (unpublished manuscript).

45. See Russell Spears, Martin Lee, & Stephen Lee, *De-Individuation and Group Polarization in Computer-Mediated Communication*, 29 British J. Soc. Psych. 121 (1990); Dominic Abrams et al., *supra* note 16, at 97, 112; Patricia Wallace, *The Psychology of the Internet* 73–6 (New York: Cambridge University Press, 1999).

46. See Lee Roy Beach, *The Psychology of Decision Making in Organizations* (1997); Harrington, *supra* note 44.

47. A third possibility, raised recently by Heath and Gonzales, is that hearing other similar opinions produces greater confidence in individual positions, opening members to a more extreme judgment in the same direction. See Chip Heath and Richard Gonzales, *Interaction with Others Increases Decision Confidence but Not Decision Quality: Evidence against Information Collection Views of Interactive Decision Making*, 61 Organizational Behavior and Human Decision Processes 305–26 (1997).

In the same vein, it seems reasonable to think that part of the reason for choice shifts and group polarization is that individuals begin by moderating their judgments, seeking what appears to be a middle ground; they are emboldened by the stated positions of (some) others and hence there is a change toward a more extreme point in the direction indicated by original predispositions.

48. See H. Burnstein, *Persuasion As Argument Processing, in*, Group Decision Making (H. Brandstetter, J. H. Davis, and G. Stocker-Kreichgauer eds., 1982).

49. Brown, *supra* note 32, at 225.

50. Amiram Vinokur & Eugene Bernstein, *The Effects of Partially Shared Persuasive Arguments on Group-Induced Shifts*, 29 J. Personality & Social Psych. 305 (1974).

51. Vinokur & Bernstein, *supra*, at 884.

52. See David Schkade et al., *Deliberating About Dollars: The Seventy Shift*, 100 Col. Rev. 1139 (2000).

53. See R. T Riley and T. F. Pettigrew, *Dramatic Events and Attitude Change*, 34 J. Personality and Social Psych 1004 (1976).

54. Myers, *supra* note 33, at 135.

55. See Timur Kuran, *Ethnic Norms and Their Transformation through Reputational Cascades*, 27 J. Legal Stud. 623, 648 (1998).

56. See *id.*

57. See *id.* at 650–1.

58. See Lawrence Lessig, Code and Other Laws of Cyberspace 186 (New York: Basic Books, 1999); Andrew Shapiro, The Control Revolution 124–32 (New York: Public Affairs, 1999).

59. See Donald Jacobs, *Race, Media, and the Crisis of Civil Society*, 144 (New York: Cambridge University Press, 2000).

60. See Wallace, *supra* note 45, at 73–84.

61. See Syracuse Peace Council v. F.C.C., 867 F.2d 654 (D.C. Cir. 1989).

62. *Id.*

63. Thomas W. Hazlett & David W. Sosa, *Was the Fairness Doctrine a "Chilling Effect"? Evidence from the Postderegulation Radio Market*, 26 J. Legal Stud. 279 (1997) (offering an affirmative answer to the question in the title).

64. The term comes from Nicholas Negroponte.

65. See Brown, *supra* note 32, at 227–9 (collecting studies).

66. *Id.* at 239.

67. See Richard L. Revesz, *Environmental Regulation, Ideology, and the D.C. Circuit*, 83 Va. L. Rev. 1717, 1755 (1997); Frank Cross and Emerson Tiller, *Judicial Partisanship and Obedience to Legal Doctrine*, 107 Yale L.J. 2155 (1998).

68. The Federalist No. 68.

69. The Federalist No. 6.

70. Philip Kurland & Ralph Lerner, 3 The Founders' Constitution 542 (Chicago: University of Chicago Press, 1994).

71. See Jurgen Habermas, A Theory of Communicative Action 99 (Cambridge: MIT Press, 1984). Thus Habermas distinguishes between strategic and communicative action and stresses "the cooperatively pursued goal of reaching understanding"; compare the treatment in Gutmann & Thompson, *supra* note 1, at 52–94, emphasizing the idea of reciprocity, which emphasizes the desire to justify one's position by reference to reasons.

72. James Wilson, Lectures on Law, 1 The Works of James Wilson 291 (Chicago: Callahan, 1890).

73. See Harrington, *supra* note 44, at 28–30.

74. See the discussion in Sunstein, *supra* note 1, at 22.

75. See Christenson & Abbott, *supra* note 3, at 273.

76. *Id.* at 274.

77. C. C. Kirchmeyer & A. Cohen, *Multicultural Groups: Their Performance and Reactions with Constructive Conflict*, 17 Group and Organization Management 153 (1992).

78. See Letter to Madison (Jan. 30, 1798), *reprinted in* The Portable Thomas Jefferson 882 (M. Peterson ed., New York: Viking Press, 1977).

79. See Speech to the Electors (Nov. 3, 1774), *reprinted in* Burke's Politics 116 (Ross Hoffman ed., New York: Knopf, 1949).

80. See *id.*

81. See The Federalist No. 10.

## Chapter 2

1. Stephen Breyer, *The Federal Sentencing Guidelines and the Key Compromises upon Which They Rest*, 17 Hofstra L. Rev. 1, 14–9 (1988).

2. As quoted in New Republic, June 6, 1994, p. 12.

3. Lochner v. New York, 198 U.S. 48, 69 (1908) (Holmes, J., dissenting).

4. See Henry Sidgwick, The Methods of Ethics 96–104 (7th ed.) (New York: Dover, 1966).

5. This is the tendency in Ronald Dworkin, Law's Empire (Cambridge: Harvard University Press, 1985).

6. Here I follow John Rawls, Political Liberalism (Cambridge: Harvard University Press, 1996).

7. National Coalition for Gay and Lesbian Equality v. Minister of Justice, 1998 B.C.L.R. 1517, 1998 S.A.C.L.R. LEXIS 36 (1998).

8. I discuss this in more detail in Cass R. Sunstein, Legal Reasoning and Political Conflict (Oxford: Oxford University Press, 1996).

9. See Cass R. Sunstein, One Case at a Time (Cambridge: Harvard University Press, 1999) for more detailed discussion.

*Chapter 3*

1. See Lawrence Lessig, Code and Other Laws of Cyberspace (New York: Basic Books, 1999).

2. The Constitutional Court of South Africa, Shaballala and Others v. Attorney General of the Transvaal and Another, 1996 South Africa 725 (C.C.) at paragraph 26.

3. See, e.g., Government of South Africa v. Grootboom, 2000 (11) B.C.L.R. 1165 (CC).

4. See Gordon Wood, The Radicalism of the American Revolution (New York: Random House, 1991).

5. Lochner v. New York, 198 U.S. 45, 56 (1905) (Holmes, J., dissenting).

6. *Id.*

7. Griswold v. Connecticut, 381 U.S. 479 (1965).

8. 405 U.S. 438 (1972).

9. 410 U.S. 113 (1973).

10. 478 U.S. 186 (1986).

11. Michael H. v. Gerald D., 490 U.S. 505 (1985).

12. See Cruzan v. Director, 497 U.S. 261 (1990); Washington v. Glucksberg, 521 U.S. 702 (1997).

13. See Washington v. Glucksberg, 117 S.Ct. 2258 (1997).

14. Cruzan v. Director, at 287–292 (O'Connor, J., concurring).

15. Romer v. Evans, 517 U.S. 620, 630 (1996).

16. See Hilary Putnam, Renewing Philosophy (Cambridge: Harvard University Press, 1992).

17. John Rawls, A Theory of Justice (Cambridge: Harvard University Press, 1971).

18. Cass R. Sunstein, Legal Reasoning and Political Conflict (Oxford: Oxford University Press, 1996).

19. Anthony Kronman, *Precedent and Tradition*, 99 Yale L. J. 1029, 1066 (1990).

20. See Government of South Africa v. Grootboom, 2000 (11) B.C.L.R. 1165 (CC).

21. *Id.*

22. *Id.*

23. An excellent overview is David Currie, The Constitution of the Federal Republic of Germany (Chicago: University of Chicago Press, 1994).

24. *Id.* at 229–30.

25. New York Times v. Sullivan, 376 U.S. 254 (1964).

26. 198 U.S. 45 (1905).

27. See Cass R. Sunstein, The Partial Constitution ch. 2 (Cambridge: Harvard University Press, 1993); Ronald Dworkin, Taking Rights Seriously (Cambridge: Harvard University Press, 1976); John Hart Ely, Democracy and Distrust (Cambridge: Harvard University Press, 1981).

28. More specifically: Substantive due process is a linguistically difficult notion. By an ordinary reading of its plain terms, the due process clause is procedural, not substantive. That is, the clause seems to require procedures of a certain kind rather than a judicial evaluation of the substance of legislation. A better constitutional foundation for substantive protection of important interests would have been the privileges and immunities clause, also found in the Fourteenth Amendment. The Supreme Court concluded in an early case that this clause added nothing to the original constitution. See The Slaughterhouse Cases, 83 U.S. 36 (1873). This conclusion is most doubtful; but aggressive use of the privileges and immunities clause would have left open many of the issues discussed here: How do we know what interests count as "privileges and immunities"? Perhaps tradition would have been a key way of answering this question. I cannot discuss these complex issues in this space; I am trying to explain the origins of the use of tradition under the due process clause rather than to reach a final judgment on the legitimacy of substantive due process or what might have been, in a different form, "substantive privileges and immunities."

29. See Jack Balkin, *Tradition, Betrayal, and the Politics of Deconstruction,* 11 Cardozo Law Review 1613 (1993).

30. See Antonin Scalia, A Matter of Interpretation (Princeton: Princeton University Press, 1996).

31. My own views are set out in Cass R. Sunstein, One Case at a Time (Cambridge: Harvard University Press, 1999).

32. See Scalia, *supra* note 30.

33. See Alexander Bickel, The Least Dangerous Branch (New Haven: Yale Univ Press, 1962). I am grateful to Michael McConnell for helpful discussion of this point.

34. See Sunstein, The Partial Constitution ch. 9, for more detail.

*Chapter 4*

1. Dwight L. Dummond, The Secession Movement 1860–1861 120–1 (New York: Macmillan, 1931).

2. Thomas Jefferson, Letter to Samuel Kercheval (July 12, 1816), *reprinted in* The Portable Thomas Jefferson 558–61 (Merrill D. Peterson ed., New York: Viking, 1975).

3. James Madison, Letter to Thomas Jefferson (Feb. 14, 1790), *reprinted in* The Mind of the Founder: Sources of the Political Thought of James Madison 230–1 (Marvin Meyers ed., Bobbs-Merrill, 1973).

4. Jon Elster and Stephen Holmes have explored this idea in many places. See Jon Elster, Ulysses Unbound (Cambridge: Cambridge University Press, 2000); Stephen Holmes, Passions and Constraint (Chicago: University of Chicago Press, 1996). Elster has recently expressed doubt about the idea that constitutions arise, in fact, as precommitment strategies, and many of his arguments are convincing. See Elster, *supra.* I am interested here not in explaining why constitutions take

the form they do but in why a good constitution might take one form rather than another. My goal is normative, not descriptive.

5. I borrow here from Stephen Holmes, *Precommitment, and the Paradox of Democracy, in* Constitutionalism and Democracy 195 (Jon Elster & Rune Slagstad eds., Cambridge: Cambridge University Press, 1991), and Stephen Holmes, *Gag Rules or the Politics of Omission,* in *id.* at 19.

6. See generally Jon Elster, The Cement of Society (Cambridge: Cambridge University Press, 1989); Edna Ullmann-Margalit, The Emergence of Norms (Oxford: Oxford University Press, 1977).

7. See, for example, Gibbons v. Ogden, 22 U.S. 1 (1824).

8. For an especially helpful discussion, overlapping with the argument here, see Allen Buchanan, *Toward a Theory of Secession,* 101 Ethics 322 (1991). The credibility of the moral case makes it especially troublesome to suggest that military force should be used to stop secession—a difficult problem that I cannot discuss in detail here. Sometimes military force will be justified because the ground for secession is itself weak or involves oppression, as in the case of the American Civil War. Sometimes such force will deter other secession movements, and this will justify force when the secession movements are not, all things considered, legitimate ones. But the consequences of the use of military force are generally unpredictable and often worse than first anticipated. In this light the question whether a nation should be kept together through official violence cannot be sensibly answered in the abstract. At any rate, one need not and should not extrapolate from the American experience the proposition that civil war is always preferable to secession.

9. Thomas Jefferson, Letter in W. Lynn Ford (June 20, 1816), quoted in Lee Buchbet, Session (New Haven: Yale Univ. Press 1978).

10. This is the ambiguous and controversial right of self-determination. The principle of self-determination, recognized in the United Nations Charter and in numerous U.N. declarations, came to have great importance in the era of decolonization, though the contours of the right—particularly with respect to armed intervenion by third parties intent on furthering the right—remain unclear. See also the United Nations Declaration on Principles of International Law Concerning Friendly Relations and Co-operation Among States in Accordance with the Charter of the United Nations, which proclaims "The principle of equal rights and self-determination of peoples." ("[A]ll peoples have the right freely to determine, without external interference, their political status . . . and every State has the duty to respect this right in accordance with the provisions of the Charter.") U.N. Res. 2625 (Oct. 24, 1970), in 13 United Nations Resolutions, Series I (General Assembly Resolutions) 337, 339 (Dusan J. Djonovich ed., New York: Oceana, 1976).

*Chapter 5*

1. For criticism of originalism, see Cass R. Sunstein, One Case at a Time (Cambridge: Harvard University Press, 1999).

2. See Richard A. Posner, An Affair of State (Cambridge: Harvard University Press, 1999).

3. 1 Max Farrand, ed., The Records of the Constitutional Convention of 1787, 104 (New Haven: Yale University Press, 1937).

4. 2 Max Farrand, ed., The Records of the Constitutional Convention of 1787, 64 (New Haven: Yale University Press, 1937).

5. *Id.* at 65.

6. *Id.* at 65.

7. *Id.* at 65.

8. *Id.* at 67.

9. *Id.* at 66; see also 68.

10. *Id.* at 68.

11. *Id.* at 69.

12. *Id.* at 550.

13. *Id.* at 550.

14. *Id.* at 550.

15. *Id.* at 551.

16. See *id.*

17. See The Federalist No. 65 (Alexander Hamilton).

18. 2 Founders' Constitution 165 (Philip B. Kurland & Ralph Lerner eds., Chicago: University of Chicago Press, 1987).

19. *Id.* at 165.

20. *Id.* at 166.

21. *Id.* at 179.

22. See David A. Strauss, *Common Law Constitutional Interpretation*, 63 U. Chi. L. Rev. 877 (1996).

23. See Myers v. United States, 272 U.S. 52 (1926).

24. See William H. Rehnquist, Grand Inquests: The Historic Impeachments of Justice Samuel Chase and President Andrew Johnson (New York: Free Press, 1992).

25. Aaron Fellmeth, *A Divorce Waiting to Happen*, 3 Buff. J. Intl. L. 413, 486 (1996–97).

26. See Ex parte Milligan, 71 U.S. 2, 120–1 (1866) (stating that constitutional guarantees are to be upheld and protected by the courts "at all times and under all circumstances," irrespective of whether the nation is "in peace or war"). For factual details see William Rehnquist, *Civil Liberty and the Civil War: The Indianapolis Treason Trials*, 72 Ind. L. J. 927 (1997).

27. See Youngstown Sheet & Tube Co. v. Sawyer (The Steel Seizure Case), 343 U.S. 579 (1952).

*Chapter 6*

1. See John Hart Ely, Democracy and Distrust: A Theory of Judicial Review 132–3 (Cambridge: Harvard University Press, 1980).

2. See, for example, Bowen v. Georgetown University Hospital, 488 U.S. 204, 208–9 (1988) (stating that a congressional delegation of authority will be understood as granting the power to make retroactive rules only if the Congress specifically said so).

3. See, for example, Muscogee (Creek) Nation v Hodel, 851 F2d 1439, 1444–5 (D.C. Cir. 1988) (stating that "canons of construction applicable in Indian law" require that "[s]tatutes are to be construed liberally in favor of the Indians, with ambiguous provisions interpreted to their benefit").

4. I discuss the idea of judicial minimalism in detail in Cass R. Sunstein, One Case at a Time (Cambridge: Harvard University Press 1999).

5. The specific term is used and discussed in Amalgamated Meat Cutters v. Connally, 337 F. Supp. 737, 745–7 (D. D.C. 1971).

6. The Brig Aurora, 11 U.S. (7 Cranch) 382, 387–8 (1813) (recognizing the nondelegation principle but upholding a disputed legislative act because it was a

revival of a legislative act and not merely a presidential proclamation); Field v. Clark, 143 U.S. 649, 692 (1892) (noting the "universally recognized" principle that "Congress cannot delegate legislative power to the President"); United States v. Grimaud, 220 U.S. 506, 521 (1911) (quoting Field); J. W. Hampton, Jr., & Co. v. United States, 276 U.S. 394, 406–7 (1928) (collecting cases discussing delegation).

7. See Field, 143 U.S. at 692–3; The Brig Aurora, 11 U.S. at 388; Grimaud, 220 U.S. at 510.

8. A. L. A. Schechter Poultry Corp. v. U.S., 295 U.S. 495 (1935). The only other decision invalidating agency action on nondelegation grounds is Panama Refining Co. v. Ryan, 293 U.S. 388 (1935).

9. Schechter Poultry, 295 U.S. at 537.

10. See Mistretta v. U.S., 488 U.S. 361 (1989); U.S. v. Southwestern Cable Co., 392 U.S. 157 (1968); Lichter v. U.S., 334 U.S. 742 (1948); Yakus v. U.S., 321 U.S. 414 (1944).

11. See David Schoenbrod, Power Without Responsibility 180 (New Haven: Yale Univ. Press, 1993); Gary Lawson, *The Rise and Rise of the Administrative State,* 107 Harv. L. Rev. 1231, 1240–1 (1994); Ely, *supra* note 1, at 132.

12. Some questions emerge about this conventional view from David Epstein & Sharyn O'Halloran, Delegating Powers: A Transactions Cost Politics Approach to Policy Making Under Separate Powers 237–9 (Cambridge: Cambridge University Press, 1999); the analysis there emphasizes the role of committtees in fashioning specific terms when delegation is unavailable.

13. The Nazi experience might provide a lesson here. One of the earlier decisions by the German legislature, under Hitler, was to authorize Hitler to rule "by decree," and the resulting experience helped inspire an explicit nondelegation principle in the German constitution. See David P. Currie, The Constitution of the Federal Republic of Germany 125–6 (Chicago: University of Chicago Press, 1994). See also German Const. Art. 80, § 1, requiring that the content, purpose, and extent of the legislative authorization be specified in the statute itself. Note also that the Constitutional Court of South Africa has embarked on enforcement of a nondelegation principle, at least in extreme cases. See Executive Council, Western Cape Legislature v. President of the Republic South Africa 1995 (4) S.A. 877, 898–906, 918–19 (Const. Ct.).

14. James Madison referred to both but spoke of the former as the more serious danger: "[I]n our Governments the real power lies in the majority of the Community, and the invasion of private rights is chiefly to be apprehended, not from acts of government contrary to the sense of its constituents, but from acts in which the Government is the mere instrument of the major number of the constituents." Letter from Madison to Jefferson (Oct. 17, 1788), *in* 11 The Papers of James Madison 298 (R. Rutland & C. Hobson eds., Charlottesville: University of Virginia Press, 1977).

15. 1 Stat. 95 (1789).

16. 1 Stat. 137 (1790).

17. See the excellent treatment in Jerry L. Mashaw, Greed, Chaos, and Governance: Using Public Choice to Improve Public Law 131–57 (New Haven: Yale University Press, 1997).

18. See Epstein and O'Halloran, *supra* note 12, at 206–31.

19. See Cass R. Sunstein & Edna Ullmann-Margalit, *Second-Order Decisions,* 110 Ethics 5, 16 (1999).

20. See Epstein & O'Halloran, *supra* note 12.

21. *Id.* at 237.

22. *Id.*

23. *Id.*

24. 467 U.S. 837 (1984).

25. See, for example, Bowen v. Georgetown University Hospital, 488 U.S. 204, 208–9, 212–3 (1988) (noting a canon against interpreting a statute to be retroactive and denying judicial deference to an agency counsel's interpretation of a statute when the agency itself has articulated no position on the question).

26. See Rust v. Sullivan, 500 U.S. 173, 191 (1991).

27. See National Association of Regulatory Utility Commissioners v. F.C.C., 880 F.2d 422 (D.C. Cir. 1989).

28. Bowen v. Georgetown University Hospital, 488 U.S. 204, 208 (1988).

29. See, for example, Usery v. Turner Elkhorn Mining, 438 U.S. 1, 14–20 (1976) (holding that the Black Lung Benefits Act of 1972 does not violate the Fifth Amendment due process clause by requiring employers to provide retrospective compensation for former employees' death or disability due to employment in mines).

30. E.E.O.C. v. Arabian American Oil Co., 499 U.S. 244, 248 (1991).

31. See Ramah Navajo Chapter v. Lujan, 112 F.3d 1455, 1461–2 (10th Cir. 1997) (grounding a canon of statutory construction favoring Native Americans in "the unique trust relationship between the United States and the Indians"); Williams v. Babbitt, 115 F.2d 657, 660 (9th Cir. 1997) (noting in dicta that courts "are required to construe statutes favoring Native Americans liberally in their favor"); Tyonek Native Corp. v. Secretary of Interior, 836 F.2d 1237, 1239 (9th Cir. 1988) (noting in dicta that "statutes benefiting Native Americans should be construed liberally in their favor").

32. United States Department of Energy v. Ohio, 503 U.S. 607, 615 (1992).

33. United States v. Wells Fargo Bank, 485 U.S. 351, 354 (1988).

34. Michigan Citizens for an Independent Press v. Thornburgh, 868 F.2d 1285, 1299 (D.C. Cir. 1989) (Ginsburg dissenting) (noting the "accepted rule" that antitrust exemptions must be narrowly construed); Group Life & Health Insurance v. Royal Drug Co., 440 U.S. 205, 231 (1979) (noting the "well settled" rule that antitrust exceptions "are to be narrowly construed").

35. King v. St. Vincent's Hospital, 502 U.S. 215, 220 n. 9 (1991).

36. See Industrial Union Department, A.F.L-C.I.O. v. American Petroleum Institute, 448 U.S. 607, 644 (1980) (plurality) (holding that in promulgating OSHA, Congress "intended, at a bare minimum, that the Secretary [of Labor] find a significant risk of harm and therefore a probability of significant benefits before establishing a new standard"); Corrosion Proof Fittings v. E.P.A., 947 F.2d 1201, 1222–3 (5th Cir. 1991) (vacating the EPA's proposed rulemaking under the Toxic Substances Control Act and its ban on asbestos, partially on the grounds that the agency's own figures suggested that enforcing the regulation might cost as much as $74 million per life saved); Alabama Power Co. v. Costle, 636 F.2d 323, 360–1 (D.C. Cir. 1979) (stating that "[u]nless Congress has been extraordinarily rigid, there is likely a basis for an implication of de minimis authority to provide exemption when the burdens of regulation yield a gain of trivial or no value"); Monsanto Co. v. Kennedy, 613 F.2d 947, 954–55 (D.C. Cir. 1979) (allowing the commissioner of Food and Drugs not to apply the strictly literal terms of the statute and to make de minimis exceptions).

37. See Public Citizen v. Young, 831 F.2d 1108, 1122 (D.C. Cir. 1987) (finding no de minimis exception under the Delaney Clause, which barred the use of carcinogens in food additives). In a famous essay, Karl Llewellyn contended that

the canons of construction were indeterminate and unhelpful. See Karl N. Llewellyn, *Remarks on the Theory of Appellate Decision and the Rules or Canons about how Statutes Are To Be Construed,* 3 Vand. L. Rev. 395 (1950). There has been a vigorous debate over whether Llewellyn was right. See, for example, Antonin Scalia, A Matter of Interpretation 26–7 (Amy Gutmann ed., Princeton: Princeton University Press, 1997) (rejecting Llewellyn's claim). Even if Llewellyn is right, his argument does not undermine the nondelegation canons, which go in a single direction: against agency discretion. Of course it will be possible that other canons, for example those involving syntax, will support the agency's view of the statute.

38. See Stephen Breyer, Breaking the Vicious Circle 10–7 (Cambridge: Harvard University Press 1993) (discussing the problem of "the last 10%").

39. Consider Hampton v. Mow Sun Wong, 426 U.S. 88, 114–7 (1976) (holding that the Civil Service Commission could not decide to exclude aliens from the civil service but leaving open the question whether Congress or the president could do so).

40. See Richard A. Posner, Federal Courts 285 (Cambridge: Harvard University Press, 1997).

*Chapter 7*

1. On humiliation, see the important discussion in Avishai Margalit, The Decent Society (Cambridge: Harvard University Press, 1996).

2. See, e.g., Allgeyer v. Louisiana, 165 U.S. 578 (1897).

3. Clark Nadinelli & Curtis Simon, *Customer Racial Discrimination in the Market for Memorabilia: The Case of Baseball,* 105 Quart. J. Econ. 575 (1990).

4. See Edmund S. Phelps, *The Statistical Theory of Racism and Sexism,* 62 Am. Econ. Rev. 659 (1972).

5. See David Strauss, *The Myth of Colorblindness,* 1986 Supreme Court Review 99.

6. Jon Elster, Sour Grapes (Cambridge: Cambridge University Press, 1983) is an extended argument on the point.

7. M. Wollstonecraft, A Vindication of the Rights of Women (C. Poston ed., New York: Norton, 1975) (1792).

8. *Id.* at 43.

9. See Mill, The Subjection of Women (Cambridge: MIT Press, 1970) (1869), writing against the claim that the existing desires of women are a product of consent.

10. See Amartya Sen, Commodities and Capabilities 82 (Oxford: Oxford University Press, 1999).

11. See, e.g., Califano v. Goldfarb, 430 U.S. 199 (1977); Califano v. Webster, 430 U.S. 313 (1977); Rostker v. Goldberg, 453 U.S. 57 (1981); Michael M. v. Sonoma County Superior Court, 450 U.S. 464 (1981).

12. Michael M. v. Sonoma County Superior Court, 450 U.S. 464 (1981).

13. Rostker v. Goldberg, 453 U.S. 57 (1981)

14. Califano v. Webster, 430 U.S. 313 (1977).

15. See Craig v. Boren, 429 U.S. 190 (1976).

16. See Washington v. Davis, 46 U.S. 229, 246–8 (1976).

17. 430 U.S. 313 (1977).

18. See Geduldig v. Aiello, 417 U.S. 484 (1974).

19. See the discussion of differences in Janet Radcliffe Richards, The Skeptical Feminist, 165–71 (London: Penguin, 1984); Catharine MacKinnon, Feminism Unmodified (Cambridge: Harvard University Press, 1985); Martha Minow, Making All the Difference (Ithaca: Cornell University Press, 1990).

20. Gerald Rosenberg, The Hollow Hope 212 (Chicago: University of Chicago Press, 1991).

21. See Lenore Weitzman, The Divorce Revolution (New York: Free Press, 1987).

22. See, e.g., Amartya Sen, Development as Freedom (New York: Knopf, 1999); Martha Nussbaum, Women and Human Development: The Capabilities Approach (New York: Cambridge University Press, 2000).

23. See Avishai Margalit, The Decent Society (Cambridge: Harvard University Press, 1996).

24. Compare on this score such accidents of birth as great strength or intelligence or ability to produce products that the market rewards. These accidents may be entangled with nonaccidental factors; promoting them brings about desirable incentives and also is associated with a range of valuable social goals, like increased productivity. Of course it would be possible to say that when people do not like people of certain races, there is a productivity loss from forbidding them to indulge their "taste"; sometimes this may even be true; but that productivity loss seems inadequate to overcome the basic case offered in text.

25. U.S. Congress 1873–74, 22.

26. *Id.* at 983 (emphasis in original).

27. Cong. Globe, 39th Cong., 1st Sess. 2766 (1866).

28. 163 U.S. 532, 559 (1896) Harlan, J., dissenting).

29. Dred Scott v. Sandford, 60 U.S. 393 (1857).

30. The high-water mark of the anticaste understanding was probably Loving v. Virginia, 388 U.S. 1 (1967), with its reference to "White Supremacy." The triumph of the antidifferentiation idea can be found in Washington v. Davis, 426 U.S. 229 (1976), and City of Richmond v. Croson, 488 U.S. 469 (1989).

31. See Craig v. Boren, 429 U.S. 190 (1976); City of Richmond v. Croson, 488 U.S. 469 (1989); Cleburne v. Cleburne Living Center, 473 U.S. 432, 440 (1985).

32. I am putting to one side the distinction between "strict scrutiny," used in the racial context, and "intermediate scrutiny," used in the context of sex discrimination. An interesting development is the Court's own recent emphasis on its failure to choose between intermediate and strict scrutiny for gender, see J. E. B. v. Alabama 511 U.S. 127 (1994), though it is not clear that there is much difference here.

33. *Id.*

Chapter 8

1. 478 U.S. 186 (1986) (upholding a homosexual's criminal conviction for sodomy).

2. National Coalition for Gay and Lesbian Equality v. Minister of Justice, 1998 B.C.L.R. 1517, 1998 S.A.C.L.R. LEXIS 36 (1998); National Coalition for Gay and Lesbian Equality v. Minister of Justice, 1998 (6) B.C.L.R. 726 (W); 1998 S.A.C.L.R. LEXIS 6 (1998).

3. See John H. Ely, Democracy and Distrust, 15–8 (Cambridge: Harvard University Press, 1980)

4. Edwin Cameron, *Sexual Orientation and the Constitution: A Test Case for Human Rights,* 110 S.A.L.J. 450, 464 (1993), quoted in National Coalition for Gay and Lesbian Equality v. Minister of Justice, 1998 B.C.L.R. 1517, 1998 S.A.C.L.R. LEXIS 36 (1998).

5. See, e.g., Cleburne v. Cleburne Living Center, 473 U.S. 432, 440 (1985).

6. See *id.* at 450.

7. E.g., Steffan v. Aspin, 8 F.3d 57, 70 (D.C. Cir. 1993), vacated, 1994 U.S. App. LEXIS 9977 (D.C. Cir. Jan. 7, 1994); Dahl v. Secretary of the United States Navy, 830 F. Supp. 1319, 1337 (E.D. Cal. 1993); Meinhold v. United States Dep't of Defense, 808 F. Supp. 1453, 1455 (C.D. Cal. 1993).

8. Steffan, 8 F.3d 57.

9. Dahl, 830 F. Supp. 1319; Meinhold, 808 F. Supp. 1453.

10. Bowers, 478 U.S. 186, 196 (1986).

11. Baker v. State, 744 A.2d 864 (1999).

12. 759 F. Supp. 1543, 1551 (D. Kan. 1991), rev'd on other grounds, 976 F.2d 623 (10th Cir. 1992).

13. Watkins v. United States Army, 847 F.2d 1329, 1349 (9th Cir. 1988), withdrawn, 875 F.2d 699 (9th Cir. 1989), cert. denied, 498 U.S. 957 (1990).

14. I know of no study of this phenomenon, but substantial evidence suggests that it is widespread. Consider the fact that there has been serious debate over whether "marching in a gay parade" should be taken as evidence of homosexuality. See 139 Cong. Rec. S6691, S6692 (daily ed. May 27, 1993) (remarks of Sen. Nunn)(regarding Representative Frank's proposal concerning gay men and women in the armed forces); *id.* at S11211 (daily ed. Sept. 9, 1993) (committee report).

15. Bowers v. Hardwick, 478 U.S. 186, 197 (1986) (Burger, C. J., concurring)(quoting 4 William Blackstone, Commentaries *215).

16. John Stuart Mill, The Subjection of Women 13–4 (Cambridge: MIT Press, 1970) (1869).

17. See generally Andrew Koppelman, *Why Discrimination Against Lesbians and Gay Men Is Sex Discrimination,* 69 N.Y.U. L. Rev. 197 (1994). See also Andrew Koppelman, The Miscegenation Analogy, 98 Yale L. J. 145 (1988); Sylvia A. Law, *Homosexuality and the Social Meaning of Gender,* 1988 Wis. L. Rev. 187.

18. Loving v. Virginia, 388 U.S. 1, 3 (1967).

19. 347 U.S. 483 (1954).

20. *Id.* at 495. It should be noted that *Brown,* strictly speaking, was limited to the context of public school education. Later Supreme Court cases expanded upon *Brown* and found racial discrimination unconstitutional in other contexts. See, e.g., New Orleans City Park Improvement Ass'n v. Detiege, 358 U.S. 54 (per curiam) (public parks), aff'g 252 F.2d 122 (5th Cir. 1958); Gayle v. Browder, 352 U.S. 903 (per curiam) (buses), aff'g 142 F. Supp. 707 (D. Ala. 1956); Holmes v. City of Atlanta, 350 U.S. 879 (per curiam) (public golf courses), vacating 223 F.2d 93 (1955); Mayor of Baltimore v. Dawson, 350 U.S. 877 (per curiam)(public beaches), aff'g 220 F.2d 386 (4th Cir. 1955).

21. Loving, 388 U.S. at 11.

22. State v. Walsh, 713 S.W.2d 508, 510 (Mo. 1986) (en banc).

23. See sources cited in note 17 *supra.*

24. See *id.* at 36.

25. See *id.*

26. Alexander Bickel, The Least Dangerous Branch 66 (New Haven: Yale University Press, 1962) (quoting Abraham Lincoln, speech at Peoria, Illinois (Oct.

16, 1854), in 2 The Collected Works of Abraham Lincoln 256 (Roy P. Basler ed., 1953)).

27. *Id.*

28. *Id.* at 68.

29. Cf. Lawrence G. Sager, *The Legal Status of Underenforced Constitutional Norms,* 91 Harv. L. Rev. 1212 (1978).

30. See, e.g., Robinson v. California, 370 U.S. 660 (1962).

31. See National Coalition for Gay and Lesbian Equality v. Minister of Justice, 1998 B.C.L.R. 1517, 1998 S.A.C.L.R. LEXIS 36 (1998), for an overview.


*Chapter 9*

1. See E.E.O.C. v. Catholic University of America, 856 F. Supp. 1 (D.D.C. 1994), affirmed, 83 F.2d 455 (D.C. Cir. 1994).

2. Bollard v. California Province of the Society of Jesus, 1998 U.S. Dist. LEXIS 7563 (May 15, 1998).

3. The term "religious institutions" can cover many things—from churches and temples themselves to religious schools to private sphere employers who act on their religious convictions. I am deliberately leaving the term vague here.

4. American law makes the basic prohibitions on employment discrimination inapplicable where religion, sex, or national origin is "a bona fide occupational qualification reasonably necessary to the normal operation of that particular business or enterprise." 42 U.S.C. 2000e-2(e). The prohibition is generally inapplicable "to a religious corporation, association, educational institution, or society with respect to the employment of individuals of a particular religion to perform work connected with the carrying on by such corporation, association, educational institution, or society of its activities." 42 U.S.C. 2000e-1.

5. See, e.g., Young v. Northern Illinois Conference of United Methodist Church, 21 F.3d 184 (7th Cir. 1994).

6. E.E.O.C. v. Catholic University of America, 83 F.3d 455 (D.C. Cir. 1994).

7. See Edna Ullmann-Margalit, The Emergence of Norms (Oxford: Oxford University Press, 1977).

8. Michael McConnell, *Free Exercise Revisionism and the Smith Decision,* 5/ U. Chi. L. Rev. 1109 (1990); Abner Greene, *The Political Balance of the Religion Clauses,* 102 Yale L. J. 1611 (1993).

9. Employment Division, Department of Human Services v. Smith, 494 U.S. 872 (1990). Technically, *Smith* holds that a facially neutral law will be upheld so long as it has a "rational basis," unless it is discriminatorily motivated. The Court did not overrule Sherbert v. Verner, 374 U.S. 398 (1963) (holding that a state may not deny unemployment benefits to a Seventh-Day Adventist who was fired because she would not work on Saturday) or Wisconsin v. Yoder, 406 U.S. 205 (1972) (allowing Amish teenagers to be exempted from a requirement of school attendance until the age of sixteen); but it did read those cases extremely narrowly. It should be noted that the *Smith* decision was surprising as well as controversial and that it remains an object of continuing debate, not only in political and academic circles but also within the Supreme Court itself.

10. City of Boerne v. Flores, 521 U.S. 507 (1997).

11. Boy Scouts of America v. Dale, 530 U.S. 640 (2000).

12. In E.E.O.C. v. Catholic University of America, 83 F.3d 455 (D.C. Cir. 1994), the court held, without much explanation, that *Smith* did not undermine

previous holdings that there was an exception for ministers from the general sex discrimination law.

## Chapter 10

1. See South Africa v. Grootboom, 2000 (11) B.C.L.R. 1169 (CC). For general discussion, see, e.g., Craig Scott & Patrick Mecklen *Constitutional Ropes of Sand or Justiciable Guarantees?* 141 U. Pa. L. Rev. 1 (1992); Symposium, Socio-economic Rights, 8 S.A.J.H.R. 451 (1992).

2. See Stephen Holmes & Cass R. Sunstein, The Cost of Rights (New York: W.W. Norton, 1999).

3. See Davis, The Case Against Inclusion of Socio-economic Rights in a Bill of Rights Except as Directive Principles, 8 S.A.J.H.R. 475 (1992).

4. See note 1 *supra:* see also Chaskalson et al., Constitutional Law of South Africa 41-3–41-4 (Kenwyn; Data, 2000).

5. See Stephen Holmes, Passions and Constraint (Chicago: University of Chicago Press, 1996).

6. Ex Parte Chairperson of the Constitutional Assembly, 1996 (4) S.A. 744, 1996 (10) B.C.L.R. 1243 (C.C.) at paragraph/8.

7. An exception is Hungary. See Andras Sajo, How the Rule of Law Killed Hungarian Welfare Reform S.E.E.C.A. 31 (1996).

8. I draw here from the *Grootboom* opinion. See South Africa v. Grootboom, 2000 (11) B.C.L.R. 1169 (CC).

9. Article 2.1.

10. See Holmes & Sunstein, *supra* note 2.

# Acknowledgments

In 1989, Communism began to fall in Eastern Europe. In its wake the University of Chicago created a Center on Constitutionalism in Eastern Europe, directed by Jon Elster, Stephen Holmes, and me. A good deal of this book has its origins in discussions with Elster and Holmes, and in the chance to observe, at relatively close quarters, the extraordinary developments in constitution-making in eastern Europe in the early 1990s (and also to participate, to a very modest degree, in a few of those developments). I am grateful to Elster and Holmes, and to other participants in the Center—above all Larry Lessig, Wiktor Osiatynski, and Andras Sajo—for many illuminating discussions.

In the same period, I was also lucky enough to be able to see, at multiple stages, the process of constitution-making in South Africa (which resulted, in my view, in the most admirable constitution in the history of the world). I am grateful to many South Africans for making this possible. For instructive discussions, special thanks are due to Dennis Davis, Hugh Corder, Albie Sachs, and Etienne Mureinik, an extraordinary lawyer and law professor who died much too young. My understanding of many topics here—including deliberative trouble, incompletely theorized agreements, the role of tradition, the anticaste principle, the tension between sex equality and religion—has been shaped by experiences in eastern Europe and South Africa and by discussions with the people I have just mentioned.

I am grateful to many other people for their help. For thoughts and advice at many stages, three colleagues deserve special mention: Martha Nussbaum, Richard Posner, and David Strauss. Dedi Felman has been a truly extraordinary editor, helping to shape the book at all stages and producing innumerable improvements both large and small. Three anonymous readers offered excellent advice. Lesley Wexler provided outstanding research assistance. To these people, and others whom I have not mentioned here, I am extremely grateful.

Much of this book is new. I have, however, drawn heavily on a number of previously published papers—in all cases making substantial revisions, and in some cases altering the argument in major ways. Chapter 1 grows out of Deliberative Trouble? Why Groups Go To Extremes, 110 Yale L. J. 71 (2000); chapter 2, Constitutional Agreements Without Constitutional Theories, 13 Ratio Juris 117 (2000); chapter 3, Against Tradition, in The Communitarian Challenge to Liberalism 207 (Ellen Paul et al., eds, Cambridge: Cambridge University Press, 1996) ; chapter 4, Constitutionalism and Secession, 58 U. Chi. L. Rev. 633 (1991); chapter 5, Impeaching the President, 147 U. Pa. L. Rev. 279 (1998); chapter 6, Nondelegation Canons, 67 U. Chi. L. Rev., 315 (2000); chapter 7, The Anticaste Principle, 92 Mich. L. Rev. 2410 (1994); chapter 8, Homosexuality and the Constitution, 70 Ind. L. J. 1 (1994); chapter 9, Is Multiculturalism Bad For Women? 97 (Susan Okin, Joshua Cohen, and Martha Nussbaum, eds., Princeton: Princeton University Press, 1999). I am most grateful for permission to the journals and publishers just mentioned for permission to reprint previously published material here.

# Index

abortion rights
  changing facts and values and, 85
  diversity of supporting reasons, 53
  justified as incompletely theorized
    agreement, 99
  privacy basis for, 71
  as sex equality, 90, 92
  women opponents of, 163
abstractions
  agreement on concrete outcomes vs., 3–4,
    10, 11, 50–55, 57, 60, 62
  constitutional law and, 61–62, 65–66
  in constitutional provisions, 56
  examples of high-level theories, 57
  traditionalist argument and, 77–78
  *See also* incompletely theorized agreements
accidents of birth, 172
accountability, 7, 143–45
administrative agencies, nondelegation
  doctrine and, 138–48
administrative law model, 234–35
adultery
  paternal visiting rights and, 71–72, 84
  prosecution for, 89–90, 91, 186
affirmative action, 13–14, 15, 63, 161, 180
  cascade beliefs, 20, 21
  principle vs. theory, 49, 57, 181
  social comparison and, 26
African Americans. *See* race; racial
  discrimination
agreement, 8–9, 51–58
  compromise approaches to, 53–54
  on constitutional abstractions, 11, 56
  constitutional incentives for, 101, 114
  on levels of principle, 56–58, 240
  mistaken outcome in, 65
  on process over underlying theory, 54–55

  as social goal, 65
  *See also* incompletely theorized agreement
*Alabama Power Co. v. Costle,* 255n.36
alimony determination, 166–67
All-India Institute of Hygiene and Public
  Health, 163
ambiguous legislation, interpretative
  authority, 147–49, 241
American Civil War, 172, 252n.8
Amish, 259n.9
analogies
  discrimination cases, 58, 63, 193–94, 197,
    198–99
  impeachable crimes, 128, 129
  incompletely theorized agreement, 52, 53–
    56, 60, 63
  judicial reasoning by, 63, 64, 89
  misconceptions of, 55
  in secession rights argument, 103
animus. *See* prejudice
anonymity
  deliberation effects, 35–36
  homosexual, 194
anticaste principle, 82, 91, 155–56, 169–82, 221
  antidiscrimination principle vs., 170, 178
  Civil War amendments and, 170, 172–73
  definition of, 10–11, 155, 169–70
  enforcement of, 174–76
  future for, 178–82
  institutional constraints and, 205
  interracial marriage ban and, 199–202, 204
  moral irrelevance and, 172, 173
  motivating idea behind, 170, 188, 242
  as protection against second-class
    citizenship, 98, 242
  reform proposals, 179–82
  religious liberty and, 209–19

socioeconomic rights and, 233, 235–36, 242
*See also* second-class citizenship
*City of Boerne v. Flores*, 259n.10
*City of Richmond v. Croson*, 257nn.30, 31
civility, 59
civil law, application to religious institutions, 210–18
civil rights and liberties abridgement, as secession rationale, 106, 107
civil rights movement, 32, 33, 45
Civil Service Commission, 256n.39
Civil War amendments, 170, 172–73, 180, 197. *See also* Fourteenth Amendment
clear and present danger test, 57
*Cleburne v. Cleburne Living Center*, 257n.31, 258n.5
Clinton, Bill, 37, 184, 191
  impeachment unconstitutionality, 115–16, 127–31
collective action problems, 99–100, 103, 114
collective good, self-interest vs., 99
commerce clause, 100, 101, 102
commercial speech, 65, 69, 79
commonality, 28, 59
common law, 75–76
communications market. *See* media
communism
  collapse in eastern Europe, 6, 22
  denial of travel rights, 107
  free speech principle and, 58
  U.S. party member restrictions, 4
comparative positions, 26, 44
compelling interest, 214, 215, 217
competing views, 36–37, 40–41, 47
compromise
  constitutionalism facilitating, 114
  in furthering social change, 204
  precedent over theory and, 53–54
  risk-taking vs., 24
  U.S. electoral college as, 39
conceptual descent, 51
confidence, 28, 33, 46
conflict
  group polarization and, 34–35
  silence as minimizer, 56–58
conformity tendency, 18–19, 25
Congress of the United States
  accountability in, 144
  ambiguous legislation interpretation authority, 146–47
  bipartisanship and, 36–37
  Fourteenth Amendment implementation by, 156, 175
  impeachment power, 116–17, 119, 125, 126
  member immunity, 118
  nondelegation doctrine and canons, 137–53

presidency and, 37, 39
religious liberty and, 214–15
*See also* federal legislation
consciousness raising, 33–34
consensual sexual activity, 186, 187, 196
conservatism, 46–47, 63, 64
  Burke traditionalism and, 75–76
constitutional amendments, 5, 96
Constitutional Convention, U.S., 120–23. *See also* United States Constitution
Constitutional Court of Germany, 79, 87
Constitutional Court of South Africa, 78–79, 187, 254n.13
  socioeconomic rights cases, 221, 225–37
constitutional interpretation
  bases of agreement, 50
  conventional sources of, 69–70
  impeachment power and, 117–19
  incompletely theorized agreement, 54–55, 59
  originalism and, 87–89, 117
  rules and analogies, 53–56
  sexual orientation-based discrimination and, 69–70, 72, 185–97, 215
  tradition-based, 69–72, 79–84, 117
  transformative vs. preservative, 68
constitutionalism
  abstractions and, 56, 65–66, 172
  agreement on practices over theory and, 50–51, 99
  allowance for competing positions in, 41, 44–45, 240
  anticaste principle and, 10–11, 172–73
  basic rights and, 59–60, 71, 97–99. *See also* constitutional rights
  cases and practices, 3–4, 9–10
  central goal of, 6, 240
  conservativism and, 64
  deliberative democracy linked with, 7, 44–45, 239–43
  democratic conflicts with, 10–11, 96–97, 98
  democratic facilitation by, 98–99, 102, 114
  design of good institutions by, 10–11, 43–47, 240
  disagreement in, 64–66
  equality principles and, 97–98, 156, 185, 221, 242
  impeachment provision, 116–35
  incompletely theorized agreements and, 9, 10, 50–66, 172
  Jefferson's vs. Madison's approach to, 96–97, 106
  judicial review's value in, 100
  low-level justifications, 57
  negative vs. positive rights and, 222–24
  nondelegation canon and, 148–49
  original intent and, 87–89

constitutionalism (*continued*)

as pragmatic, 10, 240–41

precommitment strategies and, 97–100, 224–25, 241

preservative vs. transformative, 67–69, 76–77, 224, 240

principles vs. theories, 49–66

public officials and, 206–7

religious liberty protections by, 218

secession rights issues and, 95–114

sources of rights, 69–72

substance of, 95–114

traditions and, 7, 10, 67–93, 240

unwritten, 6, 50, 56

worst case scenarios and, 105

*See also* South African Constitution; United States Constitution

constitutional law

affirmative action and, 180

basic rights and, 59

common law and, 75–76

convergence of principles and outcomes in, 54–55

desuetude and, 89–92

as "formal inequality" ban, 165, 166

incompletely theorized agreements and, 50–66

informational cascade effects and, 21

large-scale theory and, 61–62

low-level vs. high-level agreement, 57

narrow argument as basis, 206

nondelegation doctrine issue, 137–53

preservative, 67

prudence and, 76

religious institutions and, 212–13

rules and analogies, 53–56

sexual orientation-based discrimination and, 184–208

Smith principle, 212–13

traditionalist case-by-case judgment, 75–76

tradition-based rights in, 81–84

transformative, 68, 76–79

*See also* constitutional interpretation

constitutional rights

contemporary vs. pre-twentieth century, 221

costs of, 222–23, 234

definitions of, 70

interpretive evolution of, 89

issues of, 5, 97–98

moral rights vs., 114

national or local practices and, 73

nojusticiable, 113

secession issue and, 5, 9, 95–114, 240–41

socioeconomic inclusions, 5, 9–10, 78–79, 98, 113, 205, 221–37, 241, 242

traditional sources of, 69–72

*See also* fundamental rights; rights protection; *specific rights*

contraception. *See* birth control use

convictions

deliberative reinforcement of existing, 4–9, 15–16, 22–23, 24, 33, 35, 40, 96, 120, 239–40

incompletely theorized agreement and, 59

susceptibility to cascade effects, 20

*Corrosion Proof Fittings v. E.P.A.*, 255n.36

cosmopolitanism, 73, 75

courts. *See* constitutional interpretation; judiciary; *specific courts*

*Craig v. Boren*, 257n.31

crimes

against homosexuals, 183

impeachable, 118–19, 122, 127, 133–34

racial profiling and, 160

criminal conspiracy, 43

criminal law

application to religious institutions, 210–218

ban on retroactive application of, 149

criminal punishment, 53–54. *See also* capital punishment

criminal reforms, 180, 181

cruel and unusual punishment, 49, 97

cults, 46

cultural integrity, 102, 110–11

culturally based rights, 73

Cultural Revolution (China), 22

Czech Republic, 6

damage awards, 9, 10

severity shift in, 31–32

death penalty. *See* capital punishment

debate. *See* deliberation; deliberative democracy

Declaration of Independence (U.S.), 95

decolonization, 252n.10

Defense Department (U.S.), 191–92

Delaney clause, 255–56n.37

delegation. *See* nondelegation doctrine

deliberating enclaves. *See* enclave deliberation

deliberation, 13–47

affective factors, 28

anonymity effects, 35–36

cautious shifts in, 25

as clarifying disagreement basis, 8–9

consciousness raising in, 33–34

depolarization factors, 27–29

effects of repeated meetings, 30

enhancing polarization. *See* group polarization

exposure to competing views in, 40–41, 47, 137

factors in movement to middle ground, 29

factors in predeliberative opinion shifts, 29–30

full information as precondition, 43

high-status members and, 45–46

on impeachment, 117

incompletely theorized agreements and, 9, 10, 50–66

in-group effects, 35, 36, 155

as intensifying underlying convictions, 33, 34, 35

internal morality of, 242

justifications for, 41–43

legislative nondelegation doctrine and, 137–38

mass media and, 35–36

necessity for opposing views in, 35–36

preconditions for, 42

predeliberation tendencies and, 15, 36

principles vs. theory in, 49–66

reason-giving and, 19, 239, 240

reputational cascades in, 34

risky shifts in, 24, 25, 26

as secession rights requirement, 112, 113

social influences in, 16–19, 26–29

standard positive view of, 13, 14, 24, 44–45

as strengthening like-minded existing convictions, 4–9, 15–16, 22–27, 32–40, 96, 120, 239–40

deliberative democracy, 6–10

anticaste principle in, 11, 155–56, 169–82

aspects of ideal, 6–7, 243

beliefs of, 7, 188, 239, 240

cases and practices, 4, 9–10

constitutional conflicts with, 10–11, 96–97, 98

constitutional facilitation of, 98–99, 102, 114

constitutionally entrenched rights and, 97

constitutional purpose in, 10–11, 207, 239–43

constitutional relationship with, 6–11

delegation and, 143–45

desuetude and, 89–90

diversity as strength in, 97

as electoral college's original intent, 38, 39

facially neutral laws and, 212–13

group conforming behavior in, 18–19

group polarization implications in, 32–40

impeachment power's centrality to, 115

importance of competing views in, 36–37, 40–41

inadequacy of decisions by unelected bodies in, 4, 9

incompletely theorized agreement and goals of, 50, 59–60

internal morality of, 7, 10–11, 242

judicial powers and, 241

majority rule as subverting, 7

national traditions and, 7

negative vs. positive rights in, 223

nondelegation canons and, 151–53

nondelegation doctrine and, 137

political accountability and, 7

political disagreement and, 239–41

preservative vs. transformative constitution in, 68–69

private property rights and, 223

rules and analogies, 53–56

secession rights and, 95, 114

separation of powers as enabling, 98–99

social well-being in, 6

transformative constitutions and, 79

value conflicts in, 49–50

Democratic Party (U.S.), 36, 37, 116

Denmark, 191

depolarization, 27–30

desuetude, privacy cases and, 89–90, 91, 92

differences

anticaste principle and, 10–11, 170, 173, 175, 197

equality principle and, 170

interracial marriage ban and, 200

legal/social treatment distinctions, 164–69

sexual, 197–98

dignity, 59, 79

direct democracy

deliberative democracy vs., 7

electoral college vs., 39

disabled people, 167, 168–69, 175, 177–78

disagreement

approaches to bridging, 50–66, 240

constitutional, 64–66

*See also* deliberation; incompletely theorized agreement

discrimination

analogies in, 193–94, 197, 198–99

anticaste principle and, 178–82, 242

desuetude and, 90–92

differences-in-treatment doctrines, 164–69

equal protection clause interpretation and, 77, 85

free markets as remedy for, 157–64

against homosexuals, 183–208, 215, 242

"immutable characteristics" basis, 195–96

legal ban on statistical, 161

legal disproportionate effects and, 166

national vs. local rights guarantees and, 74–75

original intent and, 88–89

preferences and, 162–64, 198

prejudice vs., 160

discrimination (*continued*)
  principle vs. theory-based remedies, 49, 56–
    57, 58, 60, 63
  rationality review, 188–89
  South African ban on all forms of, 68
  strict vs. intermediate scrutiny of, 257n.32
  suspect classes, 176–78, 193–96
  tradition-based, 82, 87
  without caste, 178
  *See also* antidiscrimination principle; racial
    discrimination; sex discrimination
discussion. *See* deliberation
diverse societies. *See* heterogeneous societies
divorce law, 103, 166–67, 168
"Don't ask, don't tell" policy, 184, 189–92
*Dred Scott v. Sanford*, 175
due process clause, 255n.29
  equal protection clause and, 185, 187, 193
  implementation of, 156
  retroactive application of law and, 149
  substantive due process and, 80, 81, 86
  tradition and interpretation of, 70, 80, 81,
    92, 185–88
Dworkin, Ronald, 250n.5

earned income tax credit, 180
eastern Europe
  cascade effect of communism's fall in, 22
  communist denial of travel rights in, 107
  postcommunist constitutions, 5, 6, 56, 67–
    68, 222
economic guarantees. *See* socioeconomic
  rights
economic injustice, as secession rationale, 107–
  9
economic liberties, 80, 241. *See also* free
  markets; private property rights
educational policies, 180, 181
  religious sex discrimination, 209, 211
*E.E.O.C. v. Arabian American Oil Co.*, 255n.30
*E.E.O.C. v. Catholic University of America*,
  259–60nn.1, 6, 12
*Eisenstadt v. Baird*, 70–71
elections
  advantage of large districts, 45, 47
  conservative restraints on, 46–47
  constitutional assurance of democratic, 6, 7
  district malapportionment, 76
  judicial decisions on, 62
  open primaries, 40
electoral college (U.S.), 38–40
Elster, Jon, 251n.4
employment
  discrimination, 158–60, 168, 176, 194
  religion-based discrimination charges, 209
  social welfare improvement policies, 180

*Employment Division, Department of Human
  Services v. Smith*, 259nn.9, 12
enclave deliberation, 4–9, 15–16, 239–40
  advantages of, 45–46, 155
  anticaste principle and, 11
  associational right to, 215
  competing views and, 40–41, 47
  dangers of, 46–47
  extremism from, 4, 16, 22–27, 96
  by religious organizations, 210, 211
  secession movements and, 96
  suppressed voices in, 45–47, 155
endangered species, 49
England, 81, 185
  unwritten constitution, 6, 56, 67
entitlements, 173, 222
environmental movement
  cascade effect in, 21, 22, 33
  enclave deliberation facilitating, 45
  leadership as polarizers, 33
  principle vs. theory, 49
Environmental Protection Agency, 137–38
equality principle, 155–82
  anticaste principle and, 10–11, 91, 155–56,
    169–82, 197–98, 200–208, 221
  antimiscegenation laws and, 199–200, 201,
    204
  Civil War amendments and, 175
  as constitutional abstraction, 56
  constitutionally designed provisions for, 7,
    9, 42, 68, 79, 97–98, 185, 221, 242
  equal protection clause as principle
    embodiment, 77
  formal inequalities and, 165–69
  free markets and, 157–64
  incompletely theorized agreement and, 60
  internal morality approach, 10–11
  irrational/unreasonable distinctions, 164–69
  legislative guarantees, 9
  privacy cases and, 90–91, 92
  private preferences and, 162–63
  prudence in asserting, 204–8
  religious institutional conflicts with, 209–11
  sexual orientation and, 184, 187–89, 200–
    208
  South African constitutional principle of,
    68
  suspect classes and, 176–78, 193–96
  three understandings of, 157–69
  transition in conception of, 175
  women and, 179–84, 197
  *See also* antidiscrimination principle
equal protection clause, 63, 69, 70–71, 77, 81,
  85
  anticaste principle and enforcement of, 175,
    185, 200

free speech (*continued*)
  costs of, 223, 234
  high-level theory and, 61
  interpretative tools, 69
  nondelegation canon protection of, 148
  principle vs. theory, 49, 57, 58, 65
  restrictions on political, 76
  traditionalism and, 81
  transformative constitutional provisions,
    79, 87
full faith and credit clause, 99–100, 102
fundamental rights
  abridgement as justifying secession, 102
  as constitutionally entrenched, 59–60, 71,
    97–99
  judicial definitions of, 71
  nondelegation canons as guarantees for,
    138–39, 141, 146, 148, 152, 153
  traditionalism and, 78

gay rights. *See* sexual orientation
gender classification
  formal inequality and, 165, 197–98, 211
  role stereotypes, 202–4, 209, 211
  same-sex marriage bans and, 201, 202
  *See also* sex discrimination; women
general good, 99, 101, 103, 108
generalizations, race- or sex-based, 160
General Security Service (Israel), 3–4, 137
Germany
  constitutionalism, 6, 79, 87, 254n.13
  gay military service, 191
Ginsburg, Ruth Bader, 165, 179
Gorelick, Jamie, 184
government power
  anticaste principle and, 11
  constitutional checks on, 9, 41, 45, 98–99,
    101, 115, 116, 120
  diversity of democratic deliberation and, 9
  nondelegation canons and, 141, 149–50
  secession rights effects on, 102–3
  socioeconomic rights protection and, 222
  substantive due process limiting, 80
  *See also* representation; separation of powers
grand jury clause, 118
*Grisold v. Connecticut*, 70, 80, 90, 91
*Grootboom* case, 227, 229, 232–33, 234, 235,
  236
group discussion. *See* deliberation
*Group Life & Health Insurance v. Royal Drug
  Co.*, 255n.34
group membership
  conforming behavior and, 18
  defined by contrast with other groups, 33–
    34

freedom of association and, 40, 215
  in-group effects, 35, 36, 155
  lower-caste stigma from, 171
  outgroups and, 33–34
  religious sex discrimination and, 210, 211,
    213–19
  shared identity and, 27, 28, 33
  strengthening already-held convictions, 32,
    210, 218
group polarization, 8–9, 15–16, 22–47
  basic phenomenon, 22–25, 240
  cascade effects and, 19–22, 23, 32–33, 41
  choice shift and, 24
  as conflict factor, 34–35
  in constitutional design, 50–51
  constitutional design restraints on, 43–45,
    98, 100, 243
  constitutionally entrenched rights and, 97
  as deliberation effect, 23
  depolarization factors, 28–30, 40–41
  in executive branch, 137, 241–42
  experiments in, 30–32
  impeachment process and, 37, 115–16, 131
  incompletely theorized agreements as
    check on, 52, 59
  meaning of, 23
  mechanisms of, 25–27, 37
  positive aspects of, 42–43
  in public institutions, 36–40
  in religious organizations, 210, 218
  risky shifts and, 24–25, 26
  secession movements as reflection of, 96,
    104, 110–11
  special-interest media fostering, 35–36
  traditionalism as response to, 67–93
groupthink, 137
gun control, 4, 15

habeas corpus writ suspension, 126
Habermas, Jürgen, 249n.71
Hamilton, Alexander, 13, 14, 44, 45
  on electoral college, 38–39
  on impeachment, 122–23
*Hampton v. Mow Sun Wong*, 256n.39
handicapped people, 167, 168–69, 175, 177–78
Hand, Learned, 59, 60
harassment
  sexual, 190, 191–92
  unenforceable laws as, 91
Harlan, John, 172–73
hate crimes, 183
hate groups, 16, 33, 46
hate speech, 33
Head Start program, 180
health-care rights, 5, 10, 221

heightened scrutiny, 176, 177–78, 194
heterogeneous societies
  constructive use of silence in, 58–61
  deliberating enclaves, 45–47
  different treatments in, 10–11
  enclave influences in, 46
  exposure to competing views in, 40, 44–45, 47
  group polarization in, 8–9, 15–16, 34
  incompletely theorized agreement use in, 55, 62, 66
  low-status member voices in, 16, 40
  moral disapproval as legal grounds in, 193
  public sphere deliberation in, 15
  secession rights and, 95
  traditionalism and, 73–74
  value conflicts and, 50
  virtues of, 43–45, 47
high crimes and misdemeanors, 117–19, 122, 123, 127, 130, 134
high-level theory
  constitutional law and, 61–62, 66, 172
  examples of, 57
Hitler, Adolf, 254n.13
Holmes, Oliver Wendell, Jr., 70, 80
Holmes, Stephen, 251n.4
homogeneous societies
  secessionist self-determination and, 110–11
  as threat to good deliberation, 15
homosexuality. See sexual orientation
hostility
  cascade-like effects and, 32, 34
  as homosexual discrimination basis, 190, 191, 194, 196, 206, 208
House Armed Services Committee, 184
House Judiciary Committee, 115–16
housing rights, 5, 9–10, 78–79, 98, 113, 221
  South African cases, 226–29, 236
Howard, Jaius, 172
human rights, 171
  as internationally applied, 75
  judicial vs. legislative policy, 3–4
humiliation, 171, 183, 185, 186, 191
humility, 89
Hungary, 6
Hyde, Henry, 115–16

ideal democracy, aspects of, 6–7
immutable characteristics, 195–96
impeachment, 115–35
  contemporary propositions, 131–35
  historical infrequency of, 124–27
  hypothetical cases, 133–35
  original constitutional understanding of, 117–23

partisan polarization and, 37, 115–16, 131
as remedy of last resort, 116–17, 241
unconstitutionality of Clinton procedure, 116, 127–31
incest, 186
income inequality, 168
incompletely theorized agreements, 9, 10, 50–66, 89
  anticaste principle and, 172
  as avoidance of theoretical conflicts, 52, 63
  bases of agreement, 50–52
  Brown v. Board of Education as, 63
  as conservative, 63, 64
  constitutional provisions and, 99, 114, 243
  constructive use of silence in, 58–61
  critics of, 58, 61–62, 63.
  disagreement and, 64–66
  equality debates and, 60
  examples of, 51–52
  as incremental decisions, 63, 75–76
  levels of, 56–58
  by rules and analogies, 52, 53–56, 63
  same-sex marriage and, 193
  as social stability source, 51, 60, 240
  traditionalists and, 76
  virtues of, 11, 62, 65–66
incorporation movement, 74
incrementalism, 63, 75–76, 185, 193, 206
Independent Counsel Act, 132–33
independent regulatory commissions, 35, 36–37
India, 113, 163–64, 170, 180, 253n.3
  constitutionalism, 224, 225
individual judgment agreements, general theory vs., 52–53
individual rights. See fundamental rights; rights protection
individual susceptibility
  cascade effects and, 19–22, 33
  cause polarization leaders and, 33
  cautious shifts and, 25
  conformity and, 18–19, 25
  persuasive arguments and, 26–27
  social comparisons and, 26
Industrial Union Department, A.F.L.-C.I.O. v. American Petroleum Institute, 255n.36
inequality. See discrimination; equality principle
influences. See social influences
information access, 42
informational externality, 16–17
  cascade effects in, 19–22, 23, 34
  social comparison and, 26
  as strife factor, 34–35
in-group beliefs, 33–34, 35

inherently suspect classification, 194
intermediate scrutiny, 257n.32
internalized norms, 211
internal morality, 7, 10–11, 242
Internal Revenue Service, 124, 134
International Covenant on Economic, Social, and Cultural Rights, 224, 229–30
international law, 109, 110
socioeconomic rights movement and, 224, 229–30
Internet
censorship issues, 49, 61
exchanges of diverse ideas on, 41
as fostering extremism, 35, 240
importance of competing views on, 40
local cascades, 16–17
interracial marriage, 198–202, 204, 257n.30
interstate commerce, 100, 101
interstate extradition clause, 118
interstate mobility, 106, 107
Iran-Contra controversy, 125–26
Iredell, James, 123
Ireland, 185
irrationality. *See* rationality reveiw
Israel, 191
torture decision, 3–4, 9, 137, 148
unwritten constitution, 6, 50, 56

*Jantz v. Muci,* 194
Jefferson, Thomas, 46, 96, 106
Jeter, Mildred, 199
Jews, 178, 209
Jim Crow, 157
Johnson, Andrew, 125
Joint Chiefs of Staff, 191
judges. *See* judiciary
judicial activism, 3–4
judicial restraint, 80
judicial review, 100, 101
judiciary
administrability, 213
anticaste principle enforcement by, 156, 174, 175, 176
appropriate role of, 11
avoidance of abstract issues by, 4, 5, 9, 10
bipartisan multimember courts, 37
as catalytic over preclusive, 11
constitutional rights underenforcement by, 205
creative use of powers of, 241
incompletely theorized agreement by, 53, 62, 63
legal interpretation and, 54–55, 63
limited wisdom and tools of, 11
multimember polarizations, 24, 37, 40, 59

nondelegation doctrine enforcement
problems, 138, 140, 142, 145–46, 152
nonrecognition of secession right by, 113, 114
sentencing by, 53–54
separation of powers and, 98
sexual orientation discrimination
approaches by, 185, 194, 206–8
socioeconomic rights enforcement by, 225, 226, 234–37, 242
suspect classications by, 176–78
tradition-based judgments by, 82–83, 86–87
transformative vs. preservative
interpretations, 68
*See also* Constitutional Court of South
Africa; constitutional interpretation;
Supreme Court of Israel; Supreme Court
of the United States
juries
outcomes without supporting reasons, 52
predeliberation verdicts predicting final
outcomes, 36
punitive damage awards, 14, 31
just outcome, unjust consensus vs., 65

Kantian theory, 57
Kennedy, John F., 126
King, Martin Luther, Jr., 32
King, Rufus, 120
*King v. St. Vincent's Hospital,* 255n.35
Koppelman, Andrew, 198, 199, 201, 202
Korean War, 191
Kronman, Anthony, 77–78
Kuran, Timur, 34

laissez faire. *See* free markets
large-scale theory. *See* high-level theory
lawmaking. *See* federal legislation
*Lectures on Law* (Wilson), 123
legal cascades, 20
legal remedies, 161–64, 172
legislation. *See* federal legislation
legislative committees, 145
legislatures
anticaste principle enforcment by, 156, 175–76
bicameralism advantages, 5, 10, 41, 43–44, 45, 109, 115
debate-based permission to change basic
rights and, 4, 137, 148
impeachment process and, 115–16
need for deliberative diversity in, 137
nondelegation doctrine, 137–53
party-line polarizations in, 37
reasons for extremism in, 16

New Deal, 80
New Zealand, 185
Nixon, Richard, 124–25, 126
nondelegation canons, 138–39, 140, 147–53
nondelegation doctrine, 137–53
    disuse of, 138, 140
    hidden principles, 146–48
Norway, 191

obstruction of justice, 128, 129, 130
Occupational Safety and Health
    Administration (U.S.), 137–38
open primaries, 40
opinion exchanges, 13–14, 20–22
oppression
    facially neutral laws and, 213
    as secession rational, 106, 107, 110, 111
    *See also* rights protection
originalism, 87–89
    impeachment power and, 117–23
    nondelegation canons and, 153
outcome agreement
    constitutional provisions for, 99–100
    convergence means, 52–53
    disconnected from abstraction, 60
    justice and, 55
    without supporting rationale, 51–52, 60
outgroups, 28, 33–34

Palestinian state, 6
paranoia, cascade-like effects and, 32
parental leave programs, 180
parental rights, 71–72, 84
partisan politics. *See* political parties
past practices. *See* precedent; traditionalism
paternalism, 193
peer pressure, 16
perjury, 128, 129–30, 134
persuasive argument theory, 26–27, 28, 29, 43
physician-assisted suicide, 72, 91–92
Pinckney, Charles, 120, 121
*Plessy v. Ferguson*, 172–73
pluralism, value conflicts and, 50
polarization. *See* group polarization
polarization entrepreneurs, 32–33
polarization games, 30–31
political activists, 32–33, 42–43
political cascades, 20, 21, 37, 38
political disagreement. *See* disagreement
political dissent, 16, 82
political equality
    powerlessness vs., 177, 194–95
    as precondition for deliberative democracy,
        7, 9, 42
political parties
    bipartisanship advantages, 36–37

depolarization, 28
electoral college and, 39, 40
impeachment and, 115–17, 120, 125, 133–34,
    241
    internal discussion polarization, 24
    legislative polarization and, 37
political process
    constitutional precommitment strategies
        and, 97–105
    reasons for secession, 105, 108, 110–11, 114
    secession rights' effects on, 104–5
    soluble vs. insoluble issues, 99
political speech, 76, 82
poll tax, 76
popular will. *See* majority views
populism, 43
positive rights, 5, 9–10, 222–24
Posner, Richard, 118
Powell, Colin, 191
practical reasoning, 60–61
pragmatism, constitutional, 10, 240–41
precedent
    incrementalism and, 63, 75
    privacy cases and, 70–71
    same-sex marriage cases and, 202
    theory vs., 53–54, 62, 63
    traditionalism and, 77
precommitment strategies, 97–105, 241
    in South African Constitution, 224–25
    waiver of secession rights as, 101–5
predeliberation positions
    conclusions on shifts in, 29–30
    jury final verdicts and, 36
    risky shifts and, 25
    social comparison and, 26
preferences, 8, 162–64, 198, 212
prejudice
    characteristics of, 159–60
    group discussions and predispositions to,
        23
    legal challenges to, 179
    race and sex distinctions and, 165
    rulings against discrimination based on,
        188, 189
    sexual orientation and, 188–89, 190, 191,
        194, 196, 208
preservative constitutions, 67–68, 81, 224, 240
    due process clause and, 185, 188
presidential elections, 38–40
presidential impeachment. *See* impeachment
presidential powers
    impeachment based on egregious
        misuse of, 116, 117, 121, 122, 125, 127, 134–
        35
    U.S. founders' disagreement over, 120–21
press freedom, 6

principle vs. theory. *See* incompletely
   theorized agreements
prisoners' dilemmas, 99
privacy rights, 70–71, 80, 87
   applied to same-sex relations, 186–87
   as constitutionally entrenched, 97, 222
   desuetude and, 89–93
   nondelegation canon protection, 148
private preference. *See* preferences
private property rights
   as basic right, 7, 97, 99, 241
   government action and, 222–23
private self-interest. *See* self-interests
privileges and immunities clause, 251n.28
professional polarizers, 32–33
prudence, 76, 78
   in initiating immediate social change, 204–
      8
*Public Citizens v. Young*, 255–56n.37
public institutions
   constitutional design of good, 43–45
   polarization in, 32–33, 36–40
   protections from unrestrained public
      passions, 98
public policy
   nondelegation canons and, 150–51
   sexual orientation-based discrimination
      and, 207
punitive damages, 14, 15, 31–32

race
   anticaste principle and, 10–11, 157–64, 172,
      174–75
   discrimination. *See* racial discrimination
   equality principle and, 179–84
   group polarization and, 34
   legal/social treatment differences, 164–69
   midlevel bases of agreement and, 57
race-conscious programs, 180–82
racial discrimination
   as analogy for other discrimination
      categories, 60, 193–94, 198–99
   equal protection clause and, 77
   free markets as remedy for, 157–61, 162
   intermarriage bans, 198–202, 204, 257n.30
   legal protections, 178–79
   old tradition of, 81, 82, 87, 197
   remedial policies, 180–82
   strict scrutiny of, 257n.32
   as suspect classification, 177
   systematic social disadvantages and, 170–71
   systemic disadvantage and, 170
   transformative constitutions and, 68
   *See also* apartheid; racial segregation
racial hierarchy, 172, 197
racial profiling, 160, 161

racial segregation
   South Africa, 22, 68, 78, 157
   United States, 63, 179
radio. *See* broadcasting
*Ramah Navajo Chapter v. Lujan*, 255n.31
Randolph, Edmund, 121
rape, sodomy comparison, 196–97
rationale. *See* reason-giving
rationality review, 188–92
Rawls, John, 13, 14, 44, 45
Reagan, Ronald, 125–26
real-world contexts
   constitutional abstractions vs., 3–4, 10, 11,
      50–55, 57
   deliberative groups in, 14–19
   incompletely theorized agreement in, 60–
      62
reason-giving, 7, 19, 239
   full particularity agreement without, 51–52,
      60
   traditionalism and, 240
referenda, as contrary to deliberative
      democracy, 7, 9
reflective equilibrium, 76–77
reflectiveness, 7
reform. *See* social change
regulatory commissions, 35, 36–37
Religious Freedom Restoration Act of 1996,
      212, 214
religious liberty
   anticaste principle and, 209–19, 242
   associational rights linked with, 215–16
   as constitutional abstraction, 56, 222
   constitutional challenges, 76
   facially neutral laws (Smith principle) and,
      212–13, 214, 215
   incompletely theorized agreement and, 51, 99
   local ordinances and, 5, 9
   mounting protections for, 82
   nondelegation canon protection for, 148
   sexual discrimination vs., 209–19, 242
   strengthening of already-held convictions
      and, 32, 210, 218
removal from office. *See* impeachment
representation
   accountability and, 144
   Burke's conception of, 46, 47
   constitutional precommitment strategies
      and, 100, 101
   electoral college and, 38–40
   measures for equality in, 109
   provisions for subunits in, 111
   rejection of "right to instruct," 41, 45
   *See also* Congress of the United States;
      legislatures
reproduction, 197–98

Republican Party (U.S.), 36, 37, 116
reputational influences
    behavior linked with, 17, 19
    in cascade effects, 21–22, 23, 34
    group polarization and, 23
    heterogeneity and, 44
    as strife factor, 34–35
retroactive law application, 148–49, 152
retroactive rule, 253n.2
rhetorical asymmetry, 31–32
Richards, Janet Radcliffe, 257n.19
rights protection
    constitutional entrenchment, 59–60, 71, 97–
        99
    as democracy's internal morality, 7
    democratic deliberation required for, 5, 9
    incompletely theorized agreements and, 50,
        59–60
    institutional constraints on, 205
    judicial definition of fundamental rights, 71
    metaphysical realism and, 73
    narrow judicial decisions, 4
    negative vs. positive, 222–24
    nondelegation doctrine and, 137, 138
    sources of, 69–72
    subsistence guarantees debate, 221–37
    traditionalism and, 68–97
    types covered, 95, 222
    universal vs. national, 75
    written constitution and, 6
    See also constitutional rights; fundamental
        rights; specific rights
right to die, 72, 85
risky shifts, 24, 25, 26
Roe v. Wade, 53, 71, 92
Romer v. Evans, 188, 189, 206
Roosevelt, Franklin Delano, 126
Rosenberg, Gerald, 168
Ruddock, Donovan ("Razor"), 183, 203
rule of law, 141
rule of lenity, 149
rules
    constitutional avoidance of, 56
    incompletely theorized agreements and, 52,
        53–56, 59, 63
Russia, 6
Rust v. Sullivan, 255n.26

same-sex marriage
    antimiscegenation law analogy, 198–202
    constitutional issues in, 192–93, 198, 200–
        204
    federal legal discrimination against, 184
    local ordinance overturning, 5, 9
    misconceived analogy and, 55
    prudent approach to, 205, 206, 207

Scalia, Antonin, 68, 72, 80–81, 86, 87, 256n.37
Schechter Poultry Corp. v. United States, 140
school prayer, 76
school segregation, 63
search and seizure protections, 100
secession rights, 5, 9, 95–114
    case arguments for, 105–12, 114
    constitutional inappropriateness of, 96, 102–
        5, 114, 240–41
    debated for recently written constitutions,
        95–96
    Jeffersonian endorsement of, 106
    military force and, 252n.8
    as nonjusticiable, 113, 114
    qualifications and limitations, 112–14
second-class citizenship
    anticaste principle and, 155–82, 197
    constitutional protection against, 98, 242
    elimination as social goal, 179
    enclave deliberation and, 45–47
    equality principle opposing, 169–70
    formal inequality and, 165
    as gay and lesbian status, 183–84, 194
    legal remedies, 172
    race-conscious programs and, 181
    religious sex-role stereotyping and, 209
    systematic social disadvantage and, 170, 172
    as women's status, 175, 197, 211
self-determination, 101, 104, 110–12, 252n.10
    local, 74, 75
self-government
    constitutional facilitation of, 114
    constitutionalism as check on, 97
    existing preferences and, 8
    goals of, 6
    secessionist self-determination claim for,
        111
    secession rights compromising, 95, 114
    U.S. founders' intent, 120
self-incrimination protection, 97
self-insulation, 47, 87
self-interests
    collective good vs., 99
    legislative limits on, 141–42, 144
self-respect, 171, 181, 186
Sen, Amartya, 6, 163–64
"separate but equal" doctrine, 199
separation of powers, 9, 11, 39, 51
    impeachment process and, 115, 120
    positive functions of, 98–99
Seventh-Day Adventists, 259n.9
severity shift, 31–32
sex-conscious programs, 180, 181
sex discrimination, 58, 60, 63, 68, 76
    anticaste principle and, 11, 173, 197
    equal protection clause and, 77

free markets as remedy for, 157–64
intermediate scrutiny of, 257n.32
legal protections, 178–79
legal treatment of differences and, 164–69
preferences and, 162–64
privacy cases linked with, 90–91, 92
religious liberty issues, 209–19, 242
sexual harassment and, 190
sexual orientation discrimination analogy, 193–94
sexual orientation discrimination as subset of, 185, 196–97, 200–208
suspect classification, 177
systemic disadvantage and, 170–71
tradition-based, 82, 87
sex-role stereotyping, 202–4, 209, 211
sexual activity
consensual issues, 186, 187, 196
illicit, 126, 128
interracial bans, 198–202, 204, 257n.30
military concerns, 190
prosecution for, 89–90, 91
sex differences and, 198
See also adultery; sexual orientation
sexual harassment, 190, 191–92
sexually explicit materials, 79
sexual orientation, 183–208
anticaste principle and, 11, 178, 183–85, 187, 189, 194, 242
constitutional interpretations and, 69–70, 72, 185–97, 215
Court-upheld sodomy ban and, 71, 87, 91, 92, 183, 184, 186, 193, 196, 258n.15
discrimination without caste, 178, 183–85, 194
"Don't ask, don't tell" policy, 184, 189–92
enclave deliberation facilitating rights movement, 45
equality principle and, 184, 187–89
equal protection clause applications, 187–89, 192, 193
incompletely theorized agreement and, 60
local ordinances and referenda, 5, 9
rationality test for discrimination against, 188
same-sex marriage issue, 5, 9, 55, 184, 192–93, 198–207
as sex discrimination subset, 185, 196–97, 200–208
South African antidiscrimination provision, 68, 185
suspect classes of discrimination and, 193–96
shared identities, 27–30, 33, 36
shelter rights. See housing rights
Sherbert v. Verner, 259n.9

Sherman, Roger, 120
shifts
cautious, 25, 205
to more extreme position, 24–32
Sidgwick, Henry, 61
silence, constructive use of, 58–61
"similarly situated" principle, 164–69, 175
Slaughterhouse Cases, 251n.28
slavery, 68, 76, 172, 175, 197
Lincoln's approach to, 204–5, 207
Slovakia, 6
Smith principle, 212–16
smoking, 20
social change
desuetude notion and, 89
enclave deliberation facilitating, 45
by professional polarizers, 32–33
prudence in enacting, 204–8
traditionalism as cautionary note on, 76, 84–85
See also socioeconomic rights
social fragmentation, 15, 35, 36, 40, 240
social influences
access to full information and, 42
cascade effects and, 16–22, 30–31
classic experiments, 17–19
comparisons as, 26, 44
enclave pros and cons, 45–47
extremism and, 32–40
in group polarization, 15, 32, 44
heterogeneity advantages, 43
incompletely theorized agreements as check on, 52
by media and Internet, 35–36
persuasive arguments, 26–27
shared identities as, 27–30, 33, 36
social reform. See social change
social stability
enclave threats to, 46
incompletely theorized agreements providing, 51, 59, 64, 243
social welfare
anticaste principle and, 170, 179
democracy promoting, 6
judicial approach to, 205
legislative enactment and, 144
post-1950 constitutional provisions for, 68, 78, 98, 221
status of gays and lesbians, 183
tradition-based indifferences to, 82
socioeconomic rights
administrative law model, 234–35
anticaste principle and, 11
issues in constitutional inclusion of, 5, 9–10, 68, 78–79, 98, 113, 171, 205, 221–37, 241, 242